To Aliens and Exiles

# To Aliens and Exiles

*Preaching the New Testament as Minority-Group Rhetoric in a Post-Christendom World*

Tim MacBride

CASCADE *Books* • Eugene, Oregon

TO ALIENS AND EXILES
Preaching the New Testament as Minority-Group Rhetoric
in a Post-Christendom World

Copyright © 2020 Tim MacBride. All rights reserved. Except for brief quotations in critical publications or reviews, no part of this book may be reproduced in any manner without prior written permission from the publisher. Write: Permissions, Wipf and Stock Publishers, 199 W. 8th Ave., Suite 3, Eugene, OR 97401.

Cascade Books
An Imprint of Wipf and Stock Publishers
199 W. 8th Ave., Suite 3
Eugene, OR 97401

www.wipfandstock.com

PAPERBACK ISBN: 978-1-5326-9683-1
HARDCOVER ISBN: 978-1-5326-9684-8
EBOOK ISBN: 978-1-5326-9685-5

*Cataloguing-in-Publication data:*

Names: MacBride, Tim, author.

Title: To aliens and exiles : preaching the New Testament as minority-group rhetoric in a post-Christendom world / Tim MacBride.

Description: Eugene, OR: Cascade Books, 2020. | Includes bibliographical references.

Identifiers: ISBN 978-1-5326-9683-1 (paperback). | ISBN 978-1-5326-9684-8 (hardcover). | ISBN 978-1-5326-9685-5 (ebook).

Subjects: LCSH: Preaching. | Bible. N.T.—Homiletical use. | Bible—Rhetorical criticism. | Bible—Hermeneutics. | Bible. N.T.—Language, style, etc.

Classification: BV4211.2 M23 2020 (print). | BV4211.2 (ebook).

Scripture quotations are taken from the Holy Bible, New International Version®, NIV®. Copyright © 1973, 1978, 1984, 2011 by Biblica, Inc.™ Used by permission of Zondervan. All rights reserved worldwide. www.zondervan.com The "NIV" and "New International Version" are trademarks registered in the United States Patent and Trademark Office by Biblica, Inc.™

Manufactured in the U.S.A.                                    05/26/20

# Contents

*Preface* | vii
Introduction: *Preaching to Aliens and Exiles* | ix

## Part 1: Minority-Group Rhetoric and the New Testament | 1
1. The Need for Attractive Difference | 3
2. Maintaining Attractive Difference | 14

## Part 2: The General Epistles | 43
3. 1 Peter: *To Aliens and Exiles* | 45
4. Hebrews: *The City That Is to Come* | 57
5. 1 John: *They Went Out from Us* | 76
6. James: *Double-Minded* | 86
7. Revelation: *Faithful and True* | 99

## Part 3: Paul's Epistles | 119
8. Philippians: *Citizens of Heaven* | 121
9. 1 Corinthians: *Are You not Worldly?* | 128
10. 1 Thessalonians: *How You Turned from Idols* | 137
11. Colossians: *Let no-One Take You Captive* | 146

## Part 4: The Gospels and Acts | 159
12. Matthew: *Here Are My Mother and My Brothers* | 161
13. John: *If the World Hates You* | 180
14. Luke–Acts: *Most Excellent Theophilus* | 199

## Part 5: Final Words | 215

15. Wisdom from African-American Preachers: *It's Gonna Be Hard for Y'all* | 217
16. Conclusions: *What Next?* | 224

*Bibliography* | 227

# Preface

THIS BOOK HAS BEEN "in the works" for about twenty years. It began when, as a second-year seminary student, I read David deSilva's *Honor, Patronage, Purity, and Kinship* and discovered how the New Testament used the rhetoric of honor and shame to strengthen and encourage its minority group audience. For the next decade or so of pastoral ministry, this understanding shaped my preaching as I sought to equip my congregation to live as "aliens and strangers" (1 Pet 2:11) in a pluralistic and sometimes hostile world. In recent years, this has become even more front-and-center, as the Western church has become increasingly aware of its minority status—and therefore its similarities with the original audiences of the New Testament. This book is an attempt to provide not just preachers—although that is its focus—but all of us with a lens with which we can approach the New Testament to see how it speaks to our newfound minority status.

I owe several debts of gratitude, firstly to the work of David deSilva and Ben Witherington III, who have been my guides throughout the majority of the journey; it's their foundation on which this book is laid. I'm grateful to Mark Harding, former Dean of the Australian College of Theology, who gave me my first opportunity to write on this topic as a chapter in *Into All the World*. My friend and New Testament teaching colleague, David Starling, has always been generous with his time and wise advice, some of which is reflected in this book. Thanks are also due to Robert Smith Jr., and his former students, Galen Jones and Reginald Calvert, whose collective wisdom and experience is found in chapter 15. And it couldn't have been completed without the gracious gift of study leave given by my employer, Morling College.

Finally, thanks to my wife and sons for their ongoing support and encouragement throughout the writing process, and to my church, Narwee Baptist, who have given me the opportunity to preach much of what's contained in these pages.

*Tim MacBride*
Easter 2020

# Introduction: *Preaching to Aliens and Exiles*

THE LANDSCAPE HAS CHANGED for Christian preachers in Western society. And it's changed quickly, in the space of a generation.[1]

A generation or so ago, the values we preached were generally consistent with the aspirational values of the dominant culture, if not their actual practice. Now, our values are increasingly seen as regressive and dangerous. Back then, a Christian worldview could be assumed as a starting point and go largely unchallenged by a society which considered itself at least culturally "Christian." Now, we must be prepared for that worldview to face challenge, even from among the Christians in our audience. Previously, Christian ministers were accorded status as leaders in the wider community and could speak with some level of acknowledged authority. Today, their relevance is being questioned if not rejected outright, hastened by the well-publicized failings of so many clergy.[2]

In short, we can no longer preach with the assumption that we are part of the dominant culture. Increasingly, we preach conscious that we belong to a minority. Not a persecuted minority by any means, but a minority all the same—one that is being pushed unevenly yet undeniably from its former central place in society toward the margins.

Given this new landscape, *how do we now preach?*

## Waking Up to Our Minority Status

Let's begin with the obvious—or what *should* be the obvious, even though we've been slow to see it. Indeed, over the past couple of decades many

---

1. Writing in English, I speak mainly of the Anglophone societies found in places like the UK, USA, New Zealand, and my own country of Australia. The landscape in the European West changed at least a generation before that.

2. Tim MacBride, "To Aliens and Strangers."

have made this point—in far more detail and nuance than I have space for here³—but it says something about our collective blindness that it's still necessary to rehearse it once more. Our first order of business is to recognize and, to some extent, embrace our minority status. And to understand that true followers of Jesus have *always* been a minority throughout the history of the church. This isn't a new situation in which we find ourselves, even if it might feel like it.

And the reason it *feels* like it is because for many generations—really, ever since Constantine—Western society considered itself to be, in a cultural sense, "Christian." Church-based institutions were frequently at its civic core, Bible stories and phrases were an important part of its shared cultural and linguistic heritage, and Western society viewed itself as being based on "Judeo-Christian values." It blurred the line between faith communities and the wider culture so that we could choose to "tune out" our minority status. As Ben Witherington puts it, speaking of the USA:

> Our country has been suffering from truth decay for a long time. The problem with numerous of my fellow white Evangelicals is that they have mistaken civic religion for Christianity or so blended together nationalism with their understanding of the Christian faith that they can't tell the difference. So, we should all be reminded that America is not the promised land, we are not Israel . . .⁴

While this is not as stark in countries like the UK and Australia, there is still the residue of a society whose social and political structures were inextricably bound up with Christendom. For some Christians, this blurring of the lines gave the illusion of a Christian society. *How can we think of ourselves as a minority when we live in a "Christian country"?*

Over the past half century, the line has become less blurry. It's become more difficult to ignore the tension between the worldview of Christians and of mainstream society. The Western world is now "post-Christendom," a term described by Stuart Murray as

> the culture that emerges as the Christian faith loses coherence within a society that has been definitively shaped by the Christian story and as the institutions that have been developed to express Christian convictions decline in influence.⁵

---

3. See especially Frost and Hirsch, *The Shaping of Things to Come*; Fitch, *The Church of Us vs. Them*, 1–9.

4. Witherington, "Praying for the President."

5. Murray, *Post-Christendom*, 21.

It's that loss of coherence and influence that we now feel, as we become aware of how increasingly out of step we are with the views of the majority.

This has accelerated over the past decade or so, as many of the values Western society inherited from Christendom have been steadily discarded now that the underlying Christian rationale for them has been rejected. This is most obviously seen in the areas of gender and sexuality. My colleague, David Starling, puts it this way:

> When I was growing up, back in the seventies and the eighties, to be a Christian was to be viewed as a kind of goody-goody, as someone who was a little bit quaint and needlessly uptight, but basically harmless. These days, increasingly, to be a Christian— to be a Christian who is committed to a conservative view of sexual morality—is to be a kind of deviant from the established social order.[6]

This, probably more than anything, has hastened this feeling of being out of step. There is a significant difference between being seen as "a bit weird," but still an accepted member of the wider community, and being seen as subversive, or even dangerous purveyors of "hate speech." We have become the "repugnant cultural other," a phrase coined by Susan Harding to describe mainstream society's attitude toward fundamentalists,[7] but now applicable to Christians in general. Not only do we believe different things, but many of those things which we believe are now considered repugnant by the majority culture: variously regressive, oppressive, and abusive. It's *that* which has made our minority status impossible to ignore or brush over any longer.

We've always been a minority, but we've now been (re)awakened to the reality of it. *How do we now preach?*

## The rhetoric of minority

Whenever a group is aware of its minority status within the wider culture, its internal and external discourse reflects this. To survive, it needs to define the group identity, provide a rationale for its continued existence, and set the nature of its interactions with the majority. In other words, minority group rhetoric is born. (We'll discuss this in more detail in the next chapter.)

It's no different whenever Christians are conscious of their minority status. They may be in the minority simply for being followers of Jesus, or they may already belong to an ethnic or cultural minority—a situation which

---

6. Starling, "Preaching on Sex in a Post-Christendom World."
7. Harding, "Representing Fundamentalism," 373–93.

is further complicated by their faith in Jesus. Either way, this gets reflected in how they preach and speak: how they define their identity, purpose, and relationship with the wider world. But there are several trajectories this Christian minority group rhetoric can take, not all of them helpful.

The first is where Christians try to minimize the differences between their group and the dominant culture. This can take quite helpful forms, in which believers are encouraged to abandon unnecessary cultural oddities and traditions which might hinder acceptance by the majority, and to adopt, instead, some of its cultural forms and practices—following the Apostle Paul's example of becoming "all things to all people" (1 Cor 9:19–23). The message tends to be along the lines of: *we're just like you, except we also know Jesus.* This is good and, indeed, biblical insofar as it breaks down barriers to people hearing the good news of Jesus Christ (which is Paul's point). It can be a little less helpful if it encourages an "attractional" model of church, in which we think the masses will flock to us if we could just get the product and sales pitch right. And it can be downright dangerous if it conditions us to seek acceptance from the majority at the expense of what *ought to* make us different in the first place; if it provides a convenient excuse for us to soft-pedal those beliefs which the majority finds objectionable or repugnant; if it's done with a view to keeping a seat at the table, maintaining our influence and tax breaks.[8] The end result of such a rhetorical approach is, in the words of Stephen McAlpine, "a world in which no one is angry about Christianity, because Christianity is too weightless, hollow, and toothless to get angry about."[9] We become so much like the culture that our message is no longer distinctive, and ultimately, we lose our very reason to exist.

The second trajectory we can take is the opposite rhetorical strategy: to embrace the difference and see the dominant culture as the enemy which is trying to bully us into conformity. It's a circle-the-wagons, us-against-them rhetoric which rallies the troops to do battle against the godless, pagan world around us. This approach can find some degree of support in Scripture, most obviously Peter's epistles, John's Gospel, and Revelation (so long as we don't spend too long considering the differences between the rhetorical setting of their original audiences and our own). And it can serve to increase the sense of belonging and commitment members feel to the church—making it tempting for some to exaggerate the level of hostility from the majority culture in order to spur the group to greater levels of

---

8. McAlpine, "The Beguiling Technicolor of OZ," 7, notes that "Our apologetic strategy has been to stress sameness in order to receive secularism's approval and a place at its table because at an unspoken level we value the same things it does."

9. McAlpine, "The Beguiling Technicolor of OZ," 3.

resistance.[10] (We'll talk more about this in the next chapter.) The problem is, of course, that it's an unattractive rhetoric which does little to encourage converts. And it's often tinged with an attitude of entitlement that suggests the post-Christendom reality has not been fully grasped. We might remain distinctive, but we're not fulfilling our mission to the world.

The third trajectory is the most difficult one. But it's also the most biblical. It's the one consistently taken by the New Testament authors as they wrote to the small groups of Jesus-followers which were scattered throughout the Mediterranean world. Some of these groups had already been a minority due to their ethnicity, most notably the Jews of the diaspora. But all had become a minority due to their faith in Jesus. And they are addressed *as* a minority group—mostly implicitly, but sometimes quite explicitly, as in Peter's addressing of his audience as "aliens and exiles" (1 Pet 2:11). They were facing a dominant culture that treated them variously with indifference, disdain, or outright hostility. They were under significant social (and sometimes physical) pressure to conform to the majority, while at the same time fulfilling their commission to win over that majority with the good news of Jesus. They needed to define their identity, articulate their purpose, and maintain their distinctiveness—yet to do so in a way that was attractive to outsiders. They had to be *attractively different*.

As Western Christians who have recently been reawakened to our minority status, the New Testament provides us with a model of how we can engage with the majority culture while maintaining our minority group identity. Its minority group rhetoric—if appropriated carefully—can become ours, guiding how we speak among ourselves and how we present to the outside world.

That's what this book is about. And although this has implications for all of our discourse—making this a book for *all* Christians—the particular focus of application here will be on how it's used in preaching, since preaching tends to shape and define the rest of our rhetoric.

## Using the rhetoric of the New Testament

If we're going to use the minority group rhetoric of the New Testament, we first need to know how it works. The first chapter introduces us to minority group rhetoric in general, using insights from the social sciences. We'll look at why such rhetoric is needed in order to counteract pressure from the majority culture to conform; this is especially true in honor-shame based cultures, such as the ones addressed by the New Testament. Mostly, religious minority

10. See, e.g., Coser, *The Functions of Social Conflict*, 106.

groups either assimilate (and so cease to be distinctive) or isolate (making it hard to win converts). The New Testament's approach of attractive difference is a solution to this problem that plagues all minority groups.

The second chapter takes us through the strategies used by the New Testament writers to promote this attractive difference, all of which address one of six key questions:

1. **Approval:** Whose opinions do we care about and whose opinions can we ignore?
2. **Disapproval:** Why can we ignore those who disapprove of us?
3. **Identity:** Who are we and why are we distinctive?
4. **Practice:** How do we live? That is, what do we *do* that makes us distinctive?
5. **Worldview:** How do we see the world, and how does that differ from the majority?
6. **Salience:** Why is group membership so important right now?

The chapters which then follow are the heart of this book. They show how this plays out in selected writings of the New Testament, highlighting the different emphases of each and the different minority situations being addressed. As we compare the situation of the original audience with our own—and understand how the biblical author seeks to speak into that situation—we can begin to formulate interpretive and preaching strategies that bring the minority group rhetoric of the New Testament to bear on our own culture.

The final chapter is no mere afterthought. It's an acknowledgement that many of our brothers and sisters around the world have been acutely aware of their minority status far longer than white, Western Christians have. What's more, our experience of being a minority pales in comparison with many believers who—as well as being part of an ethnic or cultural minority—have experienced social and economic marginalization, and sometimes physical persecution. We have much to learn from them in many areas, not the least of which is their use of the minority rhetoric of Scripture. They have learned out of necessity to pay attention to where the Bible addresses those who are marginalized and oppressed minorities, and to use that rhetoric to speak into their own context. For this reason, the last chapter presents the reflections of some African-American pastor-theologians who were asked to give the white, Western church some of their wisdom—and they graciously obliged.

## Persecuted, marginalized, or . . . ?

Before we begin, however, this reminder of the others who have gone before us should give us pause before we hastily adopt the posture and terminology of a persecuted or marginalized group. Clearly, there's a vast difference between our experience, and that of believers around the world who stand to lose more than employment opportunities, tax breaks, the respect of the mainstream media, or friends on social media. How do we take *that* into account?

I think there are two simplistic extremes to avoid when answering this. The first extreme comes from the relative lack of *physical* persecution in the West. Keen to find relevance in this key Scriptural theme, every time someone says something a bit mean about God or Christians we make a big song-and-dance about how we're a persecuted people. We end up redefining persecution as having hurt feelings.

The second extreme is the opposite reaction. It comes from reading the descriptions of persecution recorded in the New Testament, and from hearing stories of the Persecuted Church today: beatings, imprisonment, torture, and execution. We compare that with our own "suffering" for Jesus and realize that we haven't got it that bad after all—which is perfectly true! So we then decide that the persecution texts aren't really for us, *and how dare we* even breathe the "p-word" about ourselves when people in other times and places have died for their faith!

While this shows a proper respect for those who undergo severe suffering for the name of Jesus, it misses a few important things. Firstly, it suggests that the significant percentage of the New Testament which speaks about persecution has nothing much to say to us, beyond praying for our persecuted brothers and sisters. Secondly, it forgets that most of the original readers of the New Testament writings didn't suffer the fate of Stephen and subsequent martyrs. They weren't beaten or imprisoned or killed, but they still suffered ongoing marginalization and social exclusion (e.g. "publicly exposed to insult" in Heb 10:33; or made "synagogue outcasts" in John 16:2).[11] And thirdly, it neglects the fact that the New Testament is more concerned with the perceived *shamefulness* of being persecuted, rather than the severity of the suffering involved (although that was, of course, linked). Even in the Gospels' descriptions of Jesus' death, it's the shamefulness of crucifixion that's emphasized.

So as we read these texts, let's keep a balanced perspective. We're not enduring adversity anywhere near the extent to which many first century

---

11. DeSilva, *Honor, Patronage*, 44.

Christians did. But we *are* experiencing social shaming and exclusion, as we increasingly become the "repugnant cultural other" in the eyes of the majority. Our ability to articulate our beliefs publicly without fear of consequence is slowly being eroded,[12] and we're incrementally being pushed to the margins of public discourse.

> Increasingly less and less of what we consider acceptable as a public apologetic is accepted by the public. And increasingly the orthodox Christian frame is seen not only as odd, but bad.[13]

What's more, it's all happening *unevenly*, so that anyone seeking to dismiss this notion could point to any number of individual instances of where Christians can still speak with freedom and influence. But the trajectory of the past few decades is clear. As Lyndon Bowring, Executive Chairman of CARE, put it in an interview:

> The greatest challenge . . . is the growing secularization of society, where Christianity is being increasingly squeezed out of our national life. The ultimate result of this tendency will be a society that is hostile to Christian truth and practice.[14]

What we most frequently suffer for the sake of Jesus today is this loss of respect and a sense of being pushed slowly to the margins, becoming objects of ridicule and/or disgust. Therefore, I think it's better to see "persecution" on a continuum: from severe persecution and martyrdom at one end, to occasional social exclusion or shame on the other. One is far more severe than the other, of course, but the pattern is still the same. We're being *dishonored*, to some extent, because we're faithfully following Jesus—whether they're throwing rocks, as was the case with Stephen, or only throwing shade. So I prefer to use milder terms like "marginalization" and "exclusion" for what we suffer. Yet when the Bible talks about persecution, I see it speaking to that experience, too. After all, that was the experience of most of the first readers of the New Testament.

So how can we learn from their experience as a marginalized minority of aliens and exiles? That's what this book is about.

---

12. The extent to which we should expect this freedom from consequence is the subject of much debate. It's also not helped by those who articulate their beliefs in an insensitive manner, or quote Scripture in a rhetorical setting quite unlike its original.

13. McAlpine, "The Beguiling Technicolor of OZ," 6.

14. Bowring, "At the heart of CARE," *Care Today* 20 (2010) 4, cited in Chester and Timmis, *Everyday Church*, 20.

*Part 1*

# Minority-Group Rhetoric and the New Testament

# 1

## The Need for Attractive Difference

THE PREVIOUS INTRODUCTORY CHAPTER made an assumption: that being in a minority group is a problem. Or perhaps more accurately, that being in a group whose key values are perceived as being out of step, or even at odds with the majority culture at the very least presents a difficulty that needs to be addressed, if indeed the group is to survive. In other words, we've assumed that minority group rhetoric exists to meet a very real need.

In this chapter we'll justify that assumption, looking firstly at *why* being in a minority group is a problem—both in the first-century world of the New Testament and in our own. And secondly, we'll see how minority groups typically respond to their minority status, using some insights from the social sciences. In some respects this will be the most technical chapter, but stick with it, as it lays the foundation for the "why" and "how" of the minority group rhetoric we find in the New Testament.[1]

### The first-century sense of self

If the Western world in the twenty first century truly believed its own rhetoric about morality and self-image, being part of a minority group wouldn't present a significant problem for our sense of identity. We're told to be true to ourselves, march to the beat of our own drum, and deal with any disapproval that might come our way in a manner that's at once philosophical and dismissive: "haters gonna hate . . . I'm just gonna shake it off."[2] While this observation is clearly simplistic and only presents one side of a more complex cultural narrative (more on this shortly), there *is* a significant

---

1. Much of this chapter and the next is an expansion of the material in my previously published chapter, "Aliens and Strangers," 302–05.

2. Taylor Swift, *Shake it off* (Kobalt Music Publishing, 2014). Apologies if you've now got that tune stuck in your head.

kernel of truth here, in that our sense of identity and morality is primarily *internal* and *individualistic*. We don't perceive ourselves as being dependent on others in order to understand who we are or how we ought to behave: *I* think, therefore *I* am.[3] But this is the exact opposite of how it was in the first-century world within which the New Testament was written.

To those in the ancient Mediterranean world—and in many other collectivist cultures both past and present—the individual finds his or her identity not from within but in relationship with others in the wider group. Bruce Malina describes this as a "dyadic" or "collectivistic" sense of self, in which individuals "perceive themselves and form their self-image in terms of what others perceive and feed back to them."[4] They are, in a sense, defined by the sum of their relationships; their identity is primarily the identity of the group and their role within it.

We sometimes see this reflected in the ordering of a person's names in different cultures. Coming from an individualistic culture, my given name is primary—I perceive myself as "Tim," and add the surname "MacBride" as one way of distinguishing myself from other Tims in the world; I'm the Tim who belongs to the MacBride family. In strongly collectivist cultures, the name order—and associated self-understanding—is often reversed. I would first and foremost be "MacBride" (particularly in my dealings with the outside world), and add my given name if I needed to specify which member within the family. In other words, group identity is primary.[5]

Related to this is where we derive our sense of morality: what constitutes right behavior. In our individualistic culture, our conscience is generally spoken of as being located *within* us; an internal sense of right and wrong. But in a collectivist society, this conscience is *external* and derives from the reference group of those around us. As Malina points out, the Greek and Latin words for "conscience" (*syneidēsis* and *conscientia*) are both formed from the words for "together with" and "knowledge." In other words, knowledge of right and wrong comes from making judgments *together with* others, and is then internalized.[6]

In fact, it's probably more accurate to describe this as the knowledge of what's considered honorable and what's considered shameful. This is because we're not talking so much about an abstract right-and-wrong as the expectations of a particular external reference group to whom an individual

---

3. Descartes' expression, in *Principia Philosophiae* (1634): 30–31, is foundational for the Western view of the self.

4. Malina, *The New Testament World*, 62.

5. *The New Testament World*, 63.

6. *The New Testament World*, 58–59.

belongs. That group will honor those who do what the group expects and shame those who deviate from those expectations. Behavior is judged not by an individual's own internal sense of right and wrong, or by some abstract moral code, but by the opinion of the group—the "court of reputation" as it's often been called.[7] It was thought of not in terms of *doing what is right*, but as *doing what is seen to be honorable*.

What's more, in a collectivist, "honor-shame" society, family honor is seen as the supreme good—more important than wealth, health, or even one's own life.[8] It's the irreducible foundation of human behavior,[9] with men expected to compete for it in the public sphere and women to preserve honor within the family. Exclusion from the family or, in extreme cases, honor killings are an attempt to avoid the dishonor brought by the behavior of one member being ascribed to the whole. Being adjudged to be honorable in one's court of reputation—or rather, being part of a *group* adjudged to be honorable—was the goal.

Now to be fair, this isn't entirely alien to our own culture. Although we're *told* to embrace our individuality and shake off the haters, we still look to various courts of reputation for their feedback on how we should see ourselves (although we do so primarily as individuals seeking individual identity). Early in life, our parents are our court of reputation, which slowly expands to include teachers, peers, and the wider culture. We, too, develop our *con*-science *with* others, even if we perceive it to be located within and consider it "my" conscience rather than "ours."

In recent years, social media has encouraged a more dyadic sense of self, in which "likes" are the new currency of honor for which we are to compete, and the entire world has been opened up as our potential court of reputation. Its 24/7 availability has also increased the amount of time per day children and teens can be exposed to this wider court of reputation—at the expense of the mostly more forgiving judgments of their family—undoubtedly contributing to the reported increased levels of social anxiety.[10] What's more, everything is subject to being instantly rated by everyone—whether they be contestants on reality TV shows, local

---

7. Pitt-Rivers, "Honor and Shame," 35. See also DeSilva, *Honor, Patronage*, 25.

8. See Isocrates, *Ad Demonicum* 43, "Strive by all means to live in security, but if ever it falls to your lot to face the dangers of battle, seek to preserve your life, but with honor and not with disgrace; for death is the sentence which fate has passed on all mankind, but to die nobly is the special honor which nature has reserved for the good."

9. See Seneca, *De beneficiis* 4.16.2, "All our arguments start from this settled point, that honor is pursued for no reason except because it is honor."

10. Sales, *American Girls*, 10, 62–63. For a comprehensive review of the impact of social media on the mental health of teens, see Twenge, *iGen*, 93–118.

restaurants, or even the users of ride-share services—the judgments of which are publicly available in real-time and difficult to expunge. Perhaps the most extreme example (admittedly from a more collectivist culture) is the social credit score being implemented by the Chinese government, which is essentially an attempt to centrally control and administer the honor-shame system on a grand scale.[11]

What I'm saying is, the elements of the ancient Mediterranean honor-shame world are familiar enough to us—it's just that we find them to a far greater extent in the first century. Now, as then, there is pressure to live in tune with the values of our court of reputation. (This, by the way, is one place a key connection can be built between the audience of the New Testament texts and our own, laying the foundation for how these texts might speak into our own situation, too.)

So what happens when someone belongs to a group with a different idea of what's honorable from that of the wider culture? What happens when courts of reputation clash?

## Competing courts of reputation

The short answer is: conflict.[12] Since honor is the supreme good, when a minority group has significantly different criteria for judging what is honorable, conflict is inevitable. The dominant culture sees the group's existence as a threat to its own honor, as long as the minority group continues to be seen as belonging to the wider group. For this reason it will try to shame the deviant group back into conformity using different forms of social pressure—ridicule, exclusion, loss of employment, loss of inheritance, etc.. It might also escalate into exile, forcing the group to physically relocate; or even outright persecution, imprisoning or killing group members.[13]

For its part, the minority group might respond to this pressure by giving in, so that the group either redefines its values to be more amenable to the wider culture or disbands entirely. Or it might respond in the opposite way, forming strategies to help withstand the social shaming and exclusion,

---

11. https://chinacopyrightandmedia.wordpress.com/2014/06/14/planning-outline-for-the-construction-of-a-social-credit-system-2014-2020/. This official document describes the purpose of the system in honor-shame terms as the creation of an "atmosphere in the entire society that *keeping trust* is *glorious* and breaking trust is *disgraceful*" (italics mine).

12. Moxnes, "Honor and Shame," 26–27.

13. Sound familiar? It's much like the social pressure described in Heb 10:32–34.

reframing and redefining the issue to maintain its sense of honor. In this second case, minority group rhetoric is born.

Prior to New Testament times, Jews in the diaspora found themselves in this aliens-and-exiles situation. Living by Torah maintained honor within their minority Jewish culture, but would frequently invite contempt from and exclusion by the Gentile majority culture.[14] Indeed, the Levitical food laws made some form of social exclusion inevitable by design (cf. Lev 20:22–26). Many Jewish writings from this time urged their readers to choose rightly. For example, the writer of 2 Maccabees condemns the abandonment of temple and sacrificial observance by the high priest in favor of Hellenistic pursuits such as athletic contests and the gymnasium as:

> disdaining the honors prized by their ancestors and putting the highest value upon Greek forms of prestige. For this reason heavy disaster overtook them, and those whose ways of living they admired and wished to imitate completely became their enemies and punished them. (2 Macc 4:15-16)[15]

In other words, selling out to the majority culture is both dishonorable and, ultimately, short-sighted. This is minority group rhetoric.

In the Greco-Roman world, Cynic philosophers *invited* this kind of treatment. They deliberately rejected public opinion as a source of honor and identity. And in the great tradition of philosophers who embodied their teaching, they adopted unconventional lifestyles to demonstrate it: to the extent of urinating, defaecating, and copulating in public.[16] These days, of course, we call them footballers,[17] but in the ancient world it was fueled not so much by testosterone and alcohol as by a deliberate rejection of the public court of reputation and the honor-shame system it policed. For example, when the Cynic Antisthenes was applauded in public he is said to have remarked, "I am horribly afraid I have done something wrong."[18] Socrates, upon being mocked and kicked in the marketplace for his views, similarly despised the court of public opinion by saying, "If an

---

14. DeSilva, *Honor, Patronage*, 39, cites as examples of this attitude Josephus *Against Apion* 2.121, 258; Tacitus *Histories* 5.1–5; Juvenal *Satires* 14.100–104; Diodorus of Sicily *Bibliotheca historica* 34.1–4; 40.3.4.

15. *Honor, Patronage*, 39–40. He also cites Sirach, the Wisdom of Solomon, and 4 Maccabees as examples of this rhetoric.

16. De Botton, *Status Anxiety*, 119–20.

17. I have in view Australian Rugby League players, for whom this describes a typical night out. I'll leave it to readers from other countries to determine its appropriateness for players from similar sports.

18. Diogenes Laërtius, *Life of Antisthenes*, 4.

ass had kicked me, would I bring an action against him?"[19] Again, these are micro-examples of minority group rhetoric, overturning the conventional narrative of public honor.

Followers of Jesus in the first century were in a similar position. They faced potential disapproval and persecution from two main sources: Judaism and the Roman Empire.

Firstly, Jewish believers were shamed by their fellow Jews for a variety of reasons, the most obvious being the shameful manner of Jesus' death (cf. Deut 21:23). But his radical reinterpretation of Torah wouldn't have gone down well either, especially when it related to Sabbath observance (e.g., Mark 2:28), purity laws (Mark 7:8, 18), and the Temple (Mark 11:15–17).[20] What's more, the inclusion of Gentiles into the Jesus movement—without requiring them to be circumcised or obey the Law of Moses—was a source of dishonor for Jewish believers. It led to attempts to remove this source of dishonor by withdrawing from table fellowship (Gal 2:12), or requiring Gentiles to be circumcised and obey Torah (Gal 2:14) in order to maintain group honor and avoid shame (Gal 6:12–13).[21] Thus from the Galatian letter, we see that opposition from within Judaism also impacted not just Jewish believers but Gentile converts.

Secondly, Jesus' death would also have been considered shameful in the wider, Greco-Roman world, since the manner of a person's death was viewed as the judgment of the gods upon their life. For this reason, the New Testament writers frequently seek to reinterpret this as being an heroic death on behalf of others—a great virtue in Greco-Roman society.[22] Believers were also treated with suspicion and disapproval because they refused to participate in the worship of the pantheon of pagan gods and goddesses, leaving themselves open to the charge of being "atheists." This was about more than just holding some unconventional beliefs about divine beings; participation in pagan worship was seen as "doing your civic duty" so that the gods would continue to act favorably toward everyone. Failing to do this

---

19. Diogenes Laërtius, *Life of Socrates*, 3.

20. Note how each of these examples, from Mark's "Gentile" Gospel, is softened in its stance toward the law when redacted in Matthew's "Jewish" Gospel: Matt 12:3–8 contains both mitigating circumstances for the disciples' breaking of the Sabbath and Old Testament precedent, and omits the radical statement about the Sabbath's being created for humans; Matt 15:10–19 gives a reason to ignore the Pharisees' opposition and omits the parenthetical comment about "declaring all foods clean"; in Matt 21:13 the portion of the Isaiah quote about the Temple as a house of prayer "for all nations" is omitted. In both cases the audience's court of reputation is a factor in whether discontinuity or continuity with Judaism is highlighted.

21. See DeSilva, *Honor, Patronage*, 48–49.

22. Danker, *Benefactor*, 321–23, 417–35.

had the potential to bring dishonor to the city, or even the whole empire.[23] In the same way, when followers of Jesus refused to participate in emperor-worship—and instead proclaimed Jesus as the rightful ruler over the whole world—it was viewed as a threat to the stability of society and the Roman peace under which it prospered.[24]

Thus the church, right from the start, found itself under all kinds of pressure to give up its distinctive claims and values. Its very existence was a threat to the honor of the larger group—whether Judaism or the Empire—and conflict was inevitable.

## Minority group responses

So how does a "religious" minority group like this respond? We'll look at this question firstly in the abstract, with the help of some social-scientific models. In the next chapter, we'll then use this as a basis for working out how the early church responded in the pages of the New Testament.

## Sect development

Bryan Wilson, in his pioneering study of how religious minority groups develop, categorized such groups by how they respond to their minority status in relation to the wider world. According to this model, a sect like the early church has essentially three options, given its lack of size and limited access to positions of power. The default is to slowly assimilate to the dominant culture, giving up its distinctiveness in exchange for more peaceful relations with the wider world. But this isn't compatible with allegiance to Jesus as the one true God who alone is worthy of worship. A second option is isolation, in which the group avoids contact with the dominant culture as much as possible, similar to the wilderness-dwelling Jewish groups such as the Essenes and the Qumran community. It may be a viable way of minimizing persecution and dishonor, effectively cutting themselves off from the majority group, but it's incompatible with being a "conversionist sect" like the church, as Wilson describes them[25]—a group whose very reason for existence is to make more followers of Jesus (Matt 28:18–20). To do this they need to remain in contact with the wider world.

---

23. See, for example, Isocrates, *Ad Demonicum* 13; Plutarch, *Moralia* 1125E; a fuller discussion can be found in MacMullen, *Paganism in the Roman Empire*, 40, 62–73.

24. DeSilva, *Honor, Patronage*, 45–48.

25. Wilson, "Sect Development," 10.

So there's only one true option left for a conversionist minority group, but it's the most difficult path to follow. This is because it involves balancing competing principles of being open to the world while maintaining a strong group identity, without lapsing into the (simpler) extremes of isolation or assimilation. In other words, the rhetoric of the group has to perform two competing functions.

The first function is to draw a boundary between the group and the wider world. Wilson describes it in this way:

> If the sect is to persist as an organization it must not only separate its members from the world, but must also maintain the dissimilarity of its values from those of the secular society. Its members must not normally be allowed to accept the values of the status system of the external world. The sect must see itself as marginal to the wider society . . . [and] the consciousness of the inapplicability of the standards of the outside world must be retained . . . Status must be status within the sect, and this should be the only group to which the status-conscious individual makes reference.[26]

The second function is to make this boundary permeable; that is, to make it as easy as possible for an outsider to become a member of the group. However, the group's minority status and perceived shamefulness in the eyes of the majority culture makes it a difficult sell.[27] To overcome this, the group needs to portray the values and behaviors that make them distinctive in ways outsiders will find attractive; their very distinctiveness is used to win converts.[28] In short, they need to be *attractively different*.

But it's a difficult balancing act. As Wilson concludes, "for each sect there must be a position of optimal tension, where any greater degree of hostility against the world portends direct conflict, and any less suggests accommodation to worldly values."[29] So how does such a minority group go about this? How does it maintain its distinctiveness in a way that not only ensures the survival of the group, but also increases attractiveness to outsiders?

---

26. "Sect Development," 12–13.
27. "Sect Development," 13.
28. Elliott, *A Home for the Homeless*, 108.
29. Wilson, "Sect Development," 12.

## Social Identity Theory

One helpful model is Henri Tajfel's "Social Identity Theory," looking at how persecuted or marginalized minority groups tend to respond to their inferior status if they are to withstand the pressure to assimilate to the majority culture. Some are clearly not options that were open to the early church: they were too small for a program of passive resistance to have any effect; violent revolution was not in keeping with how Jesus taught the kingdom would come; and stressing their superiority to a group that was even lower in the social hierarchy was completely at odds with the upside-down kingdom they were proclaiming. Others, however, are more instructive.

Firstly, there's a tendency for minority groups to redefine the basis of comparison so that it's more favorable to the group. Tajfel cites a series of social experiments run at a summer camp in which one group of boys was placed in clearly inferior accommodation. To compensate, the boys built a garden, and then proceeded to include the garden in their evaluation of the accommodation options.[30] While the early church didn't build any gardens that we know of, they *did* frequently point to the honor they were storing up in heaven for the age to come (e.g., 1 Pet 1:4), which needed to be included in any calculation (e.g., Rom 8:18).

Secondly, there's a tendency to redefine what had previously been viewed as a negative into a positive. Philip Esler cites as a prime example the 1960s slogan "black is beautiful."[31] At a high school near me, teachers encouraged a culture of taking their final year studies seriously by launching a (successful) #nerdherd campaign that redefined the concept of "nerd" as honorable in the teenage world.[32] In the early church we could point to Paul's redefinition of the shameful "foolishness of the cross" as being "the power of God" (1 Cor 1:18–30) in which one could ironically "boast" (Gal 6:14).[33]

These two strategies will be of great significance in how we understand and adapt the minority group rhetoric of the New Testament.

---

30. Tajfel, "Group Differentiation," 96–97.
31. Esler, "Social Identity Theory," 22.
32. www.theeducatoronline.com/k12/news/never-become-complacent-principal-shares-hsc-success-story/210163. I can't believe it worked, either.
33. Moxnes, "Honor and Shame," 27.

## Social Categorization Theory

John Turner's "Social Categorization Theory" takes this a step further, discerning two processes that are involved when such groups form their shared identity.

Firstly, there is "self-categorization," in which individuals perceive greater similarities between themselves and other group members than exist between themselves and those outside the group.[34] This doesn't have to be the reality, just the perception, which is why minority group rhetoric will focus on those characteristics that are more likely to be shared by the group and not the wider culture. Over time, group members internalize what they perceive to be the shared characteristics of the group.[35]

This leads to the second process of "depersonalization," in which group members start to see themselves as a stereotypical and, to some extent, *interchangeable* example of their group.[36] They don't (necessarily) lose their individual identity in this process; rather, they gain a new social identity.[37] Minority group rhetoric thus seeks to build a sense of group identity.

For these process to form an effective minority group, a third factor also needs to be present: something Turner calls "salience."[38] That is, group members need to perceive that this set of shared group characteristics—this group identity—is important and relevant enough to have an effect on their behavior.[39] It answers the question: *why is group membership so important right now?* When group membership is perceived as salient, it leads to increased commitment to group values, a common perception of the world, and greater cooperation between group members.

We can imagine how all this might have happened in the #nerdherd example from my local high school, mentioned above. Students who wanted to perform well in their final exams started to see a commonality with other, likeminded students (despite their many differences), beginning to self-categorize as a member of the nerdherd. By internalizing the behaviors a stereotypical nerdherd member might exhibit—like meeting in lunchtime study groups, handing work in on time, and getting enough sleep—they slowly became a stereotype themselves. (As part of the campaign, each student had their photo on a poster around the school attached to a positive

---

34. Turner et al., *Rediscovering the Social Group*, 51.
35. Esler, "Social Identity Theory," 24.
36. Turner et al., *Rediscovering the Social Group*, 50.
37. Esler, "Social Identity Theory," 25.
38. Turner et al., *Rediscovering the Social Group*, 54.
39. Esler, "Social Identity Theory," 25.

affirmation about academic achievement, providing a visual reminder of their role as interchangeable exemplar.) Without losing their individuality, they gained the social identity of the nerdherd. And all this happened because students acutely felt its salience—the pressure and significance of their final exams—leading to more strongly-held values and cooperation across the year group.

There are, of course, some dangers in all of this. When group members start to evaluate themselves and others in the group against the characteristics that have become prototypical for the group,[40] it can have the positive effect of encouraging group members to live up to group values. However, it can also provide an arena in which to compete with one another for status within the group—something Paul had to address in Corinth.

Similarly, when group members discuss values and behaviors—a regular feature of minority group rhetoric—it's been shown to increase polarization.[41] Positively, this increases adherence to group values. It was the function of what the ancients called *epideictic,* or "display" rhetoric: praising people and values deemed honorable, and shaming those that were not, in order to reinforce commonly-held values and goals and provide "cultural or group cohesion."[42] Negatively, however, it can also increase alienation from and even hostility toward the wider world, breeding a kind of "reverse elitism" that undermines the attractiveness of the group's difference.

Finally, it should be noted that forming and maintaining group identity is enhanced by placing the group within history. Condor notes that "group identities are nourished by collective memory" and that "groups plan for the future and the challenges and opportunities it will bring."[43] As we'll see throughout this book, both the shared heritage of the past (e.g., Heb 11) and the envisioned eschatological future of the people of God (e.g., Rev 7) are fundamental to the New Testament's minority group rhetoric.

These, then, are the building-blocks of minority group rhetoric; the strategies by which group boundaries are drawn, yet made permeable. Let's now turn to the pages of the New Testament to see how the writers used them to encourage God's exiled people to be attractively different.

---

40. Turner et al., *Rediscovering the Social Group,* 57.
41. Esler, "Social Identity Theory," 33.
42. Kennedy, "Genres of Rhetoric," 45.
43. Condor, "Social Identity and Time," 302–3.

# 2

## Maintaining Attractive Difference

Be attractively different.

As we've seen in the previous chapter, that's the only long-term, viable strategy for a minority group (like ours) that wishes to survive *and* win new converts. We need to draw a boundary between us and the wider society, yet make that boundary permeable—so that we have a clear and distinctive identity on the one hand, but remain accessible to the rest of the world on the other. That's the tension that needs to be worked out in our rhetoric—in how we preach and how we talk among ourselves.

This is where we look to the New Testament for guidance. Because this is the situation into which each of the authors wrote, seeking to persuade their audience to live out this *attractive difference*. How did they go about it, and how might we follow their lead in how we apply Scripture to ourselves and in our preaching?

Before we look at the New Testament writings individually, this chapter will give us the overview.[1] It will provide us with the lens through which we'll be reading the rest of the New Testament. It's not the only lens, of course, but one that will focus our attention on the minority group strategies used by the biblical authors.

To be more accurate, it provides us with six separate, yet related lenses in the form of six key questions. These were the questions that the early Christians needed to address if they were to be a minority group that was attractively different:

1. **Approval**: Whose opinions do we care about (and whose opinions can we ignore)?
2. **Disapproval**: Why can we ignore those who disapprove of us?

---

1. Along with the previous chapter, this chapter is an expansion of the material in my "Aliens and Strangers," 305–12.

3. **Identity**: Who are we? Why are we distinctive?
4. **Practice**: How do we live? What do we *do* that makes us distinctive?
5. **Worldview**: How do we see the world, and how does that differ from the majority?
6. **Salience**: Why is group membership so important right now?

We met them briefly in the introductory chapter. Now, we're going to explore them in a bit more detail, asking how the New Testament writers addressed them in *their* context, as well as how we might follow their approach in our own context. (In this chapter, a handful New Testament examples will be given to illustrate each concept sufficiently; more comprehensive examples will be given in later chapters as we deal with each of the writers individually.)

## Approval: Whose opinions do we care about?

As we saw in the previous chapter, no matter what culture we belong to, our self-image depends—at least in part—on what others think of us. In the collectivist culture of the New Testament world, this was particularly acute; but even in a Western, individualistic society the opinions of others can't easily be ignored. And this has increased exponentially in the age of social media: not only are we exposed to the opinions and judgments of others with far greater volume and diversity than before, the design of the platforms themselves encourages us to see ourselves as the sum of our "likes."[2] Whether we live in the ancient Mediterranean world or in today's global village, the way we see ourselves is greatly influenced by the way others see us—by our "court of reputation."[3]

That's why it's not enough for members of a minority group simply to be told to ignore the disapproval of the wider community and live by their own rules and sense of what is right. Their court of reputation needs to be redefined.[4] For the early Christian believers, this meant excluding the dominant culture, which could well have included their family and friends, as well as synagogue communities, Greco-Roman *collegia*, and other social groupings. Much of the minority group rhetoric in the New Testament is about replacing

---

2. It's a welcome development that during the period of writing of this book, platforms like Instagram and Facebook have experimented with removing the visible "like" counter for other people's posts due to the harm such comparisons have caused.
3. See discussion in chapter 1.
4. DeSilva, *Honor, Patronage*, 40.

the usual members of that court with the only sources of opinion that truly count: namely, God, and the people who belong to him.

## God's approval

The central figure of any Christian's court of reputation ought to be God himself. This should be obvious—and it is—but time and time again the New Testament reminds its audience of this fact because the competition is so loud and pervasive. The dominant culture sees itself as the chief arbiter of honorable behavior and resists any competition for the title. This is compounded by the fact that, much of the time, its values and worldview are diametrically opposed to God's. Members of a minority group need regular reminders of why their court of reputation needs to be different. The New Testament does this frequently, reminding believers of how God's values are starkly different from those of the world,[5] and giving reasons to seek God's approval rather than the world's.

Firstly, God is presented as the one who's truly in charge of the world, even if Rome and its emperors might think otherwise. It's why Paul describes Jesus in the savior-benefactor language normally used for the emperor (e.g., Titus 2:11–14).[6] It's why Luke narrates the spread of the apostles' witness throughout the Roman world as being through divine providence, with all human authorities—both Jewish and Roman—unable to thwart God's purposes (cf. Gamaliel's sage advice in Acts 5:38–39). And it's why John gets invited through a door in the heavens to come and see the world as it truly is: with God enthroned as the true emperor and all of the created order—apart from that beastly Roman empire, whose days are numbered anyway—giving him the worship and honor he deserves (e.g., Rev 4). The book of Revelation, in graphic terms, sends the message that *God* is in charge of this world, not some jumped-up pretender in a toga with some dead leaves on his head. Therefore, *God* should be the one whose opinion we care about; he should be the center of our court of reputation.

Secondly, God is not only in charge of the world, he's also the one who's going to judge it. While the judgments of the dominant culture may seem more relevant *right now*, the New Testament writers urge their audiences to reposition the debate to include *future* judgment that will last into eternity.[7] Or to put it in terms of the summer camp experiment from chapter 1: they are to include in their comparison the eternal garden of the Lord, not just

---

5. *Honor, Patronage*, 57.
6. Danker, *Benefactor*, 330.
7. DeSilva, *Honor, Patronage*, 55.

the temporary cabins we live in now (cf. 2 Cor 5). Since God's judgments are eternal, seeking his approval is presented as being *advantageous* in the end. This is the essence of deliberative rhetoric,[8] which urges its audience to action because it will be to their (ultimate) advantage.[9] The majority of the epistles in the New Testament are deliberative in character, contrasting the temporary disadvantage of being a marginalized minority *now* with the eternal advantage that awaits (e.g., 1 Pet 1:4–6; Heb 11:26; 12:2; 1 John 2:17).

Further, it follows that since God is in charge, those who seek *his* approval have a sure hope of vindication in the future. The New Testament frequently speaks of God's faithfulness to his people (e.g., 2 Tim 2:11–13; 1 Pet 2:23), promising future vindication in the sight of those who now shame them (e.g., Phil 1:28; 1 Pet 2:12; Rev 3:9). Not only that, he also has the power to sustain them while they wait (e.g., 1 Cor 1:8; Jude 24).[10]

## The approval of God's people

While having God as their court of reputation should be *enough*, the New Testament writers don't leave it there. In addition, they present the community of faith as another reference group for a believer's sense of honor. This is important, as it gives an "embodied other" to replace those who have been removed from the believer's court of reputation. As deSilva puts it, they are "the most visible and, in many senses, the most available reflection of God's estimation of the individual."[11] Particularly in a collectivist culture, having a community of people who share the same counter-cultural values is vital in order to survive. It reminds group members that they aren't alone, and gives them a place of safety and encouragement whenever they face rejection (e.g., Heb 10:24–25; 13:1–3). It provides a community that bases its evaluations on the same things God includes: the eschatological garden rather than the temporal cabins. It can even provide a new family for those whose biological family has cut them off because of their "dishonorable" association with Jesus; when Jesus is rejected by *his* family, he redefines his familial court of reputation as those around him whose values are in line with God's:

8. The three types of Greco-Roman rhetoric were *forensic* (which grew out of the law courts and focused on proving or disproving allegations about the past), *epideictic* (which accompanied civic occasions and sought to praise those who were worthy of honor in the present), and *deliberative* (which arose out of the city councils and attempted to persuade hearers to adopt a future course of action based on advantage).

9. Aristotle, *Ars rhetorica*, 1.3.5.

10. Elliott, "The Jewish Messianic Movement," 88.

11. DeSilva, *Honor, Patronage*, 58–59.

Pointing to his disciples, he said, "Here are my mother and my brothers. For whoever does the will of my Father in heaven is my brother and sister and mother." (Matt 12:49–50)

To give a contemporary example, a friend works in an environment that he describes as hostile to followers of Jesus. It's an all-male workplace surrounded by posters of cars and scantily-clad women, supporting a culture that judges people according to the car they drive and their sexual conquests. He attributes his survival as a Christian to his home Bible study group, which has provided him with that alternative frame of reference—a different court of reputation—by which he can be reminded of who he is and why he lives differently. He says that the times he's been seduced by the dominant culture in his workplace are the times he hasn't prioritized regular contact with that alternative court of reputation.

From Social Categorization Theory (see chapter 1), we could add that it's not just the existence of people who embody God's different values, but the fact that as a group they share a view on what is *prototypical* for a group member.[12] This means that even though each group member won't always live up to God's ideals, they nevertheless evaluate themselves—and the others within the group—according to how well they meet this ideal Jesus-following prototype. Indeed, Jesus has provided them with this prototypical example, explicitly inviting people to pattern their lives after him: "follow me" is an invitation to more than just a literal journey. Afterwards, Paul showed how believers ought to be patterns for each other:

Follow my example, as I follow the example of Christ. (1 Cor 11:1)

Join together in following my example, brothers and sisters, and just as you have us as a model, keep your eyes on those who live as we do. (Phil 3:17)[13]

## Preaching that redefines our court of reputation

In sum, the question "whose opinions do we care about?" is given the simple answer: *God, and the community that belongs to him.* Weekly preaching to a congregation is, in essence, a regular reminder of this redefined court of reputation. The *content* of this preaching should reinforce for members of our minority group that God is in charge, his judgments are the only ones that

---

12. Turner et al., *Rediscovering the Social Group*, 57.
13. See also 1 Thess 1:7, and the implicit examples of Timothy and Epaphroditus in Phil 2:19–30.

endure, and he has promised us vindication when he acts in judgment. That is, it reminds us of the eternal advantage to be found in resisting the pressure to conform to the world around us. Further, the *setting* of this preaching should be a reminder that there are other people who share this worldview, who evaluate themselves according to the same standard, and who seek to emulate the same prototype. Weekly preaching should be, at its heart, minority group rhetoric that reinforces the audience's court of reputation.

This would be all the more powerful if, as preachers, we recognized that this is inherent—and quite often explicit—in the New Testament texts from which we preach. We would then be more likely to notice the strategies being used, and preach accordingly. Just to give a few examples:

- We might look at the context of statements about God's sovereignty to see what the biblical author wants us to "do" with it. Is it an abstract theological statement to which we ought to give mental assent? Or does it (also) function as a reminder to place God at the center of our court of reputation?

- We might preach texts about judgment or reward as an appeal to eschatological advantage (i.e. God's approval in the future) and an explicit repositioning of the debate from where the world wants it to take place (i.e. its approval in the present), rather than as a means of criticizing outsiders to their face—something that's rarely the function of New Testament rhetoric.

- We might use passages about future vindication and glory to address present feelings of marginalization and shame, as a way of keeping the dominant culture out of our court of reputation—yet without it devolving into the *unattractive* difference of triumphalist judgmentalism (see below).

- We might highlight not only biblical examples, but also "those who live as we do" (Phil 3:17) in our own communities as a way of encouraging prototypical group characteristics that function as a court of reputation.

In other words, we look for the rhetorical strategies in the biblical text that address Christians *as a minority group* and adapt them for our own audience.[14]

---

14. This is part of a wider philosophy of preaching that not only reflects the content of the biblical text, but the function. See my *Catching the Wave*, as well as Craddock, *Preaching*, 28; Quicke, *360-Degree Preaching*, 131; and more recently, Kuruvilla, *A Manual for Preaching*, 27–48, 266–68; Chan, *Preaching as the Word of God*.

## Disapproval: Whose opinions can we ignore?

This second strategy is the flip-side to the first. Redefining a minority group's court of reputation helps to insulate the group from outside pressure, but it can't stop them hearing the disapproving voices that come from the majority culture. To survive, a minority group must find a way of reinterpreting the disapproval of outsiders and giving reasons the group can—and should—ignore it.

## Disapproval is a sign you're on the right track

The fundamental reason the New Testament writers give for ignoring the disapproval that comes from the majority culture is that outsiders are *ignorant*. That is, they don't know God, nor do they share the values or worldview of the believing community; consequently, their behavior is also dishonorable.[15] The reason they disapprove is that they're living by a completely different set values that a follower of Jesus ought to find shameful.

The Apostle Peter takes us through the logic of this strategy:

> They are surprised that you do not join them in their reckless, wild living, and they heap abuse on you. (1 Pet 4:4)

But it's *their* behavior that will, in a "divine reversal,"[16] ultimately bring shame:

> But they will have to give account to him who is ready to judge the living and the dead. (1 Pet 4:5)

By contrast, believers have God as their court of reputation:

> They do not live the rest of their earthly lives for evil human desires, but rather for the will of God. (1 Pet 4:2)

So while outsiders might be surprised by the fact that the believing community lives differently, believers shouldn't be surprised at the opposition they face:

> Dear friends, do not be surprised at the fiery ordeal that has come on you to test you, as though something strange were happening to you. (1 Pet 4:12)

---

15. DeSilva, *Honor, Patronage*, 62–63.
16. Elliott, "Disgraced yet Graced," 172.

Rather, disapproval by outsiders should be viewed positively, as a sign of God's approval:

> If you are insulted because of the name of Christ, you are blessed, for the Spirit of glory and of God rests on you. (1 Pet 4:14)

I recall this strategy being deployed in Australian politics. Mark Latham—a former leader of the Australian Labor Party and a somewhat controversial figure—had just published his political diaries in which he unloaded on just about everyone in his former party. One Labor politician was asked, on camera, for his response to the criticism of him in the book. His reply: "If Mark Latham is criticizing me, it's a sign I must be doing something right." That's essentially the response the New Testament (particularly 1 Peter) encourages believers to have when they find themselves on the receiving end of disapproval and abuse from the wider society: *if those who don't know God and don't act his way disapprove of you, it's probably a sign you're on the right track!*

Indeed, the very fact that they were warned about it in advance reinforces the narrative of the minority group (e.g., John 15:18–25; 1 Pet 4:12; 1 John 3:13). In his study of the social world of the first Christians, Wayne Meeks puts it this way:

> If a sect expects the larger society to be hostile toward it, and if society obliges by attacking the sect, the experience is a very strong reinforcement of the group's boundaries . . . The convert who does eventually experience hostility, even in such mild forms as perhaps the jibes of friends and relatives, readily understands it as confirming the sect's picture of the way the world is.[17]

The rhetorical strategy is thus: *Jesus—and the rest of the New Testament writers—told us we'd face disapproval and look, they were right! So keep going, knowing that God's still got this under control.*

> So then, those who suffer according to God's will should commit themselves to their faithful Creator and continue to do good. (1 Pet 4:19)

---

17. Meeks, *The First Urban Christians*, 96.

### Disapproval is an opportunity

As well as being a sign of being on the right track, disapproval is also cast as an opportunity to display loyalty (e.g., 1 Pet 1:6–7).[18] After all, it's easy to claim to belong to a group when there's little or no cost involved. The true test comes when opposition arises, giving group members the chance to put their money where their mouth is, so to speak. The New Testament writers frequently describe the minority group's existence as a struggle or contest. Suffering disapproval should be seen not just as a necessary and expected evil to be endured; it should be welcomed as a chance to become "battle-hardened" and display courage and endurance.[19]

While seeing disapproval as an opportunity to display loyalty is common enough among minority groups, a uniquely *Christian* extension of this is understanding it as an opportunity to *endure shame* in imitation of Jesus.[20] In future chapters we'll see this theme emerge throughout the New Testament as the various authors encourage their audiences to a cruciform life. That is, a life in which the command to "deny themselves and take up their cross daily and follow me" (Luke 9:23) is primarily understood as embracing the *dishonor* experienced by the one they've followed, epitomized by the shameful manner of his death:

- Both Paul and Peter describe this variously as "imitation of," "sharing in," and "participation in" Christ's sufferings (e.g., 1 Thess 1:6–7; Rom 8:17; Phil 3:10–11; 1 Pet 4:13).
- In Acts, Luke notes how the apostles, after they had been flogged, went away "rejoicing because they had been counted worthy of suffering *disgrace* for the Name" (5:41). He goes on to narrate Stephen's martyrdom in a way that draws out the similarities with Jesus' own innocent death.
- In Hebrews, Jesus not only endures the shame of the cross but *despises it* (Heb 12:2). He rejects the validity of the court of reputation that judges it shameful—an attitude believers are exhorted to imitate, joining him "outside the camp" (Heb 13:13).
- The apocalyptic parable in Revelation 11 describes the martyrdom of the "two witnesses"—representing the church—in Jesus-like terms,

---

18. Elliott, "Disgraced yet Graced," 172.

19. DeSilva, *Honor, Patronage*, 68.

20. Elliott, "Disgraced yet Graced," 172. See also chapter 15 for some insights on how African-American believers have viewed suffering in this way.

including how the majority culture *dishonored* their corpses and rejoiced over their death.[21]

It's important to note that in each of these cases, not only is the suffering and shame experience reinterpreted as honorable, it's also linked with the promise of future vindication and honor (glory).[22] The rhetorical strategy can be summed up in this way: *Jesus suffered innocently, rejected the verdict of "shameful" meted out by the court of public opinion, and was ultimately vindicated by God through his resurrection and ascension; honorable followers of Jesus will do likewise, reinterpreting their own innocent suffering as honorable, and looking forward to their own vindication at the resurrection.*

## Conflict can be positive

In the previous chapter, we noted that whenever there are rival courts of reputation, conflict is inevitable. The majority culture will seek to shame the minority back into conformity through social and sometimes physical pressure. But this doesn't have to be an entirely negative development, depending on the response of the minority group.

Conflict can actually be good for the group, providing the impetus to set up clear boundaries between insiders and outsiders. This involves a reaffirmation of the group's identity, focusing on the differences between the values of the group and those of the majority culture,[23] which forms a clear "negative reference group" against which the minority can be distinguished.[24] Deviation from group values becomes more strictly monitored and enforced, as group structures tighten in the face of conflict and members become more accepting of internal discipline.[25] In other words, disapproval from the majority culture doesn't *necessarily* lead to pressure to conform. If handled correctly by the group, it can have the opposite effect. Conflict can harden resolve and bring into sharp focus the distinctiveness of the group, reminding members of the benefits of belonging—of how *attractive* their difference is.[26] It provides an opportunity: "Persecution will

---

21. See discussion on this text in chapter 8 for more details.

22. For a fuller discussion of this point, see my "Imitators of the Lord in Severe Suffering."

23. Coser, *The Functions of Social Conflict*, 38.

24. Elliott, *A Home for the Homeless*, 116.

25. Georg Simmel, "The Sociology of Conflict," trans. Kurt H. Wolff (Glencoe, IL: Free Press, 1955), *American Journal of Sociology* 9 (1903) 490–525, summarized in Elliott, *A Home for the Homeless*, 113.

26. Elliott, *A Home for the Homeless*, 114.

at times weaken affiliation to a religious group, but it can also confirm and reinforce the bonds between the persecuted faithful."[27] Minority group rhetoric uses the opportunity afforded by conflict and disapproval to focus the group on its distinctiveness.

Conflict can also have a positive effect on group unity as members are forced to cooperate more closely and rely on each other in the face of outside pressure and isolation.[28] This is why sports coaches and business managers take their teams on group bonding experiences, where they're taken out of their comfort zones and forced to rely on each other while they endure hardship and perform challenging tasks.[29] It's such a powerful phenomenon that some groups will exaggerate the external threat or even seek out conflict in order to assert control and build unity.[30] The writers of the New Testament don't invent threats and urge their audiences not to seek out conflict (e.g., 1 Tim 2:2; Heb 12:14; 1 Pet 2:12–13), but they do present the very real danger of persecution and marginalization in strong terms (e.g., Heb 2:1–3; 3:12–13; 1 Pet 2:11).

Conflict doesn't only help a group mark out its boundaries and define its differences from the wider world. It also provides opportunities for group members to have interactions with members of the majority culture in which the distinctives of the group are on the agenda. As Coser puts it, it "binds antagonists" so that "the stranger may become familiar through one's struggle with him."[31] In other words, it provides opportunities for evangelism in which group members might be well be asked to "give a reason for the hope that they have" (1 Pet 3:15).

This is an important point to grasp: minority group rhetoric doesn't just insulate the group against external disapproval; it's also a necessary step to making converts. When the dominant culture notices the minority because of its differences, *the minority has the opportunity to show just how attractive those differences are.*

---

27. Carrier, *The Sociology of Religious Belonging*, 218.
28. Von Harnack, *The Expansion of Christianity in the First Three Centuries*, 95.
29. The one team bonding adventure I was forced to endure ended up being quite effective, as the recently merged management group bonded over its dislike of the hapless instructor and gleeful subversion of every activity he set up.
30. Coser, *The Functions of Social Conflict*, 106.
31. *The Functions of Social Conflict*, 121–23.

## Preaching in the face of disapproval

Contemporary preaching perhaps needs to be reminded of this aspect of the New Testament's minority group rhetoric. It's an antidote by which to insulate our hearers from the disapproval of the wider society.[32] Except it needs to be done carefully. What we *don't* want is a return to the kind of preaching that gathered the faithful in order to vent our pious anger against the godless and corrupt world that exists "out there"—a world that wants to drag you and your children away from the faith, brainwashing you with its lies. We've had enough of that isolationist rhetoric that bears little resemblance to that of the New Testament.

However, we *do* need to be reminded of the significant differences that exist between the values of the secular culture in which we live, and the values of Jesus:

> And that is what some of you were. But you were washed, you were sanctified, you were justified in the name of the Lord Jesus Christ and by the Spirit of our God. (1 Cor 6:11)

> You are all children of the light and children of the day. We do not belong to the night or to the darkness. So then, let us not be like others, who are asleep, but let us be awake and sober. (1 Thess 5:5–6)

> As a result, they do not live the rest of their earthly lives for evil human desires, but rather for the will of God. (1 Pet 4:2)

This is the kind of difference of which we shouldn't be ashamed. And the recent increase in disapproval and marginalization we've seen has put some of those differences front-and-center in public discourse. This conflict gives us the opportunity not only to display our loyalty, to reaffirm our values, and to unite and organize in response to opposition—it also allows us to show how our differences are attractive.

For at least a few decades now, many churches have focused on minimizing the differences between the church and the world. Insofar as it removed unnecessary barriers put up by church culture, rather than by the content of the gospel itself, this has been a good thing. Indeed, such incarnational strategies are based on Paul's principle of becoming "all things to all people" (1 Cor 9:22), not wanting to place a cultural stumbling block in anyone's way (1 Cor 10:32–33). We've tried to send the message to the world, "hey, we're just like you, *but we've also got Jesus. Are you interested?*"

---

32. Material in this section is an expansion of some points I make in "Preaching to Aliens and Strangers," 10.

But there have been unintended consequences.

Firstly—and I think I've been guilty of this in the past—it's led to the naïve hope that if we just (a) get the marketing, sales pitch, and church "product" just right (for those with an "attractional" approach), or (b) deconstruct the church into the right model of authentic, organic faith communities (for those with a "missional" approach), then the world will finally be able to see the message of Jesus stripped of its "churchy" baggage and convert *en masse*. Now that's a bit of an exaggeration, I suppose. But for a while there it looked almost attainable—back when the main criticism of the church seemed to be that it was a bit outdated and quaint; or, at worst, irrelevant. Now, it seems, the world *has* seen that message and—to our great surprise—it's found the gospel offensive and our values subversive. This isn't a reason to retreat into a weird churchy ghetto once more. But it's shown that there's a limit both to how much we can minimize our differences from the world, and to what we can achieve by doing so.

Secondly, minimizing our differences may have encouraged Christians to hold a higher view of the surrounding culture than we should. Moreover, if we want to participate in public debate, we're subtly pressured into arguing within the pluralistic worldview of the dominant culture. We feel we need to adopt as our starting point the presumption that all cultures and worldviews are of equal worth, and all contain a similar degree of enlightenment. Now this is probably quite necessary in secular debates; indeed we see something of the kind modelled by Paul in Athens (Acts 17:16–34). But the danger comes when we begin to use this, even unconsciously, as a starting point for our own internal discussions of group identity and values. This is at odds with the Bible's teaching on fallen humanity and the complete "otherness" of God's wisdom that can only be understood with the help of his Spirit (1 Cor 2:11–14). We run the risk of giving implicit acceptance of some of the unbiblical assumptions of our culture, and so undermine our essential distinctiveness—or even faith itself.

This is not for a moment to allow even a hint of arrogance or disrespect toward the world to creep into our preaching (1 Pet 3:15), whether we're speaking with outsiders *or* insiders. (And in the days of podcast and livestreamed sermons, we're *always* in a place to be overheard by outsiders.) Nor is it a call to imitate the manner of some of the more confronting anti-majority rhetoric we find in the New Testament. Most of that is found within a culture of Asiatic rhetoric that expected bombast and personal attacks, and was delivered *in-house* for the consolation of a powerless, persecuted minority.[33] That's not appropriate for our context on both counts.

---

33. Esler, *The First Christians*, 14, notes that "the denunciation is for the benefit of

Rather, this is a call to preach in a way that prepares our congregation to counter the pluralistic assumptions of our age. We need to remind them of the reasons we can ignore both the world's opposition to God and his values, and resist the pressure it places on us to abandon—or at least "soft pedal"—what makes us different.

Again it needs to be stressed, *this is not just done to insulate ourselves from external pressure.* As we've seen, conflict with the majority culture is missional. When we preach the minority group rhetoric of the New Testament faithfully, we model how to disagree respectfully with the dominant culture—how to do it in a way that's attractive and invites dialogue. In other words, we model how to talk about our attractive difference. And we do so in a way that both refuses to give unnecessary offence *and* refuses to pursue a strategy that makes us the smallest possible target. To err on either side is not missional.

## Identity: Who are we?

In the first two questions we've looked at, we've seen the importance of having a shared group identity: our court of reputation is redefined to include those who share our group identity, and exclude those who don't. But discussions of group identity go beyond the definition of group boundaries to the creation of a group consciousness: a collective identity which defines *who we are* as a group, and *who I am* as a result of being a member of that group.

### Language, rituals, and symbols

The use of language is fundamental to the creation of such an identity. The most obvious example is the New Testament writers' addressing of their audiences using the language of "fictive kinship" to depict the believing community as a family: for example, "brothers and sisters," "God's children," and "God's household."[34] This has the effect of bringing group members under the mutual obligations that exist within a family. And it

---

the members of the new group; it is not intended to be directed at the old."

34. Examples of the first two terms can be found in numerous places throughout the New Testament. The concept of "God's household" occurs both in Paul (Eph 2:19; 1 Tim 3:15; Titus 1:7) and Peter (1 Pet 4:17); the significance of the Ephesians reference is that he is attempting to create a superordinate identity to which both Jewish and Gentile believers can embrace. "Fictive kinship" is used by sociologists to refer to relationships with the character and language of kinship, without actual blood-ties; compare this with the use of "Auntie" and "Uncle" for close family friends, and more broadly within Australian indigenous cultures.

suggests that the group has taken the place of its members' natural families as "the chief place of identity, security, acceptance, and belonging."[35] Paul also appropriates the "body imagery" of Greco-Roman politics, using it to refer not to the city or empire, but to the inter-dependent community of believers (Rom 12; 1 Cor 12; Col 1:18).

Group identity is also created by referring to common rituals. For example Paul describes both baptism and the Lord's Supper as a source of group identity and unity:

> For we were all baptized by one Spirit so as to form one body—whether Jews or Gentiles, slave or free—and we were all given the one Spirit to drink. (1 Cor 12:13)

> Because there is one loaf, we, who are many, are one body, for we all share the one loaf. (1 Cor 10:17)

Similarly, common symbols (such as the cross) and stories (a crucified-yet-risen Messiah) also have a unifying and group-defining effect.

## Exclusivity

This is especially the case if only group members can truly comprehend the meaning of the symbols and stories:

> For the message of the cross is foolishness to those who are perishing, but to us who are being saved it is the power of God. (1 Cor 1:18)

This claim to privileged knowledge (e.g., 1 Pet 1:12) through a special revelation from the Spirit (1 Cor 2:6–16) is a powerful strategy,[36] especially when accompanied by terms of exclusivity such as "elect" and "holy ones."

Indeed, social psychologist Robert Cialdini has shown how marketers use the principle of scarcity to great effect: something is perceived to be more desirable if customers are told it's in short supply, available for a limited time, or that information about it is only known to a select few. He tells of an experiment performed by a beef wholesaler, who told some customers of an impending short supply of beef, resulting in those customers ordering twice as much as the others did. The wholesaler told yet another group of customers that the "exclusive" information he was giving them *about* the

---

35. Elliott, "Social-Scientific Criticism," 353–54.
36. Meeks, *The First Urban Christians*, 85–93; Elliott, "The Jewish Messianic Movement," 80–84.

impending short supply was itself known only to a few—and they promptly ordered *six times as much*.³⁷ Scarcity is a powerful motivator.

Brian Wilson's study of how religious groups develop agrees, particularly if the limited good is painted in terms that imply status and privilege:

> The more fully the sect sees itself as a chosen remnant, the more fully will it offer resistance . . . Such resistance is more likely to be successful, however, if the sect has an aristocratic ethic concerning salvation—if it sees itself as a chosen elect.³⁸

In the Old Testament, we see God encouraging Israel—itself a minority group—to appreciate its privilege in being the recipients of God's revelation (Deut 7:6), and to see itself as a "royal priesthood" (Exod 19:6). This is appropriated in the New Testament by Peter to describe the church (1 Pet 2:9).

Now I hope this is setting off some alarm bells for you, raising at least two questions. Firstly, does this suggest the New Testament writers were just using manipulative marketing strategies? And secondly, how is this talk of privilege and status *attractively* different?

In answer to the first, I like to make the distinction between manipulation and persuasion; between marketing spin and honest exhortation. Manipulation is where a speaker tries to distort the truth in a deceptive way to convince their audience to do something which is for the speaker's benefit. Persuasion is where the speaker highlights the truth in an appealing way to convince their audience to do something which is for *their own* or *everyone's* benefit.³⁹ The psychological principles which are evident—such as that of scarcity—might be the same, but the means and the ends are both different. In the case of the New Testament, the writers draw attention to the truth that belonging to the people of God is a privilege not shared by all. And they do this to encourage joining or continuing in membership of that group, which is to the audience's eternal benefit.

In answer to the second, I think there *is* a real danger of this language being used badly. It can easily devolve into a "holier than thou" religious elitism which becomes pharisaic and judgmental; or into an even weirder sectarianism that you just know will end in a shootout with law enforcement in a remote farmhouse. More subtly, the circumstances of our own minority status aren't quite the same as those of the first believers, so a bunch of white

---

37. See Cialdini, *Influence*, 192.
38. Wilson, "Sect Development," 13.
39. For a fuller discussion, see MacBride, *Preaching the New Testament as Rhetoric*, 171–74; Hogan, "Rethinking Persuasion," 3–6. I include the manipulative marketing examples because they are a clear and familiar illustration of the power of such techniques, but not of their responsible use!

people talking about their privileged status as Christians isn't going to play well without a whole lot of context, and then some.

But still. This has been God's strategy right from the start, when he chose one person to bless—and later, one people group to bless—*so that all people groups on earth would be blessed through that choice* (Gen 12:1–3). It's a case of privilege and exclusivity being used as a means to attract and invite everyone.

Cialdini gives us another example, this time an experiment on two-year-old boys. They were placed in a room with two toys, one in front of a Perspex barrier, and one behind. When the barrier was only a foot high, meaning both were easily accessible, the boys showed no preference for either toy. But when it was two feet high, presenting a very real barrier they had to walk around, the boys accessed that toy three times more quickly than in the first scenario. We desire something more when it's perceived as less available.

In a sense, God put his blessing behind a Perspex barrier that's just the right height to intrigue the nations around. To be sure, most of the time Israel smudged the glass and tried to break the toy, but on some occasions the strategy worked (e.g., Rahab, Josh 2:10–11; Ruth 1:16). With the coming of Jesus, the glass was wiped clean, so that this previously hidden "mystery"—something into which the prophets and angels longed to see (1 Pet 1:10–12)—is now entrusted to the care of this tiny minority group called the church, in the hope that the nations might, at long last, be attracted by it (see Eph 3:1–13). This isn't a case of manipulation, making God's favor appear more desirable than it is, but of persuasion, making God's favor appear as desirable to us as it really is.[40]

In other words, the rhetorical strategy is something like: *although we don't deserve it, we've been chosen to have this long-hidden mystery revealed to us, so that the whole world might see and want it, too.* And to the outside world, it's even simpler: *we've been made special by God; you can become special, too.* This difference can be attractive, particularly to those who themselves feel marginalized—hence Christianity's enduring appeal among the poor and oppressed. This will need to be far more nuanced in more egalitarian cultures (such as my own) that respond negatively to any suggestion of having *higher* status; instead, a greater emphasis needs to be placed on the humility that comes from having an *undeserved* privilege.

---

40. Compare this with John Piper's discussion of "magnifying God" not with a microscope, which makes small things appear bigger, but with a telescope, so people who are far away can see him for how great he really is (Piper, *Don't Waste Your Life*, 32–33).

## Belonging to something bigger

The result of this strategy should, all going well, be an increase in the number of people in the minority group. This makes another strategy possible, that of highlighting the size of the group. While the previous strategy worked because something in scarce supply is seen as being more desirable, this strategy takes the opposite approach. It uses social validation, in which something is desirable because lots of people have it or are doing it.

Again, Cialdini points us to how advertisers have been doing this for generations, depicting their products as being popular, "number one," a "leading brand"—with accompanying imagery of large groups of people using their technology, wearing their clothes, or eating in their restaurant. Especially (but not only) in a collectivist culture where the group sets the standard, this is extremely powerful. Just how powerful is illustrated in the experience of public health campaigns trying to curb social problems like drug use and suicide: early advertisements focused on showing how widespread the problem was, but resulted in an *increase* in the behavior they were trying to discourage, because the message received was "lots of people are doing this." More recent strategies tend to avoid this; for example, depicting the isolation and social rejection that comes with drug taking and binge drinking.[41]

The New Testament writers regularly remind their audiences that they belong to a much larger group than they might think. Although they might only see their fellow believers in Corinth, Paul sends greetings from brothers and sisters throughout the network of churches he founded, including one from "all the churches" (Rom 16:16). Peter addresses his audience as "God's elect" who are scattered throughout several provinces, and sends greetings from the church in Rome (1 Pet 1:1; 5:13). John greets his church from "the children of your sister" (2 John 13).

The group they belong to is not only in the present. As we discussed in the previous chapter, group identity can also be located in time. Group members share in the group identity of those who have gone before: the "cloud of witnesses" who similarly disregarded temporal acceptance in their earthly cities in order take hold of the city that is to come (Heb 11:1–12:1).[42] They also share in an eschatological future, being part of "a great multitude that no one could count, from every nation, tribe, people and language" (Rev 7:9).[43]

---

41. Cialdini, "The Science of Persuasion," 78.
42. See chapter 4.
43. Meeks, *The First Urban Christians*, 107.

For many minority groups, there's also the vexed issue of the parent group they left, which potentially involves a loss of the group identity they once had. In situations like this, the parent group is usually depicted as being responsible for the separation. For the early church, mainstream Judaism is held responsible for rejecting its own Messiah and expelling Jewish believers from the synagogues (e.g., 1 Thess 2:14–15). The newly-formed minority, now also including Gentiles, is described as being in continuity with the "true" form of the parent religion (1 Pet 2:9; Rev 2:9). The language, symbols, and promises relating to the parent group are appropriated as being now the rightful property of the breakaway minority group.[44]

This happened with the wider empire, too. As we've already noted, imperial rhetoric is appropriated by the writers of the New Testament. The majority culture hailed the emperor as a savior, the one who grants citizenship, the head of the body politic, and the bringer of peace. But the Jesus-following minority now claims to await the royal visit of a greater savior who brings a superior citizenship (Phil 3:20); he's not only head of the church (Col 1:18), but the one who brings a universal peace—both peace with God and peace between a divided humanity (Col 1:20–21; Eph 2:11–14).[45]

The New Testament also reminds its audience that they belong to something far bigger: a growing church all across the empire. This community is one with a shared heritage stretching back to Abraham and beyond, and a shared future involving the entire created order—a future that's far superior to the present, earthly empire, and one in which they're no longer a minority group, but part of an incalculable multitude.

## Preaching group identity today

Group identity today is just as important as it was for the original audiences of the New Testament. Granted, the relationship between Christianity and synagogue Judaism might not be as pressing a concern in most contexts, although perhaps it should. An understanding of the church as belonging to the much longer story of God's people—a story that began with a minority group called Israel, continued with those among that group who embraced Jesus as their Messiah, and now seeks to gather from all nations of the world followers for him, a people being transformed into his likeness and being prepared to inherit a world set right—may still be a word on target to those

---

44. Elliott, "The Jewish Messianic Movement," 84–85.

45. For a full treatment of Paul's appropriation and subversion of the rhetoric of the Empire, see Walsh and Keesmaat, *Colossians Remixed*. We also deal with this in our chapters on Philippians and Colossians.

in a contemporary Western culture who experience a sense of alienation and a longing for community and purpose!

The New Testament language of kinship and unity, as well as our shared stories, symbols, and heritage are still powerfully relevant. This kind of New Testament preaching on *identity*—not so much individual identity or self-image, but being part of a shared group identity with a distinctive and transcendent purpose—may well be what strikes a chord with the values of Millennials and younger.[46]

## Practice: How do we live?

This sense of group identity is all well and good in the abstract, but it also needs to find a more tangible expression by way of group values and behavioral codes. Since this is who we are, *how do we now live?* Group survival requires, to some extent, a distinctive culture which marks it out from the wider society.[47] And that alternative way of life needs to be maintained and guarded, with incompatible behaviors discouraged.[48] In other words, the minority group needs its own rhetoric of honor and shame.

### An attractively different way of life

At a most basic level, this involved promoting a way of life that was consistent with what Jesus taught, regardless of how it might make group members out-of-step with the majority. Most obviously, this meant avoiding idolatry or being associated with it (e.g., 1 Cor 10:14–22; 1 John 5:21), even though it might become a barrier to attending civic festivals or having a meal with friends. It also included abstaining from the sexual immorality which often accompanied idolatrous practices (e.g., 1 Pet 4:3; Rev 2:14; and the Jerusalem Council's instruction to Gentile believers in Acts 15:29).[49] This was more problematic than we might first think, as idol food and cultic practices were so embedded in the social fabric of the empire that Christians could end up being socially marginalized in much the same way the Levitical food laws isolated Jewish communities.

---

46. See Greenberg and Weber, *Generation We.*
47. Meeks, *The First Urban Christians*, 84.
48. DeSilva, *Honor, Patronage*, 41.
49. Meeks, *The First Urban Christians*, 91. For the view that the council decree was about avoidance of idol temples and associated practices, see Witherington, *Acts*, 460–66.

Living out Jesus' values also meant rejecting the way in which the wider culture made judgments on the basis of a person's status, wealth, and outward appearance (e.g., 1 Cor 3:3; 1 Tim 2:8; Jas 2:1–4). Jesus' followers were not to participate in society's all-consuming competition for honor in the eyes of others, but trust in God's eventual vindication (1 Pet 4:15).[50] By contrast, they were to embrace the counter-cultural values that Jesus taught and demonstrated—where "the first shall be last," leaders are loving servants (Mark 10:42–45; 1 Pet 5:2–3), and group members submit to one another (Eph 5:21).[51] Loving, serving, and forgiving one another was to be the hallmark,[52] something especially prominent in the Johannine writings (e.g., John 13:35; 2 John 5; and possibly Rev 2:4).

Two millennia of Western society's ideals' being shaped—if only aspirationally—by Jesus' teaching can blind us to how sharply this ethic contrasted with the prevailing culture. It didn't just give the Christian minority a distinctive set of behaviors, but much of it was potentially attractive to outsiders. Especially to those outsiders who weren't "winning" in the struggle for honor and status, and could see among Jesus' followers an attractively different way of living. Moreover, the fact that a group lived consistently by its beliefs, even if they were a bit weird, was also considered worthy of respect (see 1 Pet 2:15; 3:16). This, too, had the potential to win converts (1 Pet 3:1–2, 15).[53]

## The rhetoric of honor and shame

The New Testament writers urged this attractively different way of life through direct commands and exhortations (e.g., 1 Pet 4; 1 John 2; Heb 13) but also through the rhetoric of honor and shame: a type of rhetoric known as *epideictic*.[54] This kind of speech—often given at civic occasions like festivals, funerals, and the visit of important people—sought to praise and honor those who were judged to be examples of the values and behaviors which society deemed honorable. (The counterpoint was also to shame those who deviated from them.) The purpose was to reinforce

---

50. DeSilva, *Honor, Patronage*, 74–76.
51. Elliott, "The Jewish Messianic Movement," 87.
52. DeSilva, *Honor, Patronage*, 79.
53. Elliott, "The Jewish Messianic Movement," 85.
54. The other two types, as noted earlier, were *deliberative*, in which the audience was urged to adopt a future course of action because it was to their advantage, and *forensic*, in which the audience was persuaded to make a right judgment, usually about something in the past.

already held values, promoting a renewed commitment to them in emulation of those being praised.[55]

In the New Testament, the supreme example to emulate is, quite naturally, God himself. Ephesians is essentially epideictic in character, honoring God and living in imitation of him:

> Praise be to the God and Father of our Lord Jesus Christ . . . to the praise of his glory. (1:3–14)

> I urge you to live a life worthy of the calling you have received. (4:1)

> You were taught, with regard to your former way of life, to put off your old self . . . and to put on the new self, created to be like God in true righteousness and holiness. (4:22–24)

Christ himself, of course, is also eulogized in this way (e.g., 1 Pet 2:21; Heb 12:2; 1 John 4:11; Rev 11:8), along with those who have followed the pattern he laid down. In Hebrews, the "cloud of witnesses" is invoked as being worthy of emulation (11:1–12:1), along with the audience themselves in the recent past (10:32–35). In Revelation, faithful witnesses like Antipas (2:13) are commended, along with the martyrs under the altar (6:9) and the "blameless" ones who refuse to worship the beast (Rev 14:1–5). In 1 Thessalonians, the recipients themselves are presented as a model for others (1:6–8) as well as a reputation they are urged to add to "all the more":

> As for other matters, brothers and sisters, we instructed you how to live in order to please God, as in fact you are living. Now we ask you and urge you in the Lord Jesus to do this more and more. (4:1)

> And in fact, you do love all of God's family throughout Macedonia. Yet we urge you, brothers and sisters, to do so more and more. (4:10)

> Therefore encourage one another and build each other up, just as in fact you are doing. (5:11)

A lot of our preaching has, appropriately, been focused on commanding and exhorting our audiences to godly behavior. Perhaps we *also* ought to follow the lead of the New Testament in its use of epideictic strategies. James Thompson calls this "preaching as remembering":

---

55. Kennedy, *A New History of Classical Rhetoric*, 4; Hauser, "Aristotle on Epideictic," 5.

> The appeal to the memory will connect the community with its foundational story, reaffirm the liturgical expression by which the community responds to God, *and recall the community's moral norms* [italics mine].[56]

This could involve examples—drawn both from Scripture and from those known to us personally—of those who embody the counter-cultural values of the Christian community, and presenting them in such a way that it inspires others to follow suit.[57]

Moving beyond what's said on a Sunday, our use of social media needs to recognize that its native mode of communication is essentially epideictic, reinforcing what the dominant culture values. Especially for Millennials and younger, the church needs to use social media to create an alternative visual rhetoric of honor and shame—one that promotes an attractively different lifestyle modelled by flawed-yet-faithful people who honor God, serve others, seek justice, and above all find their identity in God and his people. And as a former young adults' pastor, my advice would be to inspire and equip those generations to do that by and for themselves, rather than thinking we can do it for them. (We might think we can speak meme, but we can't. Source: my two teenage sons.)

## Worldview: How do we see the world?

If a minority group is, over the long term, to maintain an alternative court of reputation which informs a distinct identity and advocates counter-cultural practices, its members need to see the world in a particular way. Minority group rhetoric seeks to paint this worldview using its own special symbols and stories,[58] described by Elliott as: "a coherent worldview/symbolic universe integrating values, goals, norms, patterns of belief and behaviour and supplying ultimate (divine) legitimation for the sect's self-understanding, interests, programme and strategies."[59] In other words, it gives the group an overarching narrative in which to locate and understand its own story, and the language with which it can be articulated and internalized. New Testament examples of this include Peter's appropriation of the story of Israel as an elect nation of priests; John's symbolic world of starkly-defined opposites like light/darkness, from above/below, and children of God/the devil; and

---

56. Thompson, *Preaching Like Paul*, 141.
57. See my *Catching the Wave*, 40–44, for a discussion on how to preach from epideictic texts.
58. Meeks, *The First Urban Christians*, 93.
59. Elliott, "The Jewish Messianic Movement," 88.

of course the comprehensive, other-worldly, and subversive view of the universe that was revealed to John on Patmos.

We'll talk more about these in the individual chapters which follow, but their common strategy is, as Green points out, an attempt to take ownership of the narrative, the lexicon, and social conventions.[60]

## Rewriting the narrative

For example, instead of accepting how the dominant culture sought to define them as deviants from what's normal and honorable, the early church constructed a different worldview—one in which they saw themselves as belonging to a different narrative altogether. In the case of 1 Peter, they belonged to "Israel's" story, which had reached its climax in its Messiah and includes those who follow him from both Jewish and non-Jewish backgrounds. In the case of Revelation, they belonged to God's much bigger story (in time and space) in which both the empire and rebellious humanity are the deviant minority. And this isn't just about giving the minority group its own story to insulate them from pressure to conform; it's also about writing a compelling *alternative* story which is consciously at odds with that of the majority—different, yet attractive.

## Recasting the lexicon

Likewise, the meaning of words can be recast so that they have a different, often subversive significance for the minority group than for the wider culture. Green notes a few examples from 1 Peter:

- "Lord" is now Jesus, not the emperor or civic benefactors (2:13).
- "Fear" is reverent awe toward a powerful, loving Father-God, rather than "intimidation, anxious dread, or terror" in the face of a capricious tyrant (2:17).
- "Judgment" is by a just and loving God, not by one's family or local community; nor is it by Rome (4:6).

There's power in taking the words of the dominant culture that are used to demand conformity and redefining them in an attractively different way.

---

60. Green, *1 Peter*, 284–88.

## Redefining social conventions

More broadly, all of the strategies we have discussed thus far could be summed up by how they redefine social conventions. Instead of the court of public opinion being allowed to determine how the early believers saw themselves and how they behaved, that prerogative was given to God and to the fellow members of the alternative society he was creating. This adds up to a worldview in which social conventions were redefined, encouraging group members to give up the struggle to fit in with the majority. Instead, they were to embrace a new set of conventions in line with the new narrative of which they were now a part.

## Preaching an alternative worldview

A sometimes neglected function of contemporary preaching is the formation and preservation of an alternative worldview that is both different and attractive. Daniel Doriani includes it as one of his four aspects of biblical application, although he terms it *discernment*, in the sense of being able to see the world the way God does.[61] It forms the foundation from which the other three naturally flow: if someone sees the world God's way, they're more likely to do their *duty* toward God, exhibit the *character* of God in their lives, and pursue God-directed *goals* for their life.

Our preaching can help our congregation imagine this God-centered world view by following the New Testament's lead in appropriating the words and symbols of our own culture and taking ownership of the narrative. Words like "security," "freedom," and "equality" are ripe for recasting in Gospel terms; what the world longs for can truly only be found in Jesus. Similarly,

> the narratives of global terrorism, climate catastrophe, and financial meltdown can be retold not as challenges we will overcome by our own effort, but as the outworkings of a world in rebellion against its creator that will only truly be defeated when he recreates his world—with us as his firstfruits.[62]

Again, this isn't simply to give us a different narrative to reinforce our group boundaries, but to present a narrative that's a clear and attractive alternative to what the rest of the world is offering.

---

61. Doriani, *Putting the Truth to Work*, 113–16.
62. MacBride, "Preaching to Aliens and Strangers," 13.

## Salience: Why is this important right now?

In chapter 1, we learned from Social Categorization Theory that a key factor in the effectiveness of any minority group rhetoric is *salience*. This is where group members perceive group identity as being of particular importance and relevance to their present experience.[63] As Reicher and Hopkins note, "we all have a number of self-categories, but in different situations different categories will be more or less important to us."[64] Esler illustrates this by referring to his own experience as an immigrant to the UK in which his identity as an Australian was particularly salient whenever Australia was playing England in rugby.[65] Effective minority group rhetoric stresses the salience of the group's identity.

US President Dwight D. Eisenhower famously said, "I have two kinds of problems: the urgent and the important. The urgent are not important, and the important are never urgent."[66] The writers of the New Testament, however, are at pains to stress both the importance *and* urgency of belonging to the community of believers and embracing its minority group identity as a minority group. That is, they frequently remind their audience of its salience.

The most obvious are the references to God's impending judgment: it's *God's* judgment, so it's more important than any other judgment; and it's *impending*, so dealing with it can't be put off. Peter reminds his audience that all are accountable "to him who *is ready to judge* the living and the dead" in the context of their own faithful behavior for which they were being mistreated by the majority culture (1 Pet 4:4–5). Paul refers to "the coming wrath" in the same breath as he praises the Thessalonians for their rejection of the dominant culture's idolatry and embrace of Paul's pattern of living (1 Thess 1:10). The writer to the Hebrews tells the story of God's judgment at Mount Sinai when God's voice "shook the earth" in order to warn of a coming "shaking" which will be on an even greater scale (Heb 12:26). This contrasts with the secure group identity of those assembled on Mount Zion, "the church of the firstborn, whose names are written in heaven" (Heb 12:22–23). When it comes to Revelation, the presence of impending judgment is obvious; but

---

63. Turner et al., *Rediscovering the Social Group*, 54.

64. Reicher and Hopkins, *Self and Nation*, 38.

65. Esler, "Social Identity Theory," 25.

66. He was quoting Roscoe Miller, president of Northwestern University, in his address to the World Council of Churches, 19 August 1954, *The American Presidency Project*, www.presidency.ucsb.edu/node/232572. Management gurus have since used this to encourage leaders to maximize the time spent on the important-but-not-urgent, e.g., Covey, *The 7 Habits of Highly Effective People*, 150–52.

note that in the midst of that judgment, attention is drawn to how God's faithful minority receives a measure of protection, as well as a sign marking out their group membership (e.g., Rev 7:1–17; 14:1–5; 15:1–4). God's impending judgment makes group membership salient.

As the church entered the latter half of the first century, there was a danger that the sense of the imminence of Christ's return would fade. Group membership might still be important, but lack urgency. To counter this, we see the Gospel writers emphasize the motif of delay-followed-by-unexpected-return in Jesus' parables (e.g., Matt 24:48–51; 25:5–6; 19). The epistles make references to Jesus return that are too numerous to list. And again, the "soonness" of Jesus' coming in Revelation is a key motivation to remain loyal to the group and its values (e.g., Rev 1:1; 3:11; 22:7; especially 22:11–15). It also means that the *future* aspect of the group's identity is imminent: although the dominant culture doesn't see their special status as God's children, they will when Christ returns (e.g., 1 John 3:1–2). More broadly, salience is stressed by describing the group's entire existence as being in the "last days," which among other things is a motivation for right behavior, (e.g., 1 Pet 4:7) having clear group boundaries (e.g., 1 John 2:18), and regular contact with one another (e.g., Heb 10:24–25).

Group membership was also salient because of the danger of apostasy in the face of outside pressure to yield to the dominant culture's court of reputation. The New Testament writers make frequent mention of this, both as potential and as a reality (e.g., the desertion of Paul by "Demas, because he loved this world," 2 Tim 4:10). Hebrews appears to have been written to a group in which such pressure had come in the recent past (10:32–34) and was again on the horizon (12:4), occasioning numerous warnings not to leave the group and so forfeit its benefits (e.g., 2:1; 3:12; 4:1; 10:39). Peter and Paul frequently acknowledge that their audiences had experienced rejection by their culture of origin (e.g., 1 Pet 1:6; 4:12; 1 Thess 2:14–15), not to mention Paul's own suffering at the hands of both Jews and Gentiles (e.g., 2 Cor 11:26). Along with John's own exile, the letters to the seven churches near the start of Revelation function not only as warnings against compromise with the majority culture but also as reminders of the salience of the message.

In short, group membership was both urgent and important for two reasons. Firstly, Jesus' return was imminent, at which point he would judge those outside the group and reward those within the group. Secondly, there was relentless pressure from the majority culture forcing group members to choose sides: either conform, or face social sanction—or worse. The New Testament writers describe this as a present crisis to force the issue front-and-center, so that their audience would perceive the salience of their identity as God's people.

## Why is our group identity important today?

Just as the New Testament writers explicitly draw attention to the salience of minority group identity—even though for each of their audiences it was an implicit and inescapable part of their background—our preaching should similarly remind our own congregations of why it is both important and urgent. The introductory chapter was, to a large extent, an argument for this, so we won't repeat it at length here. In sum, the imminence of God's judgment is still one powerful reason that remains unchanged. And in the face of our growing position as "repugnant cultural other"—as *aliens* in our own countries—we also face the prospect of intentional apostasy, or perhaps a more insidious drift into cultural compromise. Our challenge is to remind our hearers of this in such a way as to focus their attention on the importance of group identity without sounding alarmist or provoking militance. The need to be different and the need to be attractive are both salient.

*Part 2*

# The General Epistles

So enough with the theory, let's see how this all works in practice.

The next five chapters will look at some of the General Epistles through the lens of minority group rhetoric. We'll begin with **1 Peter**, since it's in many respects the prototypical minority group letter of the New Testament, consciously addressing its audience as "aliens and exiles." **Hebrews** then follows, being a sermon (13:22) designed to prevent its hearers from "falling away" in the face of pressure from the majority culture. The **letters of John** deal with the issue of division *within* a minority group, and how such a group responds when some members leave to form their own group. **James** addresses his audience as "the twelve tribes in the dispersion," their minority status forming the background to his appeal to resist trying to have a foot in both camps—being friends with God at the same time as being friends with the world. Finally, **Revelation** is a word of comfort to seven churches as it both endures persecution and resists the temptation to syncretism in order to avoid being marginalized.

# 3

## 1 Peter
## *To Aliens and Exiles*

IN THIS CHAPTER WE'LL look at what I think is the most prototypical example of minority group rhetoric in the New Testament, 1 Peter. This is because in a number of places it explicitly addresses its minority group audience *as a minority group*. What's more, the overarching purpose of the letter is to teach this minority group how to interact with the dominant culture.[1] In other words, the audience's minority status is front-and-center throughout, rather than simply being part of the assumed setting as is the case with most of Paul's letters.

The prototypical nature of 1 Peter, however, means that a systematic analysis of its rhetorical strategies would look a lot like the previous chapter—except that all the examples would be drawn from this one epistle. For this reason I've taken a different approach with 1 Peter, instead providing a (rather unusual) sermon example, so you can see how this might look—or better, hear how this might sound—in practice.

The sermon example is unusual because it's a homiletical reading of the entire text of 1 Peter. It normally takes around 40 minutes—which is a fair bit longer than the average sermon in the churches I'd regularly preach in—so it's not something you'd do every week.[2] But it was designed as a bit of an experiment to help my congregation appreciate how ancient letters functioned as coherent, unified speeches sent at a distance.[3] Anecdotally, it

---

1. Witherington, *Letters and Homilies for Hellenized Christians*, 2, 23, describes it as "the only New Testament document that systematically addresses the issue of Christians being resident aliens within the macrostructures of the larger society."

2. Dever, *The Message of the New Testament*, 16, commends the practice of preaching an "overview sermon" at the start of a series in order to make "the point of a whole book the point of a sermon."

3. On this, see the field of NT Rhetorical Criticism, including Witherington, *N.T. Rhetoric*; and MacBride, *Catching the Wave*.

seemed to do the job, with a number of people saying afterwards, "*now* I get how epistles work!" Either way, for our purposes here it allows me to show how the theory of the previous chapter is illustrated in 1 Peter, and how such insights might spark contemporary application.

## 1 Peter: Attractively Different

Today, we're doing something very different. Normally, we read a relatively short excerpt from a book of the bible. And then we—and by "we," I mean the preacher—then we talk about it. At length. A little bit of bible. Then lots of talking.

Today, we're going to flip that around and read not just an *excerpt* from a book of the bible, but the whole letter of 1 Peter. Which, funnily enough, is how it was first meant to be experienced. Not one or two paragraphs per week, but all in one sitting. And not by *reading* printed text, but by *hearing* it read out. After all, in the first century, most people were illiterate and photocopiers hard to come by. So you had to get together to *hear* Scripture being read out; as a speech being "performed."

Now, we will have *some* explanation and application as we go. Which was the custom of Jewish teachers around the time of Jesus: to paraphrase, to explain, to apply the Scripture as they read it out (cf. Neh 8:8). So we're going to do just that with 1 Peter, listening to this word from God straight from the mouth of the apostle Peter. Now sit back—or better, lean forward in anticipation—as we take out this ancient letter and hear what it has to say to us:

> Peter, an apostle of Jesus Christ, To God's elect, exiles scattered throughout the provinces of Pontus, Galatia, Cappadocia, Asia and Bithynia . . .

Well that's a bit awkward, isn't it? After all that build-up, it's not actually addressed to us. Do we have any Galatians in the audience? Anyone live in Cappadocia? Has anyone ever . . . been to Turkey on a holiday? That's not going to cut it, is it? We're not the audience Peter has written to: people living 2000 years ago in Roman provinces located in what's called Turkey today. But maybe we're a bit like them?

After all, he calls them God's **elect**. God's chosen ones—his special people. That's like us, right? Maybe it's going to speak to us, too. But then he calls them **exiles**. The Greek word means travelling strangers: people who haven't settled in the country they're living in. They're just passing through, hoping one day to return to their homeland. And so they don't fit in. A little later in the letter he also calls them **aliens**. The Greek word literally means those "outside the household." These were immigrants: people who had permanently settled in the country, but were still treated as outsiders by those who were citizens. Again, people who don't fit in.[4] And then he describes them as **scattered**. The word there—*diaspora*—is a term used for Jews who'd been scattered throughout the Mediterranean by various invasions and wars, permanently living away from the Holy Land. So Peter may well be writing to Jewish Christians. Or, he might be using Jewish terminology to describe *all* of God's people, scattered throughout the empire.[5]

So let's get this clear, as it's the key to how we're going to hear the letter when we read it shortly. It's addressed to a minority group, explicitly *as* a minority. They are exiles, just passing through. They are aliens, excluded from citizenship. They are scattered, away from their home. Some of them, perhaps quite literally—particularly if they were Jewish Christians. But for many of them, they *did* belong where they lived. They *weren't* foreigners. They *hadn't* been scattered. Yet their decision to follow Christ had made them outcasts. Or at least, it made them feel like they no longer fitted in with the wider society. They were subtly excluded, publicly ridiculed, and out of step with the majority. These Christians found themselves very quickly marginalized.

Does that sound in any way familiar? How is that like *our* experience, as followers of Jesus in the twenty-first-century Western world? That's not a rhetorical question. Discuss that for a few minutes with the people sitting near you, and then we'll start to listen to Peter's letter.

### 1. We are different

*1 Peter, an apostle of Jesus Christ, To God's elect*[6]—that's you; *exiles*—a minority mocked and excluded by the rest of society—*scattered throughout*

---

4. Elliott, *A Home for the Homeless*, 48, shows how these words were used to describe a socio-economic reality, and argues that Peter's addressees were not merely *metaphorical* outsiders because they were now "citizens of heaven" (which imports a foreign Pauline concept from Phil 3:15), but were social outsiders in a very real way.

5. For a more technical discussion of the audience of 1 Peter, see my "Aliens and Strangers," 313–15. Witherington, *Letters and Homilies for Hellenized Christians*, 2, 36, argues that the audience was largely Jews who had been thoroughly Hellenized. By contrast, Green, *1 Peter*, 6, sees a mixed but predominantly Gentile audience focusing on their *theological* identity as "Israel."

6. In this printed sermon, Scripture is italicized so the reader can see which parts are homiletic amplification; when presented, the audience is encouraged to follow along with their Bibles, and the text is displayed on-screen. Some verses have been omitted due to time constraints. The biblical text is taken from the New International Version, 2011.

the provinces of Pontus, Galatia, Cappadocia, Asia and Bithynia, *as well as Europe, Africa, Asia, the Americas, and even remote islands like Australia. 2* who have been chosen, according to the foreknowledge of God the Father, through the sanctifying work of the Spirit to be obedient to Jesus Christ, *to be different from the world around,* and sprinkled with his blood *that sets us apart for his service:* Grace and peace be yours in abundance.

*3* Praise be to the God and Father of our Lord Jesus Christ! In his great mercy he has given us new birth into a living hope through the resurrection of Jesus Christ from the dead, *4* and into an inheritance that can never perish, spoil or fade. This inheritance is kept in heaven for you . . . *So if you've lost your "inheritance" here in this life for the sake of Christ—maybe your family's cut you out of the will, but more likely you've simply lost respect or career opportunity or friends or wealth or free time—look at this in light of the eternal inheritance that awaits. It's held not in some bank that might become insolvent; or a property portfolio that might devalue; or in shares that might crash. But it's held for you in heaven. Held for you,* 5 who through faith are shielded *from anything this world can throw at you* by God's power until the coming of the salvation that is ready to be revealed in the last time. *At which time you'll be vindicated.*

*6* In all this you greatly rejoice, though now for a little while you may have had to suffer grief in all kinds of trials. *Yes, there's eternal advantage; but there's also temporary suffering. Why* is *that?* 7 These have come so that the proven genuineness of your faith—of greater worth than gold, which perishes even though refined by fire—may result in praise, glory and honor when Jesus Christ is revealed. *These struggles as an excluded minority demonstrate your loyalty to Jesus. They give you an opportunity to put your money where your mouth is and prove your faithfulness to the one who was faithful to you.* 8 Though you have not seen him, you love him; and even though you do not see him now, you believe in him—*you pledge loyalty to him*—and are filled with an inexpressible and glorious joy, *9* for you are receiving the end result of your faith, the salvation of your souls. *So everything you're giving up to follow Jesus—how does that compare in light of the salvation God offers? I mean, think about it!*

*10* Concerning this salvation, the prophets, who spoke of the grace that was to come to you, searched intently and with the greatest care, *11* trying to find out the time and circumstances to which the Spirit of Christ in them was pointing when he predicted the sufferings of the Messiah and the glories that would follow. *12* It was revealed to them that they were not serving themselves but you, when they spoke of the things that have now been told you by those who have preached the gospel to you by the Holy Spirit sent from heaven. Even angels long to look into these things. *Generations beforehand only had* an inkling of God's plan. Even the prophets of old. Even those esteemed authors of the Old Testament. Even the angels! But you—you've now seen it all! Far from being a neglected minority, you're part of a privileged people standing in the most privileged point in the history of that people: post-Easter, post-Pentecost.[7]

*13 Therefore, with minds that are alert and fully sober, set your hope on the grace to be brought to you when Jesus Christ is revealed at his coming.* Focus on the eternal benefit, not the temporary suffering. *14 As obedient children, do not conform to the evil desires you had when you lived in ignorance.* Rather than worrying about fitting in with this world—fit in with God's plan! Don't concern yourself with what temporary status you've lost, but focus on the eternal status you've gained. *15 But just as he who called you is holy, so be holy in all you do; 16 for it is written* in Leviticus: *"Be holy, because I am holy."* Most of the time we're worried about being like everyone else, because we know that we're being judged: how we talk and how we look; how we act towards others. Instead, focus on being like God. He's the one who's set you apart for himself, just like he did with the nation of Israel thousands of years ago. He's the one whose judgment is important: *17 Since you call on a Father who judges each person's work impartially, live out your time as foreigners here in reverent fear.* Remember that you don't belong here, you belong to God. And also, remember what it cost God to make it that way.

*18 For you know that it was not with perishable things such as silver or gold that you were redeemed from the empty way of life handed down to you from your ancestors, 19 but with the precious blood of Christ, a lamb without blemish or defect. 20 He was chosen before the creation of the world, but was revealed in these last times for your sake.* You are the beneficiary of Christ's sacrifice. And you are the beneficiary of Christ's resurrection. *21 Through him you believe in God, who raised him from the dead and glorified him, and so your faith and hope are in God.* So live in light of that, not in light of the world's expectations. *22 Now that you have purified yourselves by obeying the truth so that you have sincere love for each other, love one another deeply, from the heart.* As Jesus said, that's how people will know that you belong to God: that you love one another. The fact that you're feeling different is a

---

7. If the audience is mostly Jewish, this appropriation of the language, symbols, and narrative of the parent group is a way of claiming that they are the true custodians of the parent group's identity—they stand in continuity with the "exile" of Scripture, such as Abraham, Isaac, Jacob, Moses, and all those in Babylon (cf. 5:13). If the audience is mostly Gentile, this appropriation tries to define their new identity "by inscribing them into the world of Israel's Scriptures and the record of God's relationship with his chosen people" (Green, *1 Peter*, 15).

good sign: because you *are* different. You've been changed. *23 For you have been born again, not of perishable seed, but of imperishable, through the living and enduring word of God.* Again, weigh up this temporary existence full of perishable things—weigh this against the enduring promise of that which is imperishable. As the prophet Isaiah said: *24 "All people are like grass, and all their glory is like the flowers of the field; the grass withers and the flowers fall, 25 but the word of the Lord endures forever." And this is the word that was preached to you.*

Do you get how privileged, how undeservedly favored you are? That God would do all of this—for you? Good. Because that should then motivate you to resist the temptation to fit back in with the world around you. And instead to pursue God's values. To embrace your identity as a minority group in this world. To try all the more to live differently from the rest of society.

*2:1 Therefore, rid yourselves of all malice and all deceit, hypocrisy, envy, and slander of every kind.* Don't behave like everyone else does. *2 Like newborn babies, crave pure spiritual milk, so that by it you may grow up in your salvation, 3 now that you have tasted that the Lord is good.* Just like babies cry until they get their bottle, whinge and scream until you get the Word of God into you. Don't chase the inferior existence you're told to chase by your workmates, by advertising, by the impossibly perfect life posts on social media—instead, relentlessly pursue God. Look to him as your source of what's good and right and honorable.

*4 As you come to him, the living Stone—rejected by humans but chosen by God and precious to him—* Did you spot that subtle aside? Jesus was rejected, too, by the way. You might recall the whole crucifixion thing. His wider society rejected him. Yet he was chosen and precious to God. Guess what? So are you. *5 . . . you also, like living stones, are being built into a spiritual house to be a holy priesthood, offering spiritual sacrifices acceptable to God through Jesus Christ.* Been rejected by the temple establishment or by the synagogue? Don't stress! You're now part of a greater temple. On the outer at your workplace? Ridiculed at university? Sidelined at school? Forget that: you've already got the best career, as a priest of the living God!

*6 For in Scripture it says: "See, I lay a stone in Zion, a chosen and precious cornerstone, and the one who trusts in him will never be put to shame."* All societies try to shame minority groups back into conformity, especially dangerous ones whose ideas threaten the status quo. But if we trust in Christ—the cornerstone of this new temple—we won't be put to shame. But the same can't be said for those who reject Christ. *7 Now to you who believe, this stone is precious. But to those who do not believe, "The stone the builders rejected has* become the cornerstone,"[8] *8 and, "A stone that causes people to stumble and a rock that makes them fall."* They stumble because they disobey the message—which is also what they were destined for. Although they might try to shame *you*, in the end *they* are the ones who will be put to shame.

*9 But,* in the words of God to Moses on Mount Sinai: *you are a chosen people, a royal priesthood, a holy nation, God's special possession, that you may declare the praises of him who called you out of darkness into his wonderful light.* So what if your fellow Jews have disowned you? It's in you that all God's promises to Israel will be made good. It's in you that all God's purposes for his people will be realized. In fact, so what if the Roman Empire has marginalized you? Even if you're not ethnically Israel, through Christ you now have the opportunity to become part of God's people; "children of the living God" just like the prophet Hosea said. *10 Once you were not a people, but now you are the people of God; once you had not received mercy, but now you have received mercy.* You might not feel at home in the wider world anymore, but that's OK, because you belong to the people of God. You're a living stone in a spiritual temple God's building. You're following in the footsteps of the stone that was rejected by society yet chosen and precious to God. In Christ, you belong.

## 2. Make that difference *attractive*

In light of our new identity as people who don't belong anymore to this world, but belong to God, how should we live? Peter continues: *11 Dear friends, I urge you, as aliens and exiles*—as marginalized people who no longer belong—*I urge you to abstain from sinful desires, which wage war against your soul. 12 Live such good lives among the pagans*—the wider world—*that, though they accuse you of doing wrong, they may see your good deeds and glorify God on the day he visits us.* Be different, yes. But not in a dorky Christian kind of way. Be *attractively* different. Be the kind of marginalized minority that people at the very least might grudgingly respect—if not admire.

*13 Submit yourselves for the Lord's sake to every human authority: whether to the emperor, as the supreme authority, 14 or to governors, who are sent by him to punish those who do wrong and to commend those who do right.* To prime ministers and premiers and presidents. To police and judges and bureaucrats. To bosses and teachers and parents. Why? *15 For it is God's will that by doing*

---

8. You can't fit everything into a sermon, but notice the context of the quote from Ps 118:22 in which the psalmist finds himself alone, with enemies all around him, yet puts his confidence in God as his deliverer—the one who would bring about that "divine reversal."

*good you should silence the ignorant talk of foolish people.* Even while they marginalize you, be the best citizens of your country you can be. Give them no reason—other than the gospel—to complain about you.

*16 Live as free people, but do not use your freedom as a cover-up for evil; live as God's slaves.* Demonstrate that true freedom means not living for self, but living for something far greater than self. *17 Show proper respect to everyone, love the family of believers, fear God, honor the emperor.* Don't just retreat into a Christian ghetto that deals with your minority status by ignoring the outside world. Engage with it positively, while remaining attractively different.

*18 Slaves, in reverent fear of God submit yourselves to your masters, not only to those who are good and considerate, but also to those who are harsh.* Office workers: be just as diligent whether your boss is understanding or uncaring; whether incompetent or worthy of respect. It's a sign you acknowledge authority, which ultimately comes from God. *19 For it is commendable if someone bears up under the pain of unjust suffering because they are conscious of God. 20 But how is it to your credit if you receive a beating for doing wrong and endure it?* Don't blame all of your trials at work or at school on being a marginalized follower of Jesus—maybe you're just plain lazy, or selfish, or difficult to get along with.

*But, if you suffer for doing good and you endure it, this is commendable before God. 21 To this you were called, because Christ suffered for you, leaving you an example, that you should follow in his steps.* As the prophet Isaiah said, *22 "He committed no sin, and no deceit was found in his mouth." 23 When they hurled their insults at him, he did not retaliate; when he suffered, he made no threats. Instead, he entrusted himself to him who judges justly. 24 "He himself bore our sins" in his body on the cross, so that we might die to sins and live for righteousness; "by his wounds you have been healed." 25 For "you were like sheep going astray,"* but now you have returned to the Shepherd and Overseer of your souls. So when you are mocked or left out or abused at work for being a follower of Christ, and for living by his standards, not the world's—remember, you're simply doing what Jesus did. And he trusted that God would vindicate him.

*3:1 Wives, in the same way submit yourselves to your own husbands so that, if any of them do not believe the word, they may be won over without words by the behavior of their wives, 2 when they see the purity and reverence of your lives.* Be attractively different. *3 Your beauty should not come from outward adornment, such as elaborate hairstyles and the wearing of gold jewelry or fine clothes.* Or the number of likes your new profile pic got.

*4 Rather, it should be that of your inner self, the unfading beauty of a gentle and quiet spirit, which is of great worth in God's sight. 5 For this is the way the holy women of the past who put their hope in God used to adorn themselves. They submitted themselves to their own husbands, 6 like Sarah, who obeyed Abraham and called him her lord. You are her daughters if you do what is right and do not give way to fear.* What this dynamic looks like in the twenty-first century is open to debate. (Lots of debate!) But the principle is not. Be the best twenty-first-century wife you can be in the eyes of God. Often, that will be by fulfilling—and exceeding—our culture's ideals for a wife. Sometimes it will be by being counter-cultural, living out gospel values in marriage in a world that thinks that's quaint. I'll leave it for you to work out the tension.

*7 Husbands, in the same way be considerate as you live with your wives, and treat them with respect as the weaker partner*—meaning don't use your superior physical strength to control and abuse; don't tolerate domestic violence of any kind, ever—*and treat them as heirs with you of the gracious gift of life, so that nothing will hinder your prayers.* Again, what this dynamic looks like today is open to debate. Be the best twenty-first-century husband you can be in the eyes of God. Fulfil and exceed our culture's ideals for a husband. And be counter-culturally faithful to God where you need to be.

*8 Finally, all of you, be like-minded, be sympathetic, love one another, be compassionate and humble.* Forget about marriage for a minute: be the best person, the best friend, the best co-worker you can be in the eyes of God. *9 Do not repay evil with evil or insult with insult. On the contrary, repay evil with blessing,* just as Jesus taught us, *because to this you were called so that you may inherit a blessing.* As David wrote in the Psalms, when he felt like he was in the minority—like everyone was against him—he said: *10 "Whoever would love life and see good days must keep their tongue from evil and their lips from deceitful speech . . . 12 For the eyes of the Lord are on the righteous and his ears are attentive to their prayer, but the face of the Lord is against those who do evil."*

*13 Who is going to harm you if you are eager to do good?* Not many people. But some will, of course. That's one reason you're a minority group! *14 But even if you should suffer for what is right, you are blessed.* Just as God said to Isaiah, when he was in the minority; when he was one of the few who had not bowed down to the Canaanite god called Ba'al: *"Do not fear their threats; do not be frightened." 15 But in your hearts revere Christ as Lord. Always be prepared to give an answer to everyone who asks you to give the reason for the hope that you have.* Don't just live in an attractively different way. That's just the first step. Be ready to explain why it is you're different. *But do this with gentleness and respect.* Not like some Christians, who seem to give the reason for their hope with arrogance and hostility—but do it with gentleness and respect, *16 keeping a clear conscience, so that those who speak maliciously against your good behavior in Christ may be ashamed of their slander.* Don't allow the way you present the gospel to reinforce their negative view of you as a troublesome minority. Be gracious.

*17 For it is better, if it is God's will, to suffer for doing good than for doing evil. 18 For Christ also suffered once for sins, the righteous for the unrighteous, to bring you to God. He was put to death in the body but made alive in the Spirit.* In all of this, don't forget that righteous suffering as a persecuted minority isn't an accidental by-product of the gospel. It's right at the heart of it: Christ, who righteously suffered for you.

*19 And after being made alive, he went and made proclamation to the imprisoned spirits—20 to those who were disobedient long ago when God waited patiently in the days of Noah while the ark was being built.* Jesus thus vindicated Noah in the eyes of his society; Noah, the original mocked and marginalized minority. Because they were indeed a minority: *In the ark, only a few people, eight in all, were saved through water, 21 and this water is an antitype—*a symbolic precursor—*of baptism that now saves you also—not the removal of dirt from the body but the pledge of a clear conscience toward God. It saves you by the resurrection of Jesus Christ, 22 who has gone into heaven and is at God's right hand—with angels, authorities and powers in submission to him.* So just as Noah and his family were on the winning side, rest assured that you are. Just as Isaiah prevailed against the prophets of Ba'al; just as David was kept safe from all of his enemies, so too will you. And you'll be vindicated in the eyes of all those who seek to shame you, when Christ returns.

### 3. Maintain our distinctiveness

So—in light of Jesus' example—how should we deal with being "foreigners and exiles"? How do we cope with being marginalized as the people of God? Do we give in to the pressure of the world to conform—to think and speak and act like the rest of society? No.

*4:1 Therefore, since Christ suffered in his body, arm yourselves also with the same attitude, because whoever suffers in the body is done with sin. 2 As a result, they do not live the rest of their earthly lives for evil human desires, but rather for the will of God.* We don't live for the approval of our peers or Instagram likes or the acceptance that comes from keeping up with our workmates' rate of alcohol consumption at the bar on Friday night. (And I know the pain of nursing your second beer for the evening while everyone else has had at least ten, and finds pretty much everything oh so hilarious!) *3 For you have spent enough time in the past doing what pagans choose to do—living in debauchery, lust, drunkenness, orgies, carousing and detestable idolatry. 4 They are surprised that you do not join them in their reckless, wild living, and they heap abuse on you.* Count that as a good thing! Wear it as a badge of honor. After all, they don't know God, so their disapproval is a sign you're doing the right thing. *5 But those who abuse you for this will have to give account to him who is ready to judge the living and the dead. 6 For this is the reason the gospel, God's saving plan, was preached*—by the prophets of old—*even to those who are now dead, so that they might be judged according to human standards in regard to the body, but live according to God in regard to the spirit.*

*7 The end of all things is near. Therefore be alert and of sober mind so that you may pray.* Take this stuff seriously, as the time is short and the consequences are eternal. This is both important and urgent. *8 Above all, love each other deeply, because love covers over a multitude of sins.* That's what's supposed to be attractively different about you as a minority group—you love one another, you forgive one another, you don't let hurts (whether big or small) derail your purpose or divide your community. *9 Offer hospitality to one another without grumbling.* Delight in serving others rather than seeing it as a duty.

*12 Dear friends, do not be surprised at the fiery ordeal that has come on you to test you, as though something strange were happening to you.* You knew what you were signing up for when you first followed Jesus: to be marginalized, as he was; to suffer, as he did; to take up your cross daily, just as he took up his cross for us, once and for all. In fact, this is an opportunity to share in what Christ did. So rejoice! *13 Rejoice inasmuch as you participate in the sufferings of Christ, so that you may be overjoyed when his glory is revealed. 14 If you are insulted because of the name of Christ, you are blessed, for the Spirit of glory and of God rests on you.* That kind of dishonor is supremely honorable. Redefine it in your mind, so that on Monday morning—when you get to work or school or your kids' playgroup or wherever—if someone gives you a disapproving look for mentioning you went to church on Sunday, or trots out Richard Dawkins' latest sound-byte about religion, or just excludes you because you're one of those God-botherers—that's a blessing! That's an honor! That's a sign that you belong to God!

*5:1 To the elders among you, I appeal as a fellow elder and a witness of Christ's sufferings who also will share in the glory to be revealed: 2 Be shepherds of God's flock that is under your care, watching over them—not because you must, but because you are willing, as God wants you to be; not pursuing dishonest gain, but eager to serve; 3 not lording it over those entrusted to you, but being examples to the flock.* Leaders: be attractively different in how you lead your youth, your bible study group, your ministry, your children. Don't lead the way so much of our world leads, being in it for the status or the money or the feeling of control. But be in it for the sake of those you lead. *4 And when the Chief Shepherd appears, you will receive the crown of glory that will never fade away.* This is worth far more than earthly status.

*5 In the same way, you who are younger, submit yourselves to your elders.* Be attractively different not just in how you lead, but in also how you are led. In fact, *All of you, clothe yourselves with humility toward one another, because,* as it says in Proverbs "*God opposes the proud but shows favor to the humble.*"

*8 Be alert and of sober mind. Your enemy the devil prowls around like a roaring lion looking for someone to devour.* He wants to use your sense of marginalization to keep you from God. Don't be sucked back into the majority because it's easier, or because the rewards are more immediate or more tangible. *9 Resist him, standing firm in the faith, because you know that the family of believers throughout the world is undergoing the same kind of sufferings.* You might be a minority, but you're a worldwide minority. Some of you might have lost your family to some degree, but you're now part of a much bigger family in Christ.

*10 And the God of all grace, who called you to his eternal glory in Christ, after you have suffered a little while*—at least, a little while in light of eternity—God *will himself restore you and make you strong, firm and steadfast. 11 To him be the power for ever and ever. Amen. 12 With the help of Silas, whom I regard as a faithful brother, I have written to you briefly, encouraging you and testifying that this is the true grace of God. Stand fast in it.* One last time, don't give in to the pressure of the Empire. *13 She who is in Babylon*—your fellow exiles in Rome, along with all God's people who are similarly marginalized—*chosen together with you, sends you her greetings, and so does my son Mark. 14 Greet one another with a kiss of love. Peace to all of you who are in Christ.*

Once more, I stress that this isn't a model for a regular sermon. (It may not even be a replicable model for other, similar one-off sermons, since 1 Peter is at the upper limit of the length of text for which this might work.) But I trust it's been helpful in two ways. Firstly, I hope it's given a sense of how the minority group rhetoric of the New Testament works "in the wild" rather than in the abstract captivity of the previous chapter. And secondly, I hope it's provided the starting point for a whole *series* of sermons on 1 Peter, showing the direction in which application might take if we were to appropriate its minority group rhetoric for our own contexts.

# 4

## Hebrews
### *The City That Is to Come*

IN A FAMOUS EXPERIMENT first run at Stanford University in the 1960s,[1] children were faced with a difficult choice. They were given one marshmallow, which they could eat straight away. But if they chose not to eat it and instead wait a short time (about fifteen minutes) they'd be given a second one. In the intervening time, the tester left the room. The child was left unsupervised with nothing but the uneaten marshmallow to occupy their attention. *What would they do? Would they give in to temptation now, and miss out on the future reward? Or would they resist, motivated by the promise of more?*

It was testing the child's ability to delay gratification—to endure temporary hardship in the present in order to gain more in the future. Some gave in. Others resisted. Many struggled, staring at the marshmallow—sniffing it, licking it, and eating tiny pieces off it to test the limits of what constituted "not eating it." The children were then tracked over time. As you'd probably expect, even allowing for their socio-economic background, those who were able to resist the marshmallow in the study tended to perform better as adults in areas such as educational attainment and healthy lifestyle.[2] The capacity to delay gratification is clearly important.

The exhortation we call *The Letter to the Hebrews* is essentially one long argument for its minority group audience to resist eating the marshmallow now, because there was a far greater reward on offer in the future. It urged them not to "shrink back" from being identified with Jesus and his followers just because they wanted to be accepted by the majority culture now. Instead, they were to look ahead to the "city that is to come"—the reward that

---

1. Mischel, Ebbeson, and Raskoff Zeiss, "Cognitive and Attentional Mechanisms in Delay of Gratification," 204–18.

2. For the full story and many other insights about delayed gratification, see Mischel, *The Marshmallow Test*.

awaits those who persevere.[3] Or to put it in terms of deliberative rhetoric: to embrace temporary disadvantage in the present in order to gain *eternal* advantage, repositioning the debate to include the age to come.

## A marginalized minority

It's clear that the audience was a minority group, although its precise makeup is less clear. The traditional view, reflecting the second-century title, "to the Hebrews," is that the audience was Jewish. This makes the best sense of the author's heavy use of the Old Testament and rabbinic forms of argumentation[4]—along with the assumption that his audience would understand and be persuaded by them[5]—without completely ruling out the possibility of a Gentile or mixed background.[6] It means they were quite likely a *double*-minority: they had already been monotheistic Jews living in a polytheistic, pagan world, who had become an even smaller minority when they broke away from mainstream Judaism in order to follow Jesus. Alienated from their community of exiles.

At any rate, it's clear that this minority group in was danger of "drifting away" (2:1), "turning away" (3:12), and "shrinking back" (10:39) both from the group and from Jesus himself. So the more important question isn't so much where they came *from*, but what alternative to the Christian faith, if any, they were being attracted *to*. We can rule out pagan religion, since there are no warnings against idolatry.[7] And all of the comparisons which highlight the superiority of Jesus and the new covenant point toward old covenant Judaism. This could simply be Jewish believers being

---

3. I ran a version of the marshmallow experiment when preaching from Hebrews. It was during the summer break, so the school-aged children were in church for the sermon. I gave them all marshmallows with the promise they'd get one more if they didn't eat it until the end. Nearly all passed the test, although I'm not sure the first marshmallow was all that edible after surviving 30 minutes in a tightly-clenched hand. By contrast, the high school youth either ate theirs straight away, or donated them to the one person in the row whom they designated to play "chubby bunnies," seeing how many they could fit in their mouth at once.

4. Lane, *Hebrews 1–8*, liv.

5. Johnson, *Hebrews*, 34. Further, Morrison, *Enthymemes in Hebrews*, Kindle loc. 2187–95, has shown that the unstated but implied logical premises of those arguments fit well within a Jewish worldview.

6. DeSilva, *Perseverance in Gratitude*, 2–7, notes that the Jewish nature of the letter could say more about the background of the author than the recipients, as Paul, for example, frequently uses Old Testament references and arguments to address Gentiles in letters like Galatians and Romans.

7. Koester, *Hebrews*, 48.

tempted to return to their faith of origin—for social reasons, if not theological. Or it could be Gentile believers "taking shelter in the 'camp' of Judaism" to avoid being persecuted by the Empire because they didn't participate in civic religion.[8]

However, it's probably not the case that they were being attracted *to* Judaism so much as being drawn away *from* following Jesus, since nowhere is the alternative referred to specifically. And the potential movement is described in purely negative terms—as a "shrinking back" or "turning away" *from* being identified with Jesus—rather than being *toward* anything.[9] Johnson correctly weighs the evidence:

> Above all, can we determine whether the Christian hearers are being positively drawn to something else, or are reacting negatively to their own experience? The evidence tilts towards disaffection because of negative experience rather than apostasy because of a stronger attraction . . . It may well be, however, that the Jewish cult—either as a new attraction or as a return—gains in attraction because of the negative consequences of commitment to Jesus as Messiah.[10]

So what were these negative consequences[11] that were causing the audience to think about (re)turning to Judaism? The threat of outright persecution is one important factor, with the preacher ominously saying, "you have not yet resisted to the point of shedding your blood" (12:4). But this isn't pervasive enough to be the only explanation, especially since they've already endured significant suffering in the past yet remained firm (10:32). It's more likely that they're responding to the ongoing feeling of marginalization and rejection by the majority, with "opposition from sinners" having the potential to make them "grow weary" (12:3). They're called to resist the (temporary) shaming at the hands of their culture of origin, instead "bearing the disgrace" Jesus bore (13:13–14), just like the heroes of Israel's history (e.g., Abraham leaving his homeland, 11:8–22; Moses rejecting the Egyptian court he grew up in, 11:24–26).[12]

---

8. *Hebrews*, 72; see also Bruce, *The Epistle to the Hebrews*, 382.

9. Thompson, *Hebrews*, 8–10, notes that the letter doesn't appear to be a polemic against Judaism—only once (13:9) is there a reference to an alternative teaching that needs to be corrected.

10. Johnson, *Hebrews*, 36.

11. Some commentators, e.g., Schmidt, "Moral Lethargy and the Epistle to the Hebrews," 167, have argued that it's more a "moral lethargy" causing them to drift away; however, Cockerill, *The Epistle to the Hebrews*, 118 n.8, rightly notes the frequent references to suffering and social pressure throughout (e.g., 12:4; 13:13).

12. DeSilva, *Perseverance in Gratitude*, 18.

Koester[13] traces three phases in their history that's led to their current situation. The first phase saw them embrace the message of Jesus (6:1), which led to the second, consisting of social and physical persecution:

> Remember those earlier days after you had received the light, when you endured in a great conflict full of suffering. Sometimes you were publicly exposed to insult and persecution; at other times you stood side by side with those who were so treated. You suffered along with those in prison and joyfully accepted the confiscation of your property, because you knew that you yourselves had better and lasting possessions. (10:32–34)

Although the majority tried to pressure them into giving up their beliefs, they endured it "joyfully" and were unashamed to be identified with those who had suffered in this way. This initial wave, far from having the intended effect, actually served to "galvanize solidarity within the Christian community."[14]

But after a while, this ethic of resistance had faded. In this third phase, they were coming to terms with the long-term reality of being a minority group. Some were still in prison (13:3). They were faced with ongoing shame (13:13), and an existence as "foreigners and strangers" like Israel's patriarchs (11:13)—desert wanderers who are not at home in the world (11:38). The question then became: *is following Jesus worth it, if we have to suffer ongoing dishonor and marginalization?* Some, it appears, were yearning once more to fit in with the world, leading to "a reluctance on the part of some to identify with the members of a marginal, low-status group, which would undermine their own status in society."[15] This led some to withdraw from being associated with the group (10:25) and no longer show solidarity with those who were persecuted (10:34). They were tired of being marginalized and in danger of giving up on the group.

It's not too hard to see the parallels with our own situation. In places around the world where the church experiences acute persecution it does often strengthen resolve and commitment. Perversely, over time, it can be the slow, steady, *daily* reminders that we don't fit in with the world that prove harder to resist.

We get mocked when we stand up for God's values in the world, so after a while we stop doing it; we avoid attracting attention, distancing ourselves from outspoken Christians and airbrushing our church connections from our conversation and social media. Or we get worn down by

---

13. Koester, *Hebrews*, 64–72.
14. Koester, *Hebrews*, 70.
15. DeSilva, "Despising Shame," 400.

comparing our lives that are centered on Jesus with those who are living for wealth and status and pleasure—focusing on what we're missing out on rather than what we stand to gain—so little by little, we start to live like that, too. We sniff and lick the marshmallow in front of us, and pick around the edges for a little taste, which only makes us even more hungry for it. And the longer we have to wait for Jesus to come back into the room, the harder it gets to resist.

Being out of step with the majority gets tiring over time, making the potential to "shrink back" and "drift away" from identification with Jesus very real. Yet this is what the preacher to the Hebrews[16] is trying to combat as he urges the Jesus-following minority to keep the faith.

## The supremacy of Christ

The first ten chapters of Hebrews are notoriously theologically rich and complex, but the strategy is strikingly simple. The preacher presents Jesus as superior in every way to the Judaism the audience was being tempted to fall into; he's the greater reality of which the old covenant was merely a shadow. While there might be a sociological *cause* to their wavering, the first thing the preacher does is bolster their theology. Because an accurate perception of the truth is what will protect group members from thinking the grass to be greener elsewhere.

Space doesn't allow for a detailed look at this long exercise in comparison, but in any case it's the pattern that's important. Jesus is superior to the previous revelations of God precisely because he's the son, which in the ancient world made him most qualified to make the father known (1:1–3). He's greater than angels (1:4), who in Hellenistic Jewish thought were mediators of the old covenant (2:1); as well as Moses (3:3), through whom the law was given; and the Levitical priesthood, being a priest of a higher order (7:11). The tabernacle at which he serves is a heavenly one (8:2), of which the earthly sanctuary is a mere copy (8:5); and his

---

16. Preacher to the Hebrews? It's anonymous, so the traditional way of referring to the author has been "the writer to the Hebrews." I prefer the term "preacher" as it highlights the genre of the discourse, which is self-described as a "word of exhortation" (13:22), a term for the synagogue homily (cf. the same phrase used in Acts 13:15). The preacher couldn't be there to deliver it in person, so it's been written down for a substitute—this would usually be the courier—to deliver out loud. This also explains the lack of epistolary opening. At the end of the sermon, the preacher takes the opportunity to add the customary letter greetings since it was being sent in that manner. See Witherington, *Letters and Homilies for Jewish Christians*, 20–21; Hagner, *Encountering the Book of Hebrews*, 29–30.

once-for-all sacrifice surpasses the repeated offerings made by priests (10:11–12).[17] In doing this, the preacher is using the language and stories of the parent group—Hellenistic Judaism—to show how they are completed in Christ. In other words: *if you want to (re)turn to Judaism, realize that it's been fulfilled in and superseded by Jesus.*

Throughout this series of comparisons, the preacher pauses to give exhortations based on it, making it clear what we're supposed to "do" with this theology. For example:

- If the revelation that's come through Jesus is greater than previous revelations, don't you think the disadvantage in rejecting will also be greater (2:1–4)?
- If in the household of God Jesus is the son, whereas Moses was merely a servant, doesn't it make sense to fix your thoughts on Jesus (3:1–6)?
- If there was a sabbath rest for the old covenant people, which many missed out on, how much greater will be our promised rest? So make sure you don't miss out (4:1–2)!
- If our high priest is without sin himself and permanently in the presence of God, how much more confident should we be than if we still had to go through an imperfect high priest (4:14–5:3)?

This is a reminder that the theology found in the New Testament isn't an abstraction; it's always doing something. If all we do with Hebrews is use it to construct our systematic Christology, we're missing the point. The profound Christology of Hebrews is intended to remind its minority audience of the superiority of what they're in danger of drifting away from, over against what they're tempted to (re)turn to. *Just because it will make things easier in the short term doesn't make it better. Two marshmallows are better than one. Jesus is infinitely better than what he came to fulfil.*[18] That goes for Judaism; and it also goes for any other religion or philosophy we might be tempted to drift toward. (But we'll leave that point for our discussion of Colossians in chapter 11.)

---

17. Johnson, *Hebrews*, 32.

18. This means that the *primary* application of a sermon series on Hebrews will be pretty much the same each week, if we're following the application of the original sermon. My advice, then, is either to deal with larger sections of text, focusing on the pattern a little more than the detail; or to preach a number of short series spread out over a few years. Another option is a series from 10:19 until the end (which is the more application-heavy part of the original sermon), bringing in some of the comparison material from 1–10 to illustrate.

## The advantage of not shrinking back

After the long series of comparisons, the sermon moves into a new phase (10:19) which more directly addresses the audience's minority status. It begins with a deliberative argument setting out the advantages of resisting the marshmallow of acceptance and compromise.

> Therefore, brothers and sisters, since we have confidence to enter the Most Holy Place by the blood of Jesus, by a new and living way opened for us through the curtain, that is, his body, and since we have a great priest over the house of God, *let us draw near to God* with a sincere heart and with the full assurance that faith brings, having our hearts sprinkled to cleanse us from a guilty conscience and having our bodies washed with pure water. Let us hold unswervingly to the hope we profess, *for he who promised is faithful.* (10:19–23)

It sums up the comparisons found in the previous chapters with a call to "draw near" to God, rather than drift away. In light of the advantages of living under the new covenant, it urges unswerving faithfulness to the one who has proven himself faithful.

## Maintaining the alternative court of reputation

Importantly, that "drawing near" involves a greater commitment to the group:

> And let us consider how we may spur one another on toward love and good deeds, not giving up meeting together, as some are in the habit of doing, but encouraging one another—and all the more as you see the Day approaching. (10:24–25)

As we discussed in chapter 2, this is an important part of insulating the group from being molded by the majority culture. Regular contact helps to redefine their court of reputation and *keep it* redefined; it gives them a visible alternative community in which honorable behavior is determined and encouraged. It helps to see that there are others who haven't eaten their marshmallow, either.

This has always been crucial, but even more so at this cultural moment in the West. There's a perfect storm for believers in which the values of mainstream society are diverging from Christian values, with rejection and hostility increasing as a result. Yet at the very time believers should be increasing the regularity of their contact in order to counteract that pressure, we find it decreasing in the face of at least two significant headwinds. The first is time-poverty, with long commutes and dual incomes in many cities being no longer lifestyle choices but survival necessities. And the second is the (justified) reaction against the legalism of previous generations in measuring spiritual maturity by church attendance; this has led to an overcorrection in which regular gathering is seen as just one in a number of competing life priorities. It's true that this passage in Hebrews has been used in the past to guilt people into church attendance. In the context of its minority group rhetoric, however, it should be used to highlight the importance of gathering with other group members (whatever that looks like) as a key means by which God enables us to resist the pressure to "shrink back" from identifying with him and his people. It's hard to live by an alternative court of reputation if the court is hardly ever in session.

### The disadvantage and dishonor of turning away

The preacher then switches to the negative, warning of the great *disadvantage* that will be experienced if the audience doesn't "hold unswervingly" and instead turns away. And he does this by an appeal to the stronger emotions—or *pathos,* as the speechwriting handbooks of the day called it.[19]

The first emotion is **fear**.[20] Like any good orator of the time, the preacher wants his audience to fear the consequences of the alternative. The consequences for rejecting Jesus—particularly for those who once followed him—are fearsome indeed:

> If we deliberately keep on sinning after we have received the knowledge of the truth, no sacrifice for sins is left, but only a fearful expectation of judgment and of raging fire that will consume the enemies of God . . . It is a dreadful thing to fall into the hands of the living God. (10:26-27, 31)

A little later, the preacher uses fear again. This time it's a foil for the **confident hope** his audience can have, since they aren't fearfully camped at the foot of Mount Sinai (representing Judaism) but joyfully celebrating on Mount Zion (12:18-29). Just as God's voice "shook the earth" at Sinai, there will be an even greater shaking in the future, this time involving the heavens

---

19. Aristotle, *Ars rhetorica* 1.2.5; 2.1.8; Quintilian, *Institutio oratoria* 6.2.9. See my discussion on the New Testament writers' use of *pathos* in *Catching the Wave,* 145–59.

20. Eriksson, "Fear of Eternal Damnation," 116, notes that deliberative rhetoric was most often associated with the positive emotion of hope (cf. "the hope we profess" in v. 23) and the negative emotion of fear ("fearful expectation" in v. 27; "dreadful thing" in v. 31).

as well (12:26); yet his audience can be confident, because they're receiving "a kingdom that cannot be shaken." The appropriate response to being on the "good side" of this fearsome God is "reverence and awe" (12:28).

These days, attempts to evoke fear are often derided as "fear-mongering," implying that we're trying to make something sound more frightening than it is. But the consequences of rejecting God *are* legitimately frightening. Without returning to the fire-and-brimstone preaching of generations past, a neglected aspect of minority group rhetoric is the arousing of appropriate fear at what it would mean to leave the group.

The second emotion is **indignance**.[21] The preacher wants to arouse a sense of righteous anger against those who would reject God's favor. They've counted the cost of following Jesus and decided that the benefits he brings are not worth the suffering. They no longer want to be identified with him, despite everything he's done for them. The preacher asks:

> How much more severely do you think someone deserves to be punished who has trampled the Son of God underfoot, who has treated as an unholy thing the blood of the covenant that sanctified them, and who has insulted *the Spirit of grace*? (10:29)

The preacher wants his audience to be indignant at the very thought of someone who looks at God's gift and throws it back in his face, deciding that they preferred the rewards and respect of the world. The last phrase belongs the language of patronage, in which ingratitude towards one's patron is the greatest injustice a person could commit and undying loyalty was expected.[22] Against that background, "shrinking back" merely to avoid the shaming of outsiders was dishonoring to God, who had shown nothing but generous favor and unchanging loyalty.

Fear isn't the only emotion we're tempted to downplay today. In emphasizing a loving, forgiving God we can sometimes build a picture of an easy-going "doormat" who doesn't care when we dishonor him by choosing the world's favor over his. David deSilva powerfully tries to redress the balance in commenting on this text, arousing in us an appropriate sense of indignance at our own behavior:

> If we care more about success, respect, or being wise as this world defines it, if we keep following its rules and set our ambitions on its promises, we trample upon Jesus. We set too little value on his blood if we refuse to walk in that life for which he freed us. We insult God's favor if we seek to secure the world's

---

21. See Hermogenes, *De inventione* 2.8 on how to arouse indignation in an audience.
22. See Seneca, *De beneficiis* (esp. 1.1; 5.15).

favor first and then, as far as the world will let us, God's promised benefits.

If our first thought is for keeping our neighbors' or coworkers' or fellow citizens' approval, and if we seek to live out our Christian life within the parameters of the kinds of behaviors or words that will not 'offend' the unbelievers, we show by our lives whose approval really matters to us, and we insult God.

A special danger faces the Christian in the modern, secularized world . . . Our tendency is to attend dutifully to everything else our society tells us is important and then to give religious concerns any leftover time, resources, and energy. Again, such an approach to life says to God, 'your gifts and call are not of the first order of importance in my life.'[23]

## The advantage and honor of perseverance

Having reminded them of the negative consequences of *not* persevering—if they eat the marshmallow now, there's no prospect of a second—the preacher returns to a more positive mode. Perseverance is both honorable and, ultimately, to their advantage.

To persuade them of this, he's about to give a whole list of examples from Israel's past—the honor roll of God's people who refused to buckle under the pressure from the world around them because they were looking to their eternal reward (Heb 11). But before he gets to this, the preacher reminds them of their own example:

> Remember those earlier days after you had received the light, when you endured *in a great conflict* (Greek: *athlēsis*) full of suffering. Sometimes you were publicly exposed to insult and persecution; at other times you stood side by side with those who were so treated. You suffered along with those in prison and joyfully accepted the confiscation of your property, because you knew that you yourselves had better and lasting possessions. (10:32–34)

He even casts it in terms of an athletic contest, using the word *athlēsis* rather than the usual word for trials, drawing out both the honorable nature of the struggle and their competitive spirit. Later (12:1), he'll refer to those who've gone before as a "cloud of witnesses" watching them compete. What's more, he's simply calling them to live up to their own reputation, remembering their earlier courage and perseverance. In a sense, they've already

---

23. DeSilva, *Perseverance in Gratitude*, 373.

"won the first round,"[24] and to give up now would be to "throw away" their previous efforts (10:35). (For this reason, I once preached Hebrews 10 as a locker room speech delivered by the coach at half time.) The fourth century preacher John Chrysostom commented on this passage:

> Powerful is the exhortation from deeds [already done]: for he who begins a work ought to go forward and add to it . . . And he who encourages, does thus especially encourage them from their own example.[25]

There's even an example of this strategy from about the time Hebrews was written. The historian Tacitus quotes a famous general who motivated his troops by saying:

> I would quote the examples of other armies to encourage you. As things are, you need only recall your own battle-honours.[26]

The reason for perseverance is then given, bringing to mind yet again the eternal advantage that awaits:

> So do not throw away your confidence; it will be *richly rewarded*. You need to persevere so that when you have done the will of God, you will *receive what he has promised*. (10:35–36)

And this is salient, due both to the imminence of Jesus' return and the seriousness of the consequences:

> For, "*In just a little while*, he who is coming will come and will not delay." And, "But my righteous one will live by faith. And *I take no pleasure* in the one who shrinks back." (10:37–38)

The preacher then concludes with a strategy familiar to teachers before a field trip, or some other occasion where the children will need to behave in public. After warning the class in a stern voice about the fearsome punishment that awaits those who misbehave, the tone suddenly changes: "But *we're* not going to be like that, are we, class?" And at least with younger children, they all respond, *"No . . .!"* Give them an honorable reputation to live up to, and then show them you're confident they can do it. Not much has changed in two thousand years:

---

24. *The Letter to the Hebrews in Social-Scientific Perspective*, 87–88.

25. *Nicene and Post-Nicene Fathers* 1.14:461, cited in *Perseverance in Gratitude*, 357.

26. Tacitus, *Agricola* 33–34; cited in *The Letter to the Hebrews in Social-Scientific Perspective*, 83.

"And I take no pleasure in the one who shrinks back." But *we* are not of those who shrink back and are destroyed, but of those who believe and are saved. (10:38–39)

In seeking to inspire perseverance in our own Jesus-following minority, we shouldn't neglect the power of our own past example. Celebrating how far God has already brought us is an effective way of highlighting how dishonorable it would be to give up now—not only to God, but also to our own previous efforts. And it reminds us that to persevere, we simply need to live up to who we already are; our group identity is of a people who don't conform to the relentless pressure of the world. (We'll talk more in chapter 10 about the power of giving people a reputation to live up to, in our look at 1 Thessalonians.)

## The honor of despising shame

The next chapter sees an abrupt change in mode, as the preacher shifts from a deliberative argument to an epideictic one, commending a series of honorable figures from the past. These examples are significant to the minority group audience for two reasons. The first is that they're from the Hebrew Scriptures; the preacher is using stories from the parent group, Judaism, to persuade Christ-followers not to (re)turn to it. The second is that the stories are narrated in such a way as to highlight their faithfulness to God in terms of prioritizing future reward ahead of present concerns—in particular, ahead of being accepted by the surrounding culture.[27] None of them ate the marshmallow.

It's worth going through this in some detail, to see the rhetorical effect it might have had on the hearers. It starts with a definition of "faith":

> Now faith is confidence in what we hope for and assurance about what we do not see. This is what the ancients were commended for . . . And without faith it is impossible to please God, because anyone who comes to him must believe that he exists and that he rewards those who earnestly seek him. (11:1–2, 6)

The word "faith" carries a bit more weight in Greek than in English. We have a range of words we use in English depending on the context: belief, faith, trust, and loyalty. The people listed in this chapter are commended for their *faith:* belief in who God is, and trust that he could deliver on his promises—no matter how outlandish they were. More than that, they put this trust into action through loyal obedience, despite the temporary consequences. In

---

27. Schenck, *Understanding the Book of Hebrews*, 67–68.

other words: they trusted God that there'd be far more than just an additional marshmallow awaiting them if they endured.

We then hear the roll call of those who were *faithful* throughout the history of the old covenant:

> By faith/trust Abel brought God a better offering than Cain did. By faith he was commended as righteous, when God spoke well of his offerings. And by faith Abel still speaks, even though he is dead. (11:4)

Abel displayed a trusting, loyal, obedient response by giving the *best* of his produce to God, in contrast with his brother Cain. He put loyalty to God ahead of temporary gain, refusing to keep his marshmallow for himself, so that his legacy of faithfulness still speaks today.

After commending Enoch, the preacher moves on to the archetypal shamed minority, Noah:

> By faith Noah, when warned about things not yet seen, in holy fear built an ark to save his family. By his faith he condemned the world and became heir of the righteousness that is in keeping with faith. (11:7)

What kind of fool builds a giant boat in his front yard for several years, despite the scorn and ridicule of his neighbors? The kind of fool who trusts that God knows what he's doing; the kind who's no fool at all, because he knows that loyalty to God pays off in the long term. In the end, his neighbors were the ones who were put to shame, munching on their soggy marshmallows as the flood waters rose. *Just like what will happen to those who are ridiculing you in the present for being loyal to God . . .* But we're getting ahead of ourselves.

> By faith Abraham, when called to go to a place he would later receive as his inheritance, obeyed and went, even though he did not know where he was going. By faith he made his home in the promised land *like a stranger in a foreign country* . . . (11:8–9)

That sounds like the experience of a first-century Jew living as an alien in the Greek and Roman world in the Mediterranean. Or like a Jesus-follower whose primary loyalty is to God, not Caesar; whose primary allegiance is not as a citizen of their earthly city, but a heavenly one.

> For he was looking forward to the city with foundations, whose architect and builder is God. (11:10)

A greater city; one greater than *Rome,* perhaps? Or any other city in which we might live as a faithful minority today.

> And by faith even Sarah, who was past childbearing age, was enabled to bear children because she considered him faithful who had made the promise. (11:11)

Ignoring the odd disbelieving laugh, Sarah, too, responded in faith. She trusted God despite the impossibility of the promise, and gave birth to a little baby marshmallow:

> And so from this one man, and he as good as dead, came descendants as numerous as the stars in the sky and as countless as the sand on the seashore. (11:12)

Countless packets of marshmallows, all because Abraham and Sarah trusted in God's promise, remaining loyal to God while strangers in a strange land. We then get a quick half-time recap:

> All these people were still living by faith when they died. They did not receive the things promised; they only saw them and welcomed them from a distance, admitting that they were foreigners and strangers on earth. (11:13)

This is important, because even these great heroes of faithfulness didn't see the fulfilment of the promises, only their "down-payment." By the end of his life, the only part of the Promised Land Abraham owned was his burial place. Yet they were content with their down-payment, because they were looking forward to something *beyond* this life.

> People who say such things show that they are looking for a country of their own. If they had been thinking of the country they had left, they would have had opportunity to return. Instead, they were longing for a better country—a heavenly one. Therefore God is not ashamed to be called their God, for he has prepared a city for them. (11:14–16)

People who embrace their "outsider" existence as aliens and exiles do so because they have the hope of a better place to call home. Otherwise they'd settle down and become a true part of the city they're in. Instead, they remained loyal to God's promise of a better city. And because they remained loyal—*not ashamed* to be known as followers of God—he remained loyal to them.

The preacher then takes us through the testing of Abraham's faith when he's told to sacrifice the child of the promise. Abraham responds in faith, trusting that "God could even raise the dead" if necessary. *This calls for a similar trust when your reputations, your possessions, and even your very lives are at stake.*

We're then reminded of how Isaac and Jacob both looked forward to God's promise of a land of their own. And even Joseph, who had risen to become the prime minister of Egypt, made sure his bones and those of his father would be buried back in the land. And then we get the story of Moses:

> By faith Moses' parents hid him for three months after he was born, because they saw he was no ordinary child, and they were not afraid of the king's edict. (11:23)

The implication is: *they also wouldn't be afraid of someone like Caesar, either.* (Or what the media or your neighbors might think.)

> By faith Moses, when he had grown up, refused to be known as the son of Pharaoh's daughter. (11:24)

As an exiled alien, he wasn't interested in the status he could get by joining with an oppressive foreign power—such as Roman citizenship?

> He chose to be mistreated along with the people of God rather than to enjoy the fleeting pleasures of sin. (11:25)

Just like the audience of Hebrews had been mistreated for belonging to God's people.

> He regarded disgrace for the sake of Christ as of greater value than the treasures of Egypt, because he was looking ahead to his reward. (11:26)

This is a bit anachronistically phrased, as Moses didn't know of Christ, but we get the idea: temporary treasures from the world, or a longer-lasting reward from God. *Marshmallow now, or much more later.*

> By faith he left Egypt, not fearing the king's anger; he persevered because he saw him who is invisible. (11:27)

He knew that God is more powerful than Caesar . . . I mean, Pharaoh . . .

> By faith he kept the Passover and the application of blood, so that the destroyer of the firstborn would not touch the firstborn of Israel. (11:28)

The stakes were high for Moses, just like they are today. *Do we remain faithful to God—or become like the world, and join them in their journey to destruction?*

So we've seen the example of Abraham and the other patriarchs. We've just had the example of Moses. Let's see who's the *next* great hero of faithfulness:

> By faith the people passed through the Red Sea as on dry land; but when the Egyptians tried to do so, they were drowned. (11:29)

By faith ... *the people*? In a list of the great leaders—Abraham, Isaac, Jacob, Joseph, Moses—surely *Joshua* is next, right? The one whose name means "savior"—are we not going to get a Joshua in this list?

> By faith the walls of Jericho fell, after the army had marched around them for seven days. (11:30)

A big, fortified city got destroyed by God's power without so much as a siege ramp! Maybe trusting in earthly cities for security isn't all it's cracked up to be. *Rome, we're looking at you.* (Not to mention Washington, Moscow, and Beijing.)

> By faith the prostitute Rahab, because she welcomed the spies, was not killed with those who were disobedient. (11:31)

So *Rahab* is mentioned by name—a non-Israelite, a reformed prostitute from Canaan—but not Joshua? And if you look at the next section, it looks like Rahab is the climax of this list,[28] since the rest just get a summary:

> And what more shall I say? I do not have time to tell about Gideon, Barak, Samson and Jephthah, about David and Samuel and the prophets ... (11:32)

The significance of Rahab lies in the reason she gives for hiding the spies:

> "We have heard how the Lord dried up the water of the Red Sea for you when you came out of Egypt ... When we heard of it, our hearts melted in fear and everyone's courage failed because of you, for the Lord your God is God in heaven above and on the earth below. Now then, please swear to me by the Lord that you will show kindness to my family, because I have shown kindness to you." (Josh 2:10–12)

Rahab realized Yahweh was the true God, and switched sides. She put belonging to God's people ahead of loyalty to her own city—a decision that proved to be to her advantage, as the earthly city of Jericho didn't endure.[29]

---

28. Mosser, "Rahab Outside the Camp," 384.
29. "Rahab Outside the Camp," 397.

She went on to live among God's people (Josh 6:25), experiencing his blessing—although still as a *bit* of an outsider. Because she was a Gentile, she couldn't enter the tabernacle or participate fully in worship of God. She would have had to go "outside the camp" because she was ritually impure. Just like Jesus did on our behalf:

> Let us, then, go to him outside the camp, bearing the disgrace he bore. For here we do not have an enduring city, but we are looking for the city that is to come. (Heb 13:13–14)

The rhetorical effect is: *let's put up with mistreatment by our fellow citizens, if it means getting an enduring city.* Just like Rahab, along with all the other heroes of the faith that time wouldn't let us talk about in detail:

> There were others who were tortured, refusing to be released so that *they might gain an even better resurrection*. Some faced jeers and flogging, and even chains and imprisonment. They were put to death by stoning; they were sawed in two; they were killed by the sword. They went about in sheepskins and goatskins, destitute, persecuted and mistreated—*the world was not worthy of them*. They wandered in deserts and mountains, living in caves and in holes in the ground. (11:35–38)

It's always been this way with the people of God, because living by faith means foregoing the marshmallow of security now, to get something far greater in the future. This is greater than even that which the Old Testament heroes experienced, because the fulfilment of this promise still lies in *our* future:

> These were all commended for their faith, yet none of them received what had been promised, since God had planned something better for us so that only together with us would they be made complete. (11:39–40)

These heroes of the faith didn't get what they were promised in full *in this life*. They're still waiting for their second marshmallow. Nevertheless, they remained loyal. The preacher makes the point of examples, which have been implicit up until this point, explicit:

> Therefore, since we are surrounded by such a great cloud of witnesses, let us throw off everything that hinders and the sin that so easily entangles. And let us run with perseverance the race marked out for us. (12:1)

The preacher is appealing to his audience's sense of honor: *with all of these past greats watching your performance, how can we not put in 100 percent and make it to the finish line like they did? After all, those heroes of the faith are part of our heritage as the people of God!*

And then, just as we think the honor roll has come to an end, Joshua-the-savior makes his appearance, although we know him better by the Greek form of his name:

> And let us run with perseverance the race marked out for us, *fixing our eyes on Jesus*, the pioneer and perfecter of faith. For the joy set before him he endured the cross, *despising its shame*, and sat down at the right hand of the throne of God. Consider him who endured such opposition from sinners, so that you will not grow weary and lose heart. (12:1–3)

Jesus is the ultimate example of putting future honor ahead of temporary acceptance by the world. He didn't try to prove himself honorable according to the world's way of judging. Instead, he rejected its whole system, *despising* the verdict of "shameful" that it pronounced on him. Jesus provides the most significant example of how to endure the shame of the majority. He also provides the evidence that enduring that shame will lead to future glory. And as for the Judaism to which they were being tempted—their great examples of faithfulness are merely part of a long line of which *Jesus* is the fulfilment!

David deSilva summarizes the rhetorical strategy thus:

> The author solves this problem [of being shamed by the majority] by holding up before the congregation an alternative system of honor—one familiar to them, but with regard to which they require reinforcement—which carries with it the promise of greater and lasting reward for those honored according to its standards. The author seeks to persuade the congregation to disregard the society's evaluation of honor and dishonor and to continue confidently in Christian identity and associations as a means of satisfying their desire for honor.[30]

These are "textbook" minority group strategies to counteract the attempts by the majority to shame them. The preacher convenes an alternative court of reputation consisting of Jesus and the ancients of Israel's history (along with their own past selves). He offers a reason to ignore voices outside that redefined court: like Noah's neighbors and the citizens of Jericho, they'll be on the wrong side of history. He reframes their shame and suffering as fatherly discipline, which is proof they are God's children (12:4–12). And he

---

30. DeSilva, "Despising Shame," 400.

constantly directs their eyes to the future reward that can only be attained by joining Rahab and Jesus "outside the camp":

> For here we do not have an enduring city, but we are looking for *the city that is to come.* (13:14)

Because when Jesus comes back in the room, we get to eat *all* the marshmallows we could ever want.

# 5

# 1 John
## *They Went Out from Us*

MANY YEARS AGO, A young man in his late teens turned up to our church. He'd been raised and schooled in a small fundamentalist church, but since leaving school he'd become increasingly disillusioned with the church's legalism and efforts to control every aspect of its members' lives. So he left. And his church's response was telling. They broke with their scheduled preaching program to make way for a three-week series on the evils of popular music (since our church had a band with guitars and, gasp, drums!) and the NIV translation of the Bible. It seemed like a desperate attempt to persuade the young adults who remained not to follow in their recently departed, ex-brother's footsteps. It was a classic minority group response to losing members, reinforcing group values and depicting those who've left as having sold out to the world and its evils.

This is not unlike what's going on in 1 John. Which leads to the question: is that a valid or appropriate pattern of response when people leave our minority group? To answer this question thoughtfully, we first need to look at what was going on in the background to John's letter and how John's rhetoric was intended to function in that setting. Only then can we properly identifying the similarities *and differences* with our own setting that will help us determine the extent to which we can appropriate the rhetoric of 1 John for ourselves.

### Under pressure on two fronts[1]

The first epistle of John differs from the other examples in this book as it appears to be attempting to insulate its audience on two fronts. As well as

---

1. Material in this section has been reworked from "Aliens and Strangers," 323–28.

being a minority resisting the pressure to conform to the majority culture, they're also dealing with an internal crisis: some members of the group have "gone out" from them over issues that appear to have both doctrinal and behavioral dimensions.

Scholarship has previously been focused on trying to describe or identify the rival group which left.[2] This has proven elusive, since the letter isn't written to the rival group, but to those who *hadn't* been led astray by their false teaching, and had thus remained.[3] This is why John doesn't engage in much argument against the rival group's teaching; he doesn't need to. He's more interested in those who remain, reaffirming group identity, values, and boundaries. Even when John seems to contrast true teaching with an alternative, it can't be assumed that the alternative must represent the teaching of the rival group. Greek rhetoric commonly used phrases like "if we say . . ." or "if anyone says . . ." to advance an argument against its hypothetical alternatives without there having to be actual opponents voicing the opposite.[4] In other words, we can't simply mirror-read from John's rhetoric the details of the rival group's theology. At best, we can glean that they denied either Jesus' human nature, or the saving effects of his work while in the flesh (2:22),[5] which points to a disagreement over core theology rather than secondary matters of practice or emphasis. Beyond that, the precise nature of the dispute is not overly relevant for our study of John's rhetoric.[6] As Witherington notes, "if these secessionists have gone out, then our author is neither answering nor debating them in this sermon; rather, he is trying to heal his congregation(s) and do damage control after the fact."[7] Brown

---

2. See, for example, Brown, *The Epistles of John*; Dodd, *The Johannine Epistles*; Marshall, *The Epistles of John*; Stott, *The Letters of John*.

3. Watson, "Amplification Techniques," 118.

4. Griffith, "A Non-Polemical Reading of 1 John," 258–60. Trebilco, *The Early Christians*, 280, similarly notes that in 1 John 2:3–5, the phrases "we know," "the one who says," and "anyone who keeps" are used without any indication of a change of referent.

5. Witherington, *Letters and Homilies for Hellenized Christians*, 1, 430–31.

6. There may be some relevance in how the errant theology which denied the work of the incarnate Christ (4:2–3) is linked with belonging to and being accepted by the majority (4:5). Today, we might perceive similar tendencies in which Christ's work can be stripped of its sacrificial significance, lest our culture reject it as portraying the kind of violent, vengeful God invented by superstitious pre-moderns. Or we might see it in how Christ's work can be stripped of its embodied significance, allowing us to sign up individual souls to a glorious, disembodied afterlife without having to challenge selfish behavior in the present—notably, the call to be part of a people who demonstrate radical care for one another, for the poor and oppressed, and for the physical world God will one day restore.

7. Witherington, *Letters and Homilies for Hellenized Christians*, 1, 428.

likewise concludes that the letter "was written to preserve an interpretation of the schism ... for insiders rather than to convince outsiders."[8]

What's more significant for our purposes is not the details of the disagreement but the way in which John seeks to rebuild his community after the rival group has left. At its heart, the rhetorical strategy used is *epideictic*.[9] We noted previously that this kind of rhetoric isn't intended to advance new ideas, but to reaffirm already-held beliefs and values as a means of strengthening the group's identity and boundaries.[10] This is quite clear in 1 John:

> That which was from the beginning ... (1:1)

> I am not writing to you a new command ... (2:7)

> I do not write to you because you do not know the truth, but because you do know it ... (2:21)

In the wake of the departure of the rival group, John's epistolary sermon serves as an important pastoral reminder of what the group already knows and how it already behaves.

## Refining the court of reputation

Integral to epideictic rhetoric is the idea of honor. In what's by now a familiar strategy to us, John encourages his community to keep seeking their honor from God rather than the majority culture, which is hostile both to God and his people (3:13–14). His court of reputation is the only one which counts:

> And now, dear children, continue in him, so that when he appears we may be confident and *unashamed* before him *at his coming*. (2:28)

Expressions such as "this is the last hour" (2:18) and "when Christ appears" (3:2) give an appropriate sense of urgency, and highlight the importance of being found "unashamed" when God's court is in session.

The way John's audience is to do this is to continue showing behavior that's prototypical for the group: namely, love for one another (e.g., 3:23). The frequent use of family-language (e.g., 2:1, 8, 14; 5:21) strengthens this appeal,

---

8. Brown, *The Epistles of John*, 91.

9. Watson, "An Epideictic Strategy," 144–45; Painter and Harrington, *1, 2, and 3 John*, 87.

10. Kennedy, "Genres of Rhetoric," 45.

as well as being a reminder that those who have remained form part of that alternative court of reputation in which they should seek honor.

John also uses the emotive rhetoric of praise and blame, contrasting the faithful ones who have remained with the unfaithful ones who have left. His audience is praised because they know God and have overcome evil (2:12–14). This is contrasted with a correspondingly negative depiction of the character of the rival group (2:18–27),[11] mostly using pejorative language[12] such as "antichrists" (2:18), "false prophets" (4:1) who are "of the devil" (4:3), as well as "liars" who "deny" group beliefs (2:22) and "lead astray" members of the group (2:26; 3:7); the end result is death (5:16). It's important to point out that this is at no point used *against* those who have left; it's for internal consumption only. According to Witherington, the purpose of this strong rhetoric is

> to help those remaining to let [those who have left] go and focus once more on their own spiritual well-being and belief system. It is meant to ensure that the community stops losing members and that none that remain are tempted to embrace the beliefs and behavior of the departed.[13]

This is part of John's clear delineation between "us" and "them." In a classic minority group strategy, the fact that the rival group "went out" is interpreted as a sign they did not "belong to us" (2:19). By their opposition, they showed that they didn't belong to the group, and therefore they neither belong to God nor have his approval (4:6). In fact, it's implied that their departure was tied up with seeking the approval of the majority culture:

> They are from the world and therefore speak from the viewpoint of the world, and the world listens to them. (4:5)

This rhetorical move effectively joins up the two fronts of the battle. It means that rhetorical strategies used to insulate the group against rejection and disapproval by the majority culture can equally be applied to those who have recently abandoned the group. Those who have left show by the very act of their leaving that they belong to the wider world; so their opposition should be expected (3:13) because the world is ignorant (3:14), evil (2:16), and under control of the devil (5:19). In this way, members who have left are deemed unworthy of being in the group's court of reputation, and are therefore removed.

---

11. Watson, "An Epideictic Strategy," 149, classes this as "an extended proof from pathos, the arousing of audience emotion for or against the issue and people involved."

12. "Amplification Techniques," 121.

13. Witherington, *Letters and Homilies for Hellenized Christians*, 1, 432.

### Assurance from prototypical behavior

As well as this negative depiction of the two sources of opposition (the rival group, and the majority culture), John also needs to reassure his audience that they are indeed in the right—that the verdict of God's court of reputation will be favorable. This is the explicit reason John gives for writing:

> I write these things to you who believe in the name of the Son of God *so that you may know* that you have eternal life. (5:13)

John seeks to instill this confidence by making prototypical behavior the litmus test. If they want to be confident of God's vindication, they should look no further than whether or not they display the character of the group's founder:

> This is how love is made complete among us so that we will have *confidence* on the day of judgment: in this world we are like Jesus. (4:17)

Living like Jesus, rather than the majority culture, is what gives assurance. The behavior of group members is to follow that of the group's prototype, since "whoever claims to live in him must live *as Jesus did*" (2:6) and "all who have this hope in him purify themselves, *just as he is pure*" (3:3). By contrast, group membership involves rejecting the majority culture's values and desires (2:17): they are not to "love the world or anything in the world" (2:15) and are told in closing, "keep yourselves from idols" (5:21).

Ultimately, assurance is found in obedience to God's commands. Although general obedience to Jesus' teaching is in view, John gives particular focus to group behavior that promotes solidarity and love for other members in a practical way (3:18). This behavior makes group identity concrete, and strengthens group boundaries:

> John is concerned to underline what is appropriate behavior within the community. The image of light and darkness, the concept of truth and falsehood, and the experience of forgiveness and loving one another within the circle of the fellowship of believers, all combine to strengthen the sense of community, and to define its limits.[14]

This ideal of practical love for one another is phrased not merely as an exhortation; it's also given as a command (3:23; 4:21). It's grounded in the character and example of the God who demonstrated his love in sending his son as an atoning sacrifice (4:7–12). What's more, this supreme act of love is

---

14. Griffith, "A Non-Polemical Reading of 1 John," 261.

seen as the defining symbol of the group (4:11). The atoning blood of Christ as celebrated in the Lord's Supper—along with the signs of baptism and the receiving of the Holy Spirit (5:8)—are the unique symbols and shared experience that set the audience apart from Judaism and the Greco-Roman world.[15] Group members are called to align not just their behavior but also their sense of identity with this founding action of God.

## Using John's rhetoric today

When people leave our local church or denomination today, it can be tempting to follow the kind of rhetorical response we see in 1 John—just like in the example I mentioned at the start of this chapter. It can be effective, at least in the short term, in minimizing fallout and strengthening those who remain. But in the longer term, it mostly detracts from the attractiveness of our difference; a plethora of churches and other Christian groups engaging in the rhetoric of division isn't attractive to the outside world, and in the process it undermines our own identity of loving one another. If we choose to adopt the rhetorical strategy of 1 John it must be done thoughtfully, taking into account the many differences between the original rhetorical setting and our own. (In fact, what follows is quite different from the other chapters in this book, as it amounts to an argument that most of the time we should *not* use the rhetorical tactics of 1 John, due to the overwhelming nature of those differences.)

### Is the division over core beliefs?

Most fundamentally, we noted that the issue that divided the two groups in 1 John was one of core belief. It wasn't about secondary, debatable matters, nor was it about style or emphasis. Those who left had aligned themselves with the majority culture in such a way that put the message of salvation in peril. They were denying the very means by which someone could be a member of God's people. For this reason, the rhetoric of "us" and "them" was tragically appropriate.

How many divisions in the Christian world today fall into this category? Depending on our denominational background, we can probably point to some historic points of division in which we believe this was the case. Some of those probably still stand; others may have become what David Fitch has called "banners":

---

15. "A Non-Polemical Reading of 1 John," 272.

> When distinctives become less about daily living and more about what differentiates us from other people, they in essence become banners to be waved around signaling who is in and who is out of our group. What started out as good and helpful discernment in the life of a church becomes about making enemies.[16]

Before drawing group boundaries along the lines of 1 John, we need to discern whether the division was *and still is* a core issue of salvific importance, or whether it's become merely a banner. If the source of the division doesn't seriously call into question another group's union with Christ, we simply *can't* appropriate John's "us" and "them" rhetoric. We can fiercely disagree over the issue while still affirming each other as sisters and brothers in Christ.

Of course, it's rarely that simple in practice. Normally one, if not both sides of such a division will be convinced the issue is "core" to salvation. I suspect that the fundamentalist church preaching against the NIV saw it as changing the God-given words of salvation that can only be found in the original King James, and that we risked giving the devil a foothold in our lives by bringing his musical instruments into our church.[17] I also suspect that my own denomination has elevated some issues to the status of salvific core, with arguments that are similarly convincing . . . to ourselves. We'll only be able to look beyond our cultural and denominational blind spots if each generation re-evaluates the issues which divide us, approaching with an attitude of humility, listening, and an openness to the Holy Spirit (as opposed to the Zeitgeist) if he wishes to correct us in how we've come to interpret his infallible word.[18]

## Use sectarian rhetoric with great caution

Unavoidably, there will still be some occasions when we *do* need to draw group boundaries, just like John did. There will be disputes over issues which are core to salvation, or at the very least, consequential. But there's a distinction we can make between doing *what* John was doing—insulating the group

---

16. Fitch, *The Church of Us vs. Them*, 30.

17. In my teens, I aspired to be a professional contemporary musician. A fundamentalist pastor once responded, "a Christian rock musician—isn't that a bit like being a Christian prostitute?" I told him no, it didn't pay as well.

18. By this I'm urging us to be open to correction in our interpretive judgments (rather than being the grumpy old wineskins of Matt 9:17) without adopting the shallowly-inclusive "all of the above" answer of postmodernity; without bending to culture in an attempt to remain in its favor; and without suggesting that there is any further revelation of the Spirit that corrects or mitigates the canonical Scriptures and the teaching of God's final Word contained therein.

from being similarly led astray into compromise—and imitating exactly *how* he went about it. Because the latter is more likely to contain elements that are more specific both to John's situation and culture.

Firstly, we need to appreciate the difference between our own context and that of John's community. He was addressing a group which had been rocked by the defection of some to the safety of the majority culture, having been left behind to bear the brunt of persecution from that same majority. When remaining is costly—in terms of status, livelihood, and even life itself—it can be difficult for those who stayed to show love and forgiveness to those who abandoned and perhaps even betrayed them. In times of intense persecution, the church throughout history has had to wrestle with this issue of reconciliation with temporary apostates. Forgiveness is always the goal, but there also needs to be opportunity to give voice to the hurt that comes from desertion and betrayal. Most of the time, our situation is far removed from this, dealing with disagreements between two groups of believers in the relatively safe and privileged environment of the Western church. That alone should give us pause before we employ John's sectarian rhetoric.

Secondly, we've already noted that John's us-and-them rhetoric wasn't directed at those who had left; it was for internal use only. So this *isn't* a model for attacking heretical groups; rather, it's for reinforcing the orthodox belief of the faithful. If we learn nothing else from the rhetoric of 1 John, we should learn to direct any rhetorical response to ourselves—attending to our own motivations and behaviors in the face of division and error—rather than engaging in a slanging match with our perceived opponents. What's more, we should remember (as we've observed in previous chapters) that our internal rhetoric is almost never completely internal, thanks to the internet. So any rhetorical move to shore up the belief of those *within* the group should always have one eye on the outsider who may witness it. Even when we're forced to disagree, we can be attractively different in how we go about it.

This means adhering, at the very least, to the highest ideals of our society's standards of respectful debate. In John's day, using pejorative language to characterize opponents (see above) was expected; not to do so was a signal you weren't serious,[19] which is why we see it in most of the New Testament figures, including Peter (2 Pet 2), Paul (Gal 1:7; 3:1; 4:17; 5:12; 6:12–13), and even Jesus himself (Matt 23). We should also notice that the New Testament only uses such language about false *teachers*: those who are to be held to a higher standard (Jas 3:1), who weren't simply acting out of ignorance, and who were leading others astray (Matt 23:13; 2 Tim 2:18).

---

19. Witherington, *Matthew*, 429.

While it's not unusual to see this tactic employed today—particularly when it's the current U.S. President's rhetorical bread-and-butter—it certainly falls short of cultural ideals that, for the most part, reject *ad hominem* attacks.[20] As McKnight concludes, commenting on Galatians:

> What was seen as an acceptable form of disagreement then may not be seen as acceptable today . . . The ancient world simply loved inflammatory language for expressing its differences. I can document a great deal of such language in their literature, but I have not been able to document any who thought such language was personally biased and out of line. The ancients delighted in overstatement, and overstatements were effectively countered with similar overstatements . . . Ours is not the ancient world. For this reason alone I believe we need to state our decisions more carefully and in a less inflammatory manner . . .[21]

## The rhetoric of love

Yet we can also do even better. We're called to go beyond our own society's highest ideals and show the kind of radical love exemplified by Jesus. In 1 John, the focus of that love is "one another," given the need to reaffirm the group in the wake of those who had left, and the fact that the issue that caused the defection was so significant it showed they didn't actually belong to the group. Most of our differences aren't over things that are truly core, so a radical love for those fellow believers with whom we disagree isn't optional. It's what should characterize us *even in our disagreements,* and thereby be attractively different.

Though absent in 1 John, in light of the whole canon of the New Testament we can go further than that: in how we show love to those who are not (yet) or even *no longer* part of "us" even while we're in conflict. Jesus calls us to follow his Father's example in showing love even for enemies (Matt 5:44–45), echoed by Paul (Rom 5:6–8).[22] While Paul speaks in stark terms about

---

20. It's been a disturbingly successful rhetorical tactic to energize his base, seeing off challengers like "low-energy Jeb" Bush and "lying Ted" Cruz, before defeating "crooked Hillary." That readers of the "failing" *New York Times* might object to it doesn't matter, because the pejorative characterizations are for the benefit of those already in the group. This isn't something to which Jesus-followers of any political persuasion should aspire.

21. McKnight, *Galatians*, 59–60.

22. Paul appears to be echoing the ideals of the first-century Stoic philosopher Seneca, who wrote: "If a man is a worthy one, I shall defend him even at the cost of my own blood, and share his peril" (*De beneficiis* 1.10.5), and "I shall come to his aid if he is at the point of ruin, yet not to the extent of bringing ruin upon myself, unless by so

those who live as Jesus' enemies, he does so with tears (Phil 3:18–19). If we engage in such conflict with airtight hermeneutical arguments, but have not love, we become merely the noisy gong of 1 Corinthians 13. In other words, our motivation shouldn't be a love of the fight, or of abstract truth, but a love for the people who desperately need God's truth. Radical love is the overriding rhetorical move, without compromising on truth.[23]

This calls for wisdom, holding a sometimes awkward tension, encapsulated in John's two later epistles:

> Anyone who runs ahead and does not continue in the teaching of Christ does not have God . . . If anyone comes to you and does not bring this teaching, do not take them into your house or welcome them. Anyone who welcomes them shares in their wicked work. (2 John 9–11)

> I wrote to the church, but Diotrephes, who loves to be first, will not welcome us . . . Not satisfied with that, he even refuses to welcome other believers. He also stops those who want to do so and puts them out of the church. (3 John 9–10)

As Jesus' followers, we need to have clear group boundaries. We can't accept every doctrine or behavior, or we would cease to be the people of God. But neither can we draw those boundaries too tightly. As David deSilva observes:

> 2 John reminds us that there are boundaries beyond which the faith expressed and the ethic taught are no longer Christian . . . Third John stands next in the canon to warn us against the dangers of drawing those lines so narrowly or in such a way that we find the representatives of the apostolic witness on the other side from us.[24]

---

doing I shall purchase the safety of a great man or a great cause" (*De beneficiis* 2.15.1). Paul presents God as one who goes beyond even the highest ideals of Greco-Roman moralists in radical love (laying down his life) for those who were unworthy: "Very rarely will anyone die for a righteous person, though for a good person someone might possibly dare to die. But God demonstrates his own love for us in this: While we were still sinners, Christ died for us" Rom 5:7–8. See deSilva, *Honor, Patronage*, 129.

23. It's just as unloving to tolerate sin without naming it as such, as to condemn the sinner.

24. DeSilva, *Introduction to the New Testament*, 463.

# 6

## James
## *Double-Minded*

I READ THE STORY[1] of a man who received two job offers from two different companies. Both would be located in the same building, but on different floors. So he decided to take both of them. He would get in early and start the first job at around seven a.m., before going upstairs to clock in to his second job by nine. His day would be spent travelling between floors every hour or so. If people came and found him away from his desk, they just assumed he was in a meeting. Finishing his first job early, he would then work late at the second. For six months he collected two paychecks before he was found out—and only then because someone resigned from one of his employers, got a job with the other, and recognized him. The man was promptly sacked from both.

James writes to his exiled and scattered minority audience to warn them against this: trying to work for two competing masters, God and the world. He points out the futility of trying to fool God that they're working for him full-time when every chance they get, they're sneaking off to their second job. Because God isn't fooled, and sooner or later, their double-life will come undone.

### James' audience as a double minority?

Most likely one of the earliest New Testament writings,[2] the letter of James is addressed to "the twelve tribes in the *diaspora* among the nations" (1:1). At face value, this refers to Jews outside the land of Israel (from which

---

1. It was in the newsletter of *Dilbert* cartoon creator, Scott Adams, sometime in the late 1990s, submitted by a reader. You can be the judge of its authenticity.

2. See Witherington, *Letters and Homilies for Jewish Christians*, 395–401, for a discussion of the date of composition and the related question of authorship.

James writes) who were living as a scattered minority around various parts of the Mediterranean world as a result of foreign occupation and forced migration in the past. He also addresses his readers as "believers in our Lord Jesus Christ" (2:1), which would make them a double-minority—a Messianic sect of a monotheistic, ethnic minority in a polytheistic empire.[3] As was the case with the audience of Hebrews, they would have been facing pressure on two fronts to conform: from the Jewish community, and from the majority culture.

And the nature of the exhortation in the letter suggests that it's the wider, Greco-Roman culture which was exerting the stronger pressure on James' minority audience. In particular, people of higher status[4] were being tempted to continue with "business as usual" in the social world of the empire, rather than embracing the countercultural values of Jesus (see, e.g., 2:1–14; 4:13–5:6). James responds with the same kind of minority rhetoric seen in earlier Jewish wisdom literature like *Sirach* and the *Wisdom of Solomon*. These writings essentially called their communities to live in a more overtly Jewish fashion—with an ethic informed by Torah and the wisdom tradition—in order to maintain group identity and fidelity in times of foreign influence and rule.[5] Like these predecessors, James tries to sharpen the difference of his minority audience who were in danger of forgetting their alien status.

From the outset, James alludes to this pressure to conform by referring to "trials of many kinds" (1:2) which lead to the "testing of your faith" (1:3).[6] In the world of first-century patronage, the word translated "faith"

---

3. Although some (e.g., Ropes, *James*, 120–27; McCartney, *James*, 80) have attempted to read "the twelve tribes in the dispersion" as a reference to all believers in Jesus—borrowing Israel terminology for the new covenant people—the normal usage of the term (see Adamson, *James*, 49–50), along with the Jewish flavor of the material, makes this less likely. Others (e.g., Moo, *James*, 50; Scaer, *James, the Apostle of Faith*, 28–30) have suggested narrowing the audience to Jewish Christians who had recently been dispersed as a result of the persecution mentioned in Acts 11:19; however, "in the dispersion" is more appropriate an expression for a location than for a recent event. See Witherington, *Letters and Homilies for Jewish Christians*, 418–19, esp. n.64; Blomberg and Kamell, *James*, 28–29.

4. Perdue, "Paraenesis and the Epistle of James," 250.

5. Witherington, *Letters and Homilies for Jewish Christians*, 403–04.

6. While I agree with commentators who don't want to restrict the "trials" simply to persecution, the overarching context of competing loyalties means it can't simply refer to all difficulties faced in life (contra e.g., Doriani, *James*, 19–20). Blomberg and Kamell, *James*, 29, looking at "the frequency with which James returns to the issue of wealth and poverty" conclude that the specific trials involved socioeconomic disparity; I concur, but see that as one important symptom of the underlying cause—the attempt to retain friendship with the world.

*(pistis)* had connotations of trust and loyalty, as opposed to mere "belief." So this gives us a clue that the critical question in James' letter is one of potentially divided loyalty when faced with the trials that arise when living as a minority group. *When it gets difficult, will you remain loyal to God and trust him to look after you—or will you instead try to keep yourself in the world's favor?* This introduces what I think is the key, unifying idea in James: that of *double-mindedness*.[7]

## Double-mindedness

The term "double-minded" occurs twice in James, the second clearly in the context of friendship and loyalty:

> You *adulterers*, don't you know that friendship with the world means enmity against God? Therefore, anyone who chooses to be a friend of the world becomes an enemy of God . . . Submit yourselves, then, to God. Resist the devil, and he will flee from you. Come near to God and he will come near to you. Wash your hands, you sinners, and purify your hearts, you *double-minded*. (4:4, 7–8)

In this important passage, James identifies the fundamental issue. If they continued to act like they are friends with the world, they'd be aligning themselves with everything that's opposed to God. In effect, they'd be choosing sides, becoming enemies with God.

James even goes as far as calling them "adulterers." This is an image frequently used by the prophets for Israel's flirtations with idolatry[8]—essentially an act of unfaithfulness in their relationship with God, which was meant to be exclusive. As with an extra-marital affair, they were playing a dangerous game. They were trying to serve two competing masters which, according to James' better-known brother, is impossible (Matt 6:24).

Shortly afterwards (4:8), James links their spiritual disloyalty with the description "double-minded." The fact that it stands in parallel to the term "sinners" should tell us that double-mindedness isn't about being hesitant or indecisive, as with the English expression, "to be in two minds." In the ancient world, it speaks to the context of friendship. To be friends with someone

---

7. For this unifying idea, as well as many of its implications drawn out in this chapter, I am following Johnson, *Brother of Jesus, Friend of God*, 202–20.

8. Witherington, *Letters and Homilies for Jewish Christians*, 512, notes Isa 1:21; 50:1; Jer 3:7–10; 13:27; Ezek 16:23–26; 23:45; and most famously, Hos 2:5–7. Note that idolatry was frequently associated with sexual immorality (since the key idols were those of fertility), making the "adultery" image even more pertinent.

was to be "of one mind" with them, hence Aristotle's famous definition of friendship, "one soul in two bodies."⁹ Therefore, if a person tried to be of "one mind" with both God and the world (which stands opposed to God), they were attempting the impossible task of being *double-minded*. They might have professed loyalty to one, but in their actions revealed that their true loyalty lay elsewhere—that they valued the friendship of the majority culture and the (temporal) benefits it brings over their friendship with God.

Back near the start of his letter, James first uses the term in connection with asking God for "wisdom" (1:5). In context, this wisdom refers to the ability to persevere in the loyalty-testing trials that were part and parcel of belonging to the Jesus-following minority (1:2–5). This is supported by James' own definition of "wisdom" a little later on:

> Who is wise and understanding among you? Let them show it by their *good life*, by *deeds done in the humility* that comes from wisdom. (3:13)

James contrasts this with the so-called "wisdom" of the world, which manifests itself in the "bitter envy and selfish ambition" (3:14–15) so characteristic of the majority culture. True wisdom is an understanding that enables a person to persist in living by God's values rather than the world's, despite intense pressure to the contrary. James describes the scenario of someone who asks God for this wisdom to persevere, yet doesn't trust God to deliver the help they have asked for, and so wavers in their conviction (1:6). Such a person, says James, is "double-minded and unstable in all they do" (1:8). Later, James sets this in stark contrast with the example of Abraham, whose trust in God was shown in radical obedience, meaning he could be called "God's friend" (2:23).¹⁰

The sin of double-mindedness, then, is trying to live in both worlds, serving two masters. And against this background, we can see the diverse topics addressed by James as having a common thread related to his audience's minority status. He identifies a range of ways in which they're being tempted into double-mindedness, seeking the approval of the majority culture, rather than pursuing single-minded friendship with God.¹¹

---

9. Aristotle, *Ethica Nichomachea* 9.8.2, quoting Euripedes, *Orestes* 1046. Cicero, *De amicitia* 21.80, describes a friend as "another self." See Johnson, *Brother of Jesus, Friend of God*, 213–14.

10. *Brother of Jesus, Friend of God*, 215.

11. *Brother of Jesus, Friend of God*, 216–17.

## Status and wealth

One of the most obvious examples is where James confronts the dominant culture's values around status and wealth. Early in the letter, he echoes Jewish wisdom writings[12] in stressing the temporary nature of wealth and the status that comes with it:

> For the sun rises with scorching heat and withers the plant; its blossom falls and its beauty is destroyed. In the same way, the rich will fade away even while they go about their business. (1:11)

For this reason, James' minority audience should paradoxically take "pride" in their humble position now (1:9), because of the great reversal that will take place: those who are presently rich (1:10) and therefore honored by the majority will one day be humiliated. The issue of status is thus reframed in light of the age to come, rather than limiting the comparison to the here-and-now. (In the terms of the summer camp experiment from chapter 1, their cabins will be destroyed and only the gardens will be left.)

However, James also brings this reality very much into the present when he addresses how the rich were being treated within the group:

> Suppose a man comes into your meeting wearing a gold ring and fine clothes, and a poor man in filthy old clothes also comes in. If you show special attention to the man wearing fine clothes and say, "Here's a good seat for you," but say to the poor man, "You stand there" or "Sit on the floor by my feet," have you not discriminated among yourselves and become judges with evil thoughts? (2:2–4)

This goes beyond simply not judging by appearances; it effectively subverts the underlying system of patronage that formed the social and economic foundations of the majority culture. Because giving preferential treatment to the rich wasn't optional; it was the expected *quid pro quo* in an economic model that relied upon the wealthy elite to fund public amenities, construction, festivals, and even military expenses. The main avenue for the wealthy to display their status was in lavishing benefits on the public; honor and fawning deference was the required response to such "benefactors" of the community. Jesus, however, made it clear that this wasn't to be the case among his followers, in which leaders ought to be humble:

> Jesus said to them, "The kings of the Gentiles lord it over them; and those who exercise authority over them call themselves

---

12. Compare this with Job 24:24; Ps 49:16–20; Eccles 1:3; 2:11; 4:4. Witherington, *Letters and Homilies for Jewish Christians*, 431.

Benefactors. *But you are not to be like that.* Instead, the greatest among you should be like the youngest, and the one who rules like the one who serves." (Luke 22:25–26)

James, then, is reminding his audience of the way things *should* be with them. They should reflect the values of Jesus' kingdom which favored the poor and marginalized:

Listen, my dear brothers and sisters: Has not God chosen those who are poor in the eyes of the world to be rich in faith and to inherit the kingdom he promised those who love him? But you have dishonored the poor. (Jas 2:5–6)

In essence, James isn't dealing with one, isolated issue: that of how Jesus' followers ought to treat the rich and poor. He's telling them not to participate in the status game being played by the surrounding culture.

In fact, he goes on to ask why they'd *want* to play that game when on closer inspection, these wealthy, so-called "benefactors" aren't all that beneficent! After all, it's apparently the wealthy who were exploiting them and taking them to court:[13]

Is it not the rich who are exploiting you? Are they not the ones who are dragging you into court? Are they not the ones who are blaspheming the noble name of him to whom you belong? (5:6–7)

The double-mindedness in view here is straightforward: despite claiming to be a group centered around Jesus and his values (2:1), they were continuing to play the status games of the surrounding culture so they could remain "friends" with it. By showing the expected favoritism to those who leveraged wealth to gain status, they were endorsing and enabling a corrupt system when they ought to have been displaying an attractive difference.

If we're committed to living out this kind of attractive difference today, James urges us to guard against the same temptation to double-mindedness: what games do we still play along with that allow people to display their importance, or receive preferential treatment?

Wealth is still up there, of course, where rich Christians can have a disproportionate say over what happens in our churches—especially if they're significant donors who won't give without attaching a few strings. Perhaps more frequently, a person's career and level of education can affect how

---

13. See *Letters and Homilies for Jewish Christians*, 526–27, for the various views on whether the rich were Jews or Christians (in an era in which the distinction was far from clear cut, anyway) and how they might have been exploiting the poor among James' audience.

easily they are included in our social circles, as well as determine the roles within the church that may be open to them. This is an implicit endorsement of the value system of the surrounding culture.

The cult of celebrity is particularly problematic, as in the past century it's become probably the key status indicator in society. How should we, as the church, deal with celebrity? In a way, we still worship at this altar. I've been to two funerals attended by a well-known ex-politician; he even happened to sit next to me at one of them, in a seat near the back of the auditorium. Now this is no reflection on him, as he tried to slip in and out as anonymously as possible. But both times—even though he was there in a private capacity—other people felt obliged to treat him differently, giving him a special welcome from the pulpit and making a show of introducing him to the pastor of the church. We still tend to act like some people are more worthy of our attention than others, because that's what our culture has conditioned us to do.

It gets more complicated because we can use celebrity as a means of bringing people to hear the gospel. And there's nothing inherently wrong with this. It's important that the rest of the world sees that it's not just unfashionable nobodies like me who follow Jesus; there are people who "have it all" in the eyes of the world who also call him "Lord." But we need to be careful that we don't exalt celebrity Christians to the status of "super-Christians."[14] Although their celebrity may open many doors for the gospel that remain closed for the rest of us, they are no better than anyone else in our community. In a celebrity-obsessed culture, our single-minded insistence that everyone be equally valued ought to be attractively different.

## Use of words

The next instance of double-mindedness requires far less in the way of cultural background to understand, as it relates to something common to all times and cultures: how we use our words. James famously observes how our speech is both indicative of the self-control we have over the other parts of our lives, as well as the disproportionate damage it can do if not kept under control:

> Anyone who is never at fault in what they say is perfect, able to keep their whole body in check. When we put bits into the

---

14. As I write, Kanye West, *Jesus is King* mania is in full-flight. His sense of perspective in acknowledging, "I am not a theologian—I am a recent convert," gives some hope that he might attempt to subvert our tendency to exalt celebrity Christians. (Interview with Zane Lowe on *Beats 1*, Apple Music, 24 October 2019.)

mouths of horses to make them obey us, we can turn the whole animal ... Consider what a great forest is set on fire by a small spark. The tongue also is a fire, a world of evil among the parts of the body. It corrupts the whole body, sets the whole course of one's life on fire, and is itself set on fire by hell. (3:2–3, 5–6)

Given the significance of our speech, being double-minded in this area is no small matter. Being "double-tongued" undermines what should be an attractive difference for James' audience:

> With the tongue we praise our Lord and Father, and with it we curse human beings, who have been made in God's likeness. Out of the same mouth come praise and cursing. My brothers and sisters, this should not be. (3:9–10)[15]

It's double-minded to praise the God in whose image our fellow human beings were made, yet send a completely different message with our words. This can be seen in how believers speak to one another when they disagree, or speak about one another when that person isn't around. It can also be evident in how believers engage with those outside the group, whether it be the manner in which they defend the faith and campaign for God's values in the secular world, or in how they speak of other (perhaps more) marginalized groups with judgment or disdain. Our attractive difference can be quickly undone through words which reveal a deeper double-mindedness.[16] Again, we find ourselves displaying friendship with the world by using words the same the way it does.

## Prayer

We can also approach prayer in a way that's consistent with the world's goals and values. James gives this as a reason for prayers that were not answered:

> When you ask, you do not receive, because you ask with wrong motives, that you may spend what you get on your pleasures. (4:3)

---

15. James is again calling his audience back to principles found in Jewish wisdom writings. Sirach 28:12–13 even uses the term "double-tongued" for those who use their words to "destroy the peace of many."

16. James similarly condemns the kind of double-mindedness that plays games with words in order to deceive others, referencing Jesus' teaching on oaths in the context of how they had come to be abused (5:12; cf. Matt 5:33–38; 23:16–22).

A little later, he contrasts this with the story of Elijah, whose friendship with God led him to align his prayers with God's revealed will and purposes.[17] His prayers were effective:

> The prayer of a righteous person is powerful and effective. Elijah was a human being, even as we are. He prayed earnestly that it would not rain, and it did not rain on the land for three and a half years. Again he prayed, and the heavens gave rain, and the earth produced its crops. (5:16–18)

Many years ago, I visited a large church. Just before the collection was taken up, one of the pastors read out a selection of response cards from congregation members about prayers that had been answered. They went like this: "Praise God! I got the car I wanted at the price I wanted . . . Praise God! I got the job I wanted at the salary I wanted . . . Praise God! We got the house we wanted in the suburb we wanted . . ."[18] And so on. Presenting God as a kind of Santa Claus figure who gives you everything you ask for. Or, given its (strategic?) placement in the service, a low-risk investment portfolio that gives an excellent rate of return on your tithes and offerings. Although this is an extreme example, a few moments of introspection might show a similar mindset informing our own prayers at times.

This reveals double-mindedness in two ways. Firstly, it uses prayer to chase the goals and values of the world rather than aligning ourselves with God's revealed purposes. Secondly, it approaches prayer with the quasi-transactional understanding found in the pagan religion of the majority culture in James' day,[19] as well as in the popular piety of many religions today (Christianity included). In such a model, devotion to the gods is simply to gain or even manipulate divine favor for whatever the devotee wants to pursue. To mimic this in how we use prayer may be superficially attractive to some, but it belies the essential difference of being a true friend of God.

---

17. Cf. Deut 11:11–18 and all of Deut 28.

18. I don't know whether they were representative of everyone there or whether they had been carefully chosen by the pastor, but either way, it says something.

19. See Larson, *Understanding Greek Religion*, 40–47, for a nuanced description of Greco-Roman piety which rejects a simplistic transactional model and sets it in a cultural context of reciprocity and gift-giving. The ultimate motivation for devotion, nevertheless, is seeking the gods' favor to ensure prosperity for the worshipper and their community.

### Putting words into actions

At the heart of all of this is a double-mindedness between thoughts and actions. We can hear what God says and give mental assent, but not act on it:

> Anyone who listens to the word but does not do what it says is like someone who looks at his face in a mirror and, after looking at himself, goes away and immediately forgets what he looks like. (1:23–24)

> What good is it, my brothers and sisters, if someone claims to have faith but has no deeds? Can such faith save them? Suppose a brother or a sister is without clothes and daily food. If one of you says to them, 'Go in peace; keep warm and well fed,' but does nothing about their physical needs, what good is it? In the same way, faith by itself, if it is not accompanied by action, is dead. (2:14–17)

To put it simply: our true loyalty is seen not in what we say, but in what we do. James' minority audience is only going to be attractive when outsiders see a difference in *behavior*.

### Single-mindedness

Since much of the letter is a diagnosis, our preaching from it should be similarly diagnostic. Whether preaching this text to a congregation or simply preaching it to ourselves, we can use James' insights to reveal areas of our own double-mindedness that need to be addressed if we're to maintain our attractive difference.

However, James doesn't stop at diagnosis; he also outlines the treatment. He provides a rhetorical strategy for the group that encourages single-minded loyalty to God.

### Redefining the problem as opportunity

Like most of the other instances of minority rhetoric in the New Testament, James reframes the issue. He encourages his audience to see the situation in a different light. At the start of his letter, James redefines the problem as an opportunity:

> Consider it pure joy, my brothers and sisters, whenever you face trials of many kinds, because you know that the testing of your

> faith produces perseverance. Let perseverance finish its work so that you may be mature and complete, not lacking anything. (1:2–4)

When faced with trials that test his audience's loyalty, he urges them not merely to endure it, but to see it, perversely, as a source of joy. And he gives two reasons for them to see their trials as being positive: they give them an opportunity both to *prove* and *improve* their trust in and loyalty towards God.

Firstly, enduring under trial *improves* faith in that it develops perseverance. It gives opportunities to practise being loyal to God and resisting pressure from the world. Just like practising a musical instrument, it lays down neural pathways that over time form habits, making obedience progressively more natural. Or as James puts it,

> Submit yourselves, then, to God. Resist the devil, and he will flee from you. (4:7)

Secondly, enduring under trial *proves* faith in that it gives tangible, visible expression to it, demonstrating its genuineness. If opportunity never arises to demonstrate it, trust remains in the theoretical realm. The command to sacrifice Isaac gave Abraham the opportunity for "his faith to be made complete by what he did," thereby being called "God's friend" (2:22–23).

There's been a tendency for Christians to see our increasing marginalization purely in negative terms: that it's a restriction on our rights to practise and preach our beliefs while maintaining some level of acceptance by mainstream society. And it's sometimes led to a rhetoric of doom and gloom, coupled with desperate attempts to cling on to our accustomed position closer to the center of our society.

James, however, would urge us to see things differently. He'd see our change in status as a cause for joy, because we can no longer drift along thinking we're part of the majority culture, minimizing our difference in the hope of being accepted.[20] The world's "conscious uncoupling" from its friendship with us gives us once more the opportunity to show how and why we're different. As publicly identifying with Jesus becomes more costly, our world can see how serious we are in a far more obvious and, potentially, attractive way.

This isn't just the context of the apostolic era; it's the context in which the church lived out its faith for the subsequent few centuries. They

---

20. See Dr. Galen Jones' comments on this, from an African-American perspective, in chapter 15.

maintained radical difference (without compromise) while living in the world (without withdrawing from it) in what became known as the "third way."[21] We have the opportunity to recapture some of the power of this third way now that the illusion of Christendom has faded. Our preaching ought to echo James' encouragement to find joy in the new possibilities we've been given in this time of rapid social change, rather than bemoaning our loss of (superficial) acceptance.

## God is in control

Implicit in James' instruction to consider it "joy" is a second, equally important part of his rhetorical strategy, in which he reminds his audience of the ultimate source of power: it lies not with human society, but with God. James exhorts them, as God's friends, to live like he is truly in control—not merely in thought but also in action.

As we noted earlier, the response to "trials that test your faith" (1:2–4) shouldn't simply be to try harder to persevere in loyalty. James' first movement is away from self and toward God, urging his hearers to ask him for the wisdom (i.e. the moral will) which they lack (1:5). This is the opposite of the world's wisdom, which is *self*-striving and *self*-advancing (3:14). God's wisdom comes from humility (3:13), which is the only appropriate attitude to adopt when accepting God's internal work of regeneration:

> Therefore, get rid of all moral filth and the evil that is so prevalent and *humbly accept the word planted in you*, which can save you. (1:21)

Preaching that's consistent with the letter's rhetorical strategy needs to emphasize the divine enabling with which James frames his instruction. His emphasis on works that ought to come from faith can easily become a call to moral striving if we neglect this wider context.[22] Humble acceptance of the *implanted* word should be an integral part of any exhortation to increased loyalty to God, as our attractive difference is only made possible by him. *We are to trust that God will enable us to persevere in trust.*

Typically, James requires that trust to be put into action. This means that anyone who asks God for help, yet continues to live in fear of the world's

---

21. For a discussion along similar lines to the present study, but focusing on the history of the church rather than the rhetoric of the New Testament, see Sittser, *Resilient Faith: How the Early Christian "Third Way" Changed the World*.

22. It appears that Martin Luther either missed this framing, or judged it to be insufficient, in his negative assessment of James as "straw-epistle" for its potential to be used to advance salvation by works. (Preface to *Das Newe Testament Deitzch*, 1522.)

rejection, is hopelessly "double-minded" (1:6–8). They're still trying to have it both ways, remaining friends with the world just in case God doesn't deliver on his promises. They're still seeking pleasure, security, and acceptance in the same way the majority culture does. But if God's truly in control, his followers don't need a Plan B. And the attractiveness of a people who are "all in" and performing without a safety net shouldn't be underestimated.

For James, the appropriate demonstration of trust is an acknowledgement of God's sovereignty that pervades every aspect of life. It means prayer in each and every circumstance, especially, but not only when in trouble (5:13–14). It means consciously acknowledging dependence on God for everything, something which sharply contrasts with the way the rest of society acts like they have the future in hand (4:13–6). This radical acknowledgement of God's power isn't just a comfort to those within the group who've aligned themselves with him over against the world; it's also a source of attractive difference for those outside the group who've grown tired and disillusioned with the world's claim to have everything under control. And the pandemic of 2020 has made this all the more salient.

James calls us as God's scattered people to humbly accept his work of regeneration within us, being wholly devoted to one master in thought and in action (4:8). We joyfully embrace any opposition in the knowledge that it gives us the opportunity to demonstrate our faith in action—both to God and to those who oppose us. While our single-minded trust in his sovereignty may cost us friendship with some, for others it will be attractive in its difference.

# 7

# Revelation
## *Faithful and True*

ANY CHAPTER WHICH DEALS with Revelation is a difficult exercise, given the wide variety of hermeneutical approaches to the genre. Even a full-length commentary can't approach it from multiple perspectives while adequately dealing with the text.[1] For this reason, we'll adopt the view which I think speaks most clearly to its original audience as a marginalized minority in first-century Asia Minor, and takes into account all of the aspects of its genre.

That is, Revelation is a *letter*—a situationally-specific discourse—to a group of (literal) churches (1:4, 11) who were a marginalized minority. Some of them were under threat of imminent persecution from synagogue and empire, and all of them faced the danger of compromise and syncretism.[2] It's an *apocalypse* (1:1), using symbolism and imagery to depict the world from God's perspective—a theological and political commentary on God's faithfulness to his people in the face of opposition, which comes both from the "synagogue of Satan" and the beastly Roman empire. And it's also a *prophecy* (1:3), passing judgment on the people and institutions of first-century Rome, and promising that the risen Christ is the ultimate victor; one day he'll come to enact justice and vindicate his faithful minority. This amounts to a call on its audience to resist the temptation to

---

1. Attempts such as Gregg, *Revelation, Four Views*, are helpful in giving an idea of how the different approaches might play out, but as a result, hardly scratch the surface of the text itself.

2. Although Thompson, *Apocalypse and Empire*, 174, tried to rehabilitate Domitian and sees the threat of persecution largely a creation of John's rhetoric, most subsequent commentators have rejected this as an overcorrection. It did, however, prompt a shift toward viewing the threat as primarily sociological (i.e. the power of exclusion by the majority for refusing to participate in the imperial cult) as well as, in some places, physical. See especially Yarbro Collins, *Crisis and Catharsis*, 84–107.

compromise with imperial idolatry, and instead remain faithful to Jesus and his people—something which by now we ought to recognize as minority group rhetoric.³

Even still, it's not possible to cover the full scope of the Apocalypse's minority group rhetoric in the space available. Thankfully, David deSilva has provided us with two excellent books on the subject: the comprehensive *Seeing things John's way: the rhetoric of the book of Revelation*, and at a more popular level, *Unholy allegiances: heeding Revelation's warnings*. I can't commend these highly enough, and this chapter is indebted to deSilva's approach. What's attempted here is a brief, narrative commentary on the text, retelling the story of John's celestial vision in order to point out its relevance for marginalized minority followers of Jesus—both then and, *by extension*, now. (For the best experience, have the biblical text open as you read.)

## Jesus addresses his minority group

Revelation begins with a claim to privileged knowledge which has been given to the author (1:1-2). He functions as the representative of Jesus' faithful minority group in Asia Minor, describing himself as their "brother and companion" as they endure suffering for the sake of Jesus (1:9). Through John's address, they now share in this privileged knowledge and in the promise of blessing for those who hear and obey it (1:3).

To this powerless minority, John brings greetings from no less than the eternal God (1:4) and his son, Jesus Christ. Jesus is put forward as both the prototypical "faithful witness" whom his audience is to emulate, and the sovereign ruler to whom their opponents ultimately must answer (1:5). John then reminds his audience that despite their present lowly status in the eyes of the world, they occupy a privileged position as forgiven people who've been called to priestly service (1:5-6). And he assures them of vindication in the sight of everyone—especially those who have persecuted Jesus and his followers (1:7).

The opening vision of Jesus draws heavily on Old Testament imagery, providing continuity with previous divine appearances and identifying Jesus closely with God the Father.⁴ This is Israel's God continuing Israel's

---

3. See further, MacBride, "Aliens and Strangers," 238–39.

4. Jesus is the "son of man" from Daniel's vision (Dan 7:13), yet with the appearance of the "Ancient of Days" himself (Dan 7:6). His voice is that of God the Father (Ezek 1:24), and he speaks words of divine judgment (Isa 11:4). His face shining like the sun is reminiscent of the appearance to Moses on Mt. Sinai (Ex 34:29–35), and his first words are typical of a theophany: "Fear not!"

story, no matter what synagogue opponents might say. Pointedly, Jesus is described as holding the seven churches in his hand (1:16, 20) as well as the keys to death and Hades (1:18), reminding them that *he's* the one who controls their destiny, not Rome. And despite his exalted status, Jesus isn't a rear-echelon general commanding from afar, but one who walks among his troops in solidarity (1:13, 20; 2:1), equipping them for faithful service. Jesus knows what they're going through.

This knowledge is reflected in the seven letters which follow, in which Jesus says to each of the churches: *I know! I know your deeds (2:2, 19; 3:1, 8, 15), your afflictions (2:9), and the testing environment in which you live (2:13). Your experiences haven't gone unnoticed, and neither have your responses to them.* Jesus then gives an appraisal of each church—both the good and the bad—which makes clear the concrete setting that the rest of the apocalypse is designed to address.

On the positive side, Jesus affirms those who are faithful to group values; he commends them for holding onto the truth (2:2), resisting compromise with the majority culture (3:4, 8), and suffering persecution even to the point of martyrdom (2:10, 13). It's apparent that there are some who are maintaining their attractive difference as aliens and exiles.

Yet on the negative side, we see Jesus give a stern warning to those who've compromised—or are being tempted to compromise—with the idolatrous culture of the empire (2:14, 20). As we noted in chapter 1, participating in civic religion was about "doing your bit" for the good of the civic body, lest the gods or the emperor withdraw their favor. Refusal to do so not only marked a person out as a potential danger to society, it often amounted to voluntary exclusion from social and business contact. This is because the venues for such interaction were usually connected with pagan rituals, idol food, and sexual activity—places like temples, trade guilds, and civic festivals. Fear of socio-economic exclusion, just as much as physical persecution, would have tempted Christians to compromise, and try to live in both worlds.[5] Jesus, however, likens this to episodes in Israel's history (involving Balaam and Jezebel) in which they joined in with the idolatry and sexual immorality of the surrounding nations, thereby putting their status as God's people in jeopardy. More generally, some in John's audience were failing to maintain the group's distinctiveness by taking on the character of the city around them, leading to immoral behavior (3:2) and an attitude of self-sufficiency (3:17–18).

---

5. For a discussion of emperor worship, including the emperor's role in mediating the favor of the gods, and the empire's response to Christians who refused to participate, see Smith, "The Book of Revelation," 337–55.

The fact that the letters were to be "overheard" by the other six churches reminds us of how they ought to function today. While they might not address the precise set of circumstances in which we find ourselves, they give us the opportunity to think about the similarities we might share with the seven churches as a way of diagnosing our own tendencies to compromise. For most Westerners, we're unlikely to find ourselves excluded for not participating in idolatrous rituals; but for many of the students I teach who are from Asian backgrounds this is very much a live issue; refusal to participate in practices such as the veneration of ancestors can have significant consequences for their place in the family.[6] Yet for all of us, there's the temptation to blend in with the rest of our society. We can adopt the selfish and self-sufficient attitudes of our affluent cities, and join in their idolatry of work, pleasure, and the opinions of others—lest we find ourselves on the outer. It can become quite easy to explain away behaviors such as our excess consumption, chasing of status symbols, and tolerance of sexual content in entertainment as simply "the cost of living in today's world."

To those who persist in such sin and compromise with the majority culture, both then and now, Jesus warns of judgment (e.g., 2:5, 16, 22–23; 3:16). But for those who maintain their faithfulness—or who repent from their compromise—Jesus promises a reward that far outweighs any suffering or loss they might experience in the immediate term. Those who are killed for their testimony will receive life (2:8); those who are excluded from civic festivals will instead feast on "hidden manna" and gain an entry stone into a far greater feast (2:17);[7] those whose names were blotted out of the citizenship register[8] will never have their name blotted out of God's book of life (3:5); and those to whom the door of the synagogue has been shut have an open door into the house of David (3:7–8, cf. Isa 22:21–22)[9] and will be pillars in God's house (3:12).

In rhetorical terms, the seven letters are examples of deliberative rhetoric, which argues for a future course of action based on its *advantage*. Here, Jesus contrasts the advantages of remaining faithful to the group with the disadvantages of compromising with the majority culture.

---

6. For a sample of the debate on how Asian Christians ought to respond, see Jao, "Honor & Obey," 43–56; Kwon, *1 Corinthians 1–4: For Korean-Confucian Christians Today*, 214–28; Yeo, "The Rhetorical Hermeneutic of 1 Corinthians 8 and Chinese Ancestor Worship," 294–311.

7. Witherington, *Revelation*, 103–04; Keener, *Revelation*, 126. Both writers also offer an alternative: it could be a stone used at a trial to vote for an acquittal.

8. Hemer, *The Letters to the Seven Churches*, 148, notes that this could happen to a person prior to being executed.

9. Reddish, *Revelation*, 75.

Although compromise might lead to some immediate benefit, such as gaining the world's favor and avoiding persecution, Jesus repositions the debate to include *future* reward and judgment. We'll see this numerous times throughout Revelation.

## The throne room

After the seven letters, there's a scene change (4:1) in which John is given privileged "behind the scenes" access by means of a door in the sky. The cosmology of the ancient world was a bit like a snowdome (or *The Truman Show*, if you remember the movie) with the sky above being a semi-opaque dome that stopped humans from seeing the world inhabited either by God and his angels (if you were a monotheist), or the many gods of the pagan world. All humans could see were the specks of light from these gods/angels; by reading the stars they could attempt to figure out what was happening in the spiritual world and how that might affect humans—hence astrology. By contrast, John is led up through a door in the roof so he (and his audience) can clearly see what's going on in the spiritual realm, addressed by Jesus himself (4:1) along with the occasional angelic tour-guide.

The first thing John sees is God on his throne. It's a vision that contains elements from previous divine appearances which were recorded in the Old Testament by Moses, Isaiah, Daniel, and Ezekiel, as well as in later Jewish writings.[10] This is a way of stressing continuity with Israel's story in several ways. Firstly, it's clear this is the God of the Hebrew Scriptures, and John writes as one in a long line of his prophets; but now, access to divine revelation is through Jesus, for the benefit of those who belong to him. Secondly, the God who's the Father of Jesus Christ is the same one found in Israel's Scriptures; although many Jews had rejected his Messiah, those who do accept Jesus are the ones who are being faithful to Israel's God. Thirdly, it gives confidence that just as God has been sovereign in the past, he'll continue to be so in the future; this same God will continue to judge those who oppose him and to deliver his exiled people. In short, it sets the current crisis—of being a small minority group in a hostile empire—in the wider history of the sovereign God and his chosen people.

Some features of the vision, however, are strikingly new, originating not in Old Testament visions of God but in the customs of the Roman imperial court. For example:

---

10. See Ex 19:16–25; 24:9–11; Isa 6:1–7; Dan 7:9–10; Ezek 1:4–28; *1 Enoch* 14:17–22; *Apocalypse of Abraham* 18:1–8; *Testament of Levi* 3:1–10.

> Surrounding the throne were twenty-four other thrones, and seated on them were twenty-four elders. They were dressed in white and had crowns of gold on their heads. (4:4)

While the number twenty-four has significance within Israel's story, the Roman emperor at the time John likely wrote was Domitian,[11] who was the first emperor to increase the number of his bodyguards from twelve to twenty-four.[12] He also surrounded himself with priests—dressed in white, with golden crowns—whenever he presided at sporting events at the Coliseum.[13] John notes that the elders "cast their crowns before the throne" (4:10), which was the behavior expected of kings and rulers who had been conquered by Rome, symbolically submitting their own rule to his.[14] And as they do so, the elders say "You are worthy, *our Lord and God*, to receive glory and honor and power" (4:11); Domitian was particularly fond of that title (*Dominus et Deus noster*), being one of the few emperors who actually thought of himself as divine.[15]

In some ways, this is a form of satire. The God John sees isn't just the God of Israel; he's also the one who holds power over the mighty Roman empire. In comparison with this God, the emperors—for all their pomp and pageantry—are just pale and shadowy imitations, who can only take up their crowns and rule if and when God allows them to. To John's marginalized minority, the Roman empire might *look* big and imposing, but God's the one who holds the real power. He sits not on an earthly throne, but a heavenly one, and he's the one who's in control of the future course of human history.

This is a truth that's just as important for us to recognize today. If John were to craft a twenty-first-century throne-room scene, it might look a bit like this:

> After this I looked, and there before me was the Ancient of Days seated on a leather chair behind a mahogany desk. The office

---

11. The majority view is that John wrote during Domitian's reign (see e.g., Koester, *Revelation*, 71–79). The minority view—that it was during an earlier period of persecution under Nero—tends to flow from seeing some/all of the prophecies as referring to the fall of Jerusalem, and that those prophecies must be *predictive* (e.g., Gentry, *Before Jerusalem Fell*). I'm comfortable with references to prior events and institutions as being prophetic commentary, designed to portray them in a particular light, rather than having to read them as predictive prophecy, or prophecy *ex eventu*.

12. Paul, *Revelation*, 124.

13. Koester, *Revelation and the End of All Things*, 75.

14. Aune, *Apocalypticism*, 107–08.

15. Suetonius, *Dom.* 13; Pliny, *Pan.* 52.1, 7; Dio Cassius, *Historiae romanae* 67.4. See Smith, "The Book of Revelation," 339.

was shaped like an oval, and behind him were fifty stars all bowing down before him, with seven stripes which are the seven spirits of God. On the floor before him was the picture of an eagle. The eagle was covered in eyes which were continuous live feeds from all the satellites of the earth.

Surrounding the desk were twenty-four sons of men. They were dressed in black suits and had discreet earpieces in their ears; day and night they never stopped whispering into their lapels. From the desk came flashes of lightning, rumblings, and a shock and awe campaign the likes of which the world has never seen. And I looked and I saw at his right hand a marine carrying a briefcase; in it were the launch codes for the seven judgments upon the earth.[16]

Even for the head of the most powerful nation on earth, his power is a pale imitation of the one true God's. He only rules because God has allowed him to; the fate of the world is in God's hands, not in military might or democratic institutions. And that goes not just for governments but for any source of power—any institution or human authority—that might look big and impressive, and in some cases be oppressive. God's bigger than all of them, and John invites us to imagine for ourselves a throne-room scene to remind us of that fact.

Yet if God is, indeed, in control, John's marginalized minority could be forgiven for asking: *why are we still suffering? What's God going to do about injustice in his world, and the oppression of his people?* The second half of the throne-room scene begins to answer this, when John points out a scroll in God's right hand (5:1). The scroll has writing on both sides, reminding us of the double-sided scroll Ezekiel saw, which contained "words of lament and mourning and woe" (Ezek 2:10).[17] This is a scroll that, when opened, brings judgment to a rebellious world and vindication for God's people (see Rev 6). The only problem is, no-one is worthy to break the seven seals and open it (5:2–4).

---

16. I should firstly point out that this in no way suggests the American government is oppressing Christians (like Rome was), merely that it's been the preeminent human power of our age. And if I made it about China, it could limit my future travel options. This parody was first written during the final year of the Bush administration, and happily endured throughout Obama's two terms. It may need a little rewriting for the current occupant of the throne room, whose hair is like fine orange cotton, who can't quite hold all seven stars in his medium-sized hands, and who wears a red crown inscribed with the words "Make Rome Great Again." And none of the original twenty-four elders is still there—most have resigned and a few are under indictment. My point is, when the real thing already looks like a parody, it's hard to make a parody of it.

17. Witherington, *Revelation*, 119.

At this point in the vision, Jesus appears, in the paradoxical form of a lamb (or more accurately, a little ram[18]) who was slain, but nevertheless has remained standing (5:6). He *is* worthy,[19] because he has triumphed over death on behalf of God's people. He has won the victory, and stands ready to enact God's justice and vindicate his people. Yet *how* he did it is instructive: not by being the warrior-king that Israel was expecting, but through weakness and sacrifice; the lion from the tribe of Judah has turned up in the surprising form of a slain lamb (5:5). This hints to John's audience that just as Jesus suffered for a little while before emerging victorious, this will be their experience, too. After all, it was by that very act of suffering that they were gathered from the nations and brought into God's people, being given the privilege of serving God and exercising his rule (5:9–10).

But before the scroll is opened and God's justice enacted, we pause briefly to hear the circle of those who bow before the lamb widen: it's no longer just the four living creatures and twenty-four elders, as innumerable angels join in. These are followed by *every creature*—in the sky, on the earth, and in the sea—all giving glory to Jesus and to God the Father (5:11–14). It's a picture of the cosmos with everything in order, unified in its praise of God.

Everything, that is, except for the world of human beings, which subsequent chapters will show as being out of step: those who, despite God's warnings, persist in sin and idolatry, refusing to acknowledge God (9:20–21). This is an important subversion of Rome's view of the world, in which Jesus' followers (with their curious monotheism) are the ones who are out of step because of their refusal to participate in its worship of idols. Revelation consistently turns this picture inside out, showing that idol worshippers are the deviant minority,[20] and if they don't conform to the true "majority culture"—the rest of the created order—their destiny is destruction

## Judgment, vindication, and protection

The seals to the scroll are then opened, one by one. Each seal unleashes judgments which are strikingly similar to those prophesied for the city of Jerusalem back in Ezekiel's time (Ezek 14:21; cf. Rev 6:8), prior to its original

---

18. The Greek word, *arnion*, usually just translated "lamb," conveys the strength-in-weakness paradox, being a male sheep (associated with strength) which is not yet fully grown.

19. A phrase associated with the arrival of the emperor; Mounce, *Revelation*, 135; Paul, *Revelation*, 127, notes that it's used of the emperor "whenever his acts of beneficence match the power of his office."

20. DeSilva, *Seeing Things John's Way*, 99. This is a strategy also seen in the apocryphal *1 Enoch*, 1–5.

destruction. These judgments feature the famed "four horsemen of the apocalypse," which echo the colored horses of Zechariah's vision (Zech 1:7–17), and also provide a connection with Jerusalem's promised restoration. In Zechariah's vision, an angel pleads with God, *"Lord Almighty, how long* will you withhold mercy from Jerusalem...?" God replies to the angel with "kind and comforting words" and declares judgment on the nations who oppressed his city and its presently-exiled people. In John's vision, it's the martyrs who cry out *"How long, sovereign Lord*, holy and true, until you judge the inhabitants of the land and avenge our blood?" (6:10). They are similarly comforted while they wait, and told that justice is coming (6:11).

The message for John's audience is thus: *just as rebellious Jerusalem was judged in Ezekiel's day, judgment will come against those who persist in that rebellion today. And just as suffering Jerusalem was comforted and promised vindication in the sight of her enemies, comfort and vindication is promised for God's suffering people today.* There would be further irony if, as some suggest, the seal judgments relate to the more recent fall of Jerusalem in AD70,[21] as punishment for rejecting Jesus and persecuting his followers (cf. Mt 23:34–39). Jerusalem is again being judged, but this time it's Jesus' followers who are receiving her promises of comfort and vindication.

More broadly, however, this is a picture of God at work, judging his world for its rebellion—although at this point it's only a measure of judgment, symbolized by the destruction of "a fourth" of everything (6:8). But the pressing question for John's minority is this: *what about us? Are we going to be collateral damage in all of this destruction?* Or in the closing words of the chapter, "who can withstand it?"[22] This is addressed in the next chapter, in which two scenes provide a dramatic pause between the opening of the sixth and seventh seals.

The first scene is of angels holding back the four winds, giving another angel time to seal God's people[23] for protection. This draws on a pattern from the Hebrew Scriptures and other Jewish writings in which angels press "pause" on God's judgment, to allow time to mark for protection that which belongs to God: Noah's family, by means of the ark (1 Enoch 66:1–2); the

---

21. So Pate, *The Writings of John*, 399–410; Gentry, *Before Jerusalem Fell*, 239–43. The seal judgments are also very similar to those pronounced on Jerusalem by Jesus (Mark 13). The fourth century historian, Eusebius, used the writings of Josephus and others to demonstrate the fulfilment of Jesus' prophecy in the siege and fall of Jerusalem (*Ecclesiastical History* 3.5–9).

22. Reddish, *Revelation*, 141.

23. The 144,000 may refer to all of God's people, or just symbolize Jewish believers, or even only the martyrs. At any rate, the number symbolism tells us they are the ones who bear the dimensions of the New Jerusalem (Rev 21:15–17). See Keener, *Revelation*, 232 for a discussion on this.

Israelites' firstborn sons by a lamb's blood on the doorframe (Ex 12:23); those in Jerusalem who are faithful to God by mark on the forehead (Ezek 9:4–6); and the sacred objects in the temple (2 Baruch 6:4–7).[24] The message to John's audience is: *just as God protected his people in the past, he'll continue to do so in the present.* This is an important antidote to any anxiety we might be experiencing about our renewed appreciation of our minority status; God has always looked after his own, and in far more threatening circumstances than those in which we find ourselves.

The second scene is of an innumerable multitude,[25] with language borrowed from the vision of the new heavens and new earth (esp. 21:3–4; 22:1–5). It thus appears to function as a "flash forward" to the glorious future that awaits God's people,[26] functioning as a vivid promise of their reward—a deliberative appeal to advantage through word-picture rather than logical argument. Some have described it as a kind of "transfiguration" of the church,[27] mirroring Jesus' own transfiguration in the Gospels, in which he gets a glimpse of his future glory that hardens his resolve as he sets out on the path of suffering and death. This should remind us of the power of preaching about the age to come, which has in many places become an afterthought to the here-and-now messages of individual prosperity or social reform.

The seventh seal also introduces a pause—"silence in heaven for about half an hour" (8:1)—as God and his entourage hear the prayers of his people. In the context of Revelation, these are most likely prayers for justice, as the response is a further round of judgment from the seven trumpets. This time a third is affected, symbolizing an increasing intensity—but still not the full measure—as a further warning. Yet those who survive persist in their idolatrous rebellion (9:20–21). And it leaves us wondering whether judgment-as-warning is an effective strategy, or if it's time for God to try something else.

## Commissioned to witness

In the next chapter, it looks like God did have another set of warnings in his back pocket ready to go; however, John's told not to write what the

---

24. Reddish, *Revelation*, 142.

25. Again, there's debate over whether they are the same group as the first scene, or whether they are an expansion of it (e.g., from Jewish believers to incorporating people from all nations).

26. Reddish, *Revelation*, 147.

27. E.g., Mounce, *Revelation*, 162.

seven thunders said, for "there will be no more delay!" (10:4-6).[28] *If the first two sets didn't work, let's skip straight to the end game.* But before then, God has one more strategy to enact, and he's decided that the church will be the one to do it.

John, functioning again as the representative of God's people, is told to eat a scroll (10:9).[29] This is exactly what Ezekiel was instructed to do with his judgment-filled scroll (Ezek 3:1-3), which tasted "as sweet as honey" (cf. Ps 119:103). John is then told to "prophesy again about many peoples and nations and languages and kings" (10:11), implying that his message announces and interprets the judgments contained in the scroll. John (and his audience) is to supply the previously missing ingredient: judgment needs *interpretation* in order to function as revelation. In other words, just as Ezekiel was commissioned to announce and explain God's judgment to a rebellious Israel, so the church is now sent to do likewise to a rebellious world. There's one key difference with Ezekiel, however. Although John's scroll tasted similarly sweet, it quickly turns bitter in his stomach (10:10)—suggesting either that his message won't go down well with those on the receiving end of it, or that it'll cause the messengers a fair amount of discomfort. Either way, the end result is the same: their witness meets with fierce opposition.

Or better—their *two* witnesses, as the picture parable in the next chapter introduces us to a pair of symbolic figures (11:3) reminiscent of Moses and Elijah (and Zerubbabel and Joshua). They're further described as "the two lampstands," making a strong case that they represent the church.[30] Their story is told in a way which highlights the similarities between Jesus' experience and that of his faithful witnesses: although they come with demonstrations of God's power (11:5-6), they'll be attacked in the same city where Jesus was crucified (11:7). Like Jesus, they'll be dishonored by the public display of their bodies, heightened by the gleeful celebration of the

---

28. Following Mounce, *Revelation*, 209. As usual, there's a variety of explanations as to why the seven thunders were not recorded. Aune, *Revelation 6-16*, 562-63, sees it as following an apocalyptic convention in which all but one thing is revealed; it preserves the privileged status of the author, who knows more than he's allowed to reveal, as well as sending the message that it's not our place to know *everything* about God and his plans.

29. There is debate as to whether it's the same scroll as the one in chapter 5, or a different one (the Greek word is slightly different). Ashcraft, *Revelation*, 301, sensibly points out that "it may be futile to inquire about the content of a book which no one read before John ate it." This is true, although we could wait to see what comes out, which may well be the contents of chapter 12 onwards.

30. Previously in Revelation, lampstands have symbolized churches (Reddish, *Revelation*, 211). For a discussion on the identity of the witnesses, see also Holwerda, "Suffering Witnesses," 131; Tanner, "Climbing the Lampstand-Witness-Trees," 84-86, 90; DeSilva, *Seeing Things John's Way*, 223.

majority culture,[31] which reminds us that there's more than just the physical aspect of persecution in view. The duration of their dishonor—three-and-a-half days (11:9)—connects the period of persecution by the nations (cf. Rev 11:2; 12:6, 14; Dan 12:7, 11) with Jesus' three days in the tomb.[32] The period of the church's shame, just like that of Jesus, will be finite.

The reason it's finite is that the church, too, will experience resurrection (11:11); the two witnesses are vindicated "while their enemies looked on" (11:12), stressing the reversal of dishonor by the majority that accompanies resurrection. An associated earthquake destroys a tenth of the city, including seven thousand people (11:13), with those who remain taking note and glorifying God. The proportion is a reversal of Elijah's ministry in which only a seven thousand strong minority resisted idolatry and remained faithful to God (1 Kgs 19:18).[33] It gives John's audience comfort that they won't always be a minority.

This parable is a significant turning point in the plot of Revelation; judgment alone has so far failed to produce repentance (9:20–21), whereas the interpretation supplied by the two witnesses has made that judgment effective.[34] This is important both for John's minority group and for us in several ways.[35] Firstly, it demonstrates that our testimony, no matter how bitterly it may be received by the majority culture, is an essential part of God's plan.[36] Secondly, it means that our ministry is to be shaped after Jesus' own suffering and death; effective witness means embracing the weakness and suffering of minority, not chasing after privilege or acceptance among the majority. Thirdly, it encourages us to understand our suffering as being effective, just like Jesus' own suffering; it will result in the salvation of many, more so than any displays of power.[37] And finally, it assures us of the ultimate vindication of ourselves and our message before the majority culture.

---

31. This is probably an ironic reversal of Purim, in which God's people were miraculously saved from death, celebrating by exchanging gifts and displaying the defiled corpses of their would-be persecutors (Est 9:22, 25).

32. Beale, *Revelation*, 229.

33. Koester, *Revelation and the End of All Things*, 111.

34. Trites, *The New Testament Concept of Witness*, 170.

35. MacBride, "Imitators of the Lord in Severe Suffering."

36. Trites, *The New Testament Concept of Witness*, 170.

37. Holwerda, "Suffering Witnesses," 131.

## The dragon and the beasts

Revelation's second major cycle of visions spans chapters 12–20. Its focus is on the dominant world power, Rome, and her opposition toward God's faithful minority. Using clearly pejorative imagery, it paints the key players the way God sees them, rather than perhaps the way they'd like to be seen.

It begins with a familiar image in the skies: the queen of heaven, clothed in the sun, with the moon at her feet and surrounded by stars (12:1). It's immediately recognizable to John's audience as that of a pagan goddess: Isis, in Egypt, who gave birth to the sun-god, Horus, who grows up to slay the dragon-serpent. (The Greek version of the myth involves the sun-god, Apollos, defeating Python.) In Roman times, this imagery of the queen of heaven had been appropriated by *Roma Aeterna,* the divine embodiment of the city of Rome.[38] She's the one who gives birth to the Roman emperors—who frequently styled themselves after Apollos—and demands they be worshipped as "savior" of the world because they'd defeated the enemies of the empire.[39]

Yet in John's description, it becomes clear that this is no pagan goddess. The child she gives birth to is a son who "will rule all the nations with an iron scepter" (12:5; cf. Ps 2:7–9), marking him out as the promised king from David's line. In an individual sense, that would make the woman Mary; but she's also the people of God, collectively—the messianic community.[40] John's vision is thus highly subversive, claiming that the true queen of heaven isn't Mother Rome, as Rome's public relations consultants would have us believe. The true queen of heaven is Mother Zion, the people of God. She's the one who gave birth to the real savior, who actually does rule the world. *And John's insignificant minority group are her children* (12:17).

Still today, we need to be reminded of how the claims of Christ subvert the narrative of our majority culture. The queen of heaven isn't Mother Washington, who seems to go into labor every four years in the audacious hope of squeezing out the next savior. Neither is it Mother Humanism, giving birth to its twin saviors named Tolerance and Harmony. Nor is it Mother Science, whose saviors variously promise to give us life to the full, rescue us from the fires of climate change,[41] or upload our consciousness to the cloud where we'll

---

38. A coin found in Pergamum depicts the goddess Roma as the Queen of Heaven.

39. Paul, *Revelation*, 214.

40. Witherington, *Revelation*, 167–72; Boring, *Revelation*, 152. A passage from the Dead Sea Scrolls (1QH 3:4) includes the image of a woman (representing the community) bringing forth the Messiah.

41. This isn't to deny the reality of climate change, but the narrative often associated with it: that it's humanity's primary existential threat, and that we can be our own

live forever. Why would we chase acceptance among any of these pretenders? We're children of the true queen of heaven, and worship a savior who has defeated our ultimate enemy, death—and come back to prove it!

This raises an important question, however, for those among John's audience who were still experiencing significant persecution—one that still resonates with us today. *If Jesus has defeated the dragon, why are God's people still suffering? Some days it doesn't feel like we're on the winning side!* The next part of the vision (12:7–12) explains that although the dragon has been defeated, he hasn't yet been destroyed; more than that, he's angry at being cast out of his place in heaven, and is determined to cause as much havoc as he can in the time he has left (12:12). This is a significant rhetorical move: fierce opposition isn't to be interpreted by John's minority as a sign of impending defeat; it's merely the death-throes of a vanquished opponent which have to be endured for a short time. Increasing hostility from the majority culture shouldn't unnerve us if we learn to view it as the outworking of Jesus' already-won victory, and a reminder that things will soon be put right.

Another important aspect to this vision is that it portrays the true origin of the opposition being faced by John's audience. The dragon, explicitly identified as Satan (12:9), is the one who gives the beast from the sea his power and authority (13:2). That this beast represents the emperor can be deduced from numerous clues such as the seven heads being Rome's famed "seven hills" (17:9), the allusion to the *Nero redivivus* myth (13:3), and the letters in the Greek spelling of "Nero Caesar" adding up to the number of the beast (13:18).[42] But it's what's said about the "beastly" emperor that's even more significant: his rule is blasphemous (13:1, 6) because he has usurped God as the object of worship (13:4b); in fact, worship of the emperor is the worship of Satan (13:4a), who's the real power behind the throne.[43] And although the emperor was worshipped for bringing peace and stability to the empire, the reality is that the renowned Roman Peace was a pretext for waging war against God's people (13:7).

---

savior. In a Christian worldview, it's merely one symptom of our rebellion against our creator, which resulted in our being subject to death, and from which we're incapable of saving ourselves.

42. Number games with people's names, called *gemmatria*, were common. Granted, this can also be done by using the ASCII values of the letters in Bill Gates' name, and (I'm told) with the children's character Barney the Dinosaur. But Bill and Barney weren't known to John's audience, so I'm going with Nero. What moves this beyond mere co-incidence is the small number of New Testament manuscripts which have six hundred and sixteen as the number of the beast—reflecting a scribal "correction" which is the result of adding up the *Latin* spelling of Nero Caesar. See Witherington, *Revelation*, 176–79.

43. Reddish, *Revelation*, 250.

The second beast, arising from the land (13:11), represents the cult of emperor worship, which was particularly strong in Asia Minor.[44] Its description counters Rome's party line that emperor worship was a voluntary expression of gratitude from the people: it speaks with Satan's voice (13:11), participation is compulsory (13:12), and it deceives the people as to its nature (13:14). Lack of compliance is punishable by death (13:15) as well as socio-economic exclusion (13:16–17). John's vision seeks to unmask the emperor and the cult around him. *Don't be seduced by Rome's rhetoric. Behind all the splendor of the imperial court, he's just a hideous beast who does the work of Satan, setting himself up as a god in the place of the one true God. He's to be resisted, not appeased. There can be no compromising with the devil!*

In the West today we tend not to have autocrats who demand to be worshipped as gods after the manner of the Roman emperors (or North Korean dictators).[45] But to some extent, humanity has become the beast,[46] making ourselves into gods and declaring a Human Peace; we can solve our own problems and overcome our existential threats, if we put aside our differences and act collectively. We've even verged on creating our own civic religions: a celebration of the human spirit at the Olympics; memorial services (rightly) honoring military sacrifice without acknowledging the self-sacrificing God whose image it reflects;[47] or Christmas as the idolatry of family, consumption, or peace on earth *produced by* people of good will. Our imperial cults have become far less organized and obvious. In our age, the beast from the land has grown a hipster beard, clipped on a man-bun, and started an advertising agency. He's "deceived the inhabitants of the earth" (13:14) into worshipping possessions, body image, and celebrities. He's convinced us that we desperately want that which ends up enslaving us—worshipping our own passions and desires, rather than the one who created us.

Our difficulty, of course, is that there's nothing inherently wrong with things like sport, health, family, commerce, and harmonious relations—all of which are God's good gifts to us. And there's often no obvious, visible

---

44. *Revelation*, 258.

45. Perhaps with some exceptions.

46. Boring, *Revelation*, 157, argues that "all propaganda that entices humanity to idolize human empire is an expression of this beastly power that wants to appear Lamb-like."

47. Each year, hundreds of Australians flock to a WWI sacred site in Turkey to recite the passion narrative of Gallipoli, and to glorify the ANZAC (Australian and New Zealand Army Corps) Spirit that lives on in us all. A poem by Dame Mary Gilmore, recited at many such events, encapsulates the quasi-religious sentiment and *Hero redivivus* myth: "They are not dead; not even broken. // Only their dust has gone back home to the earth; // For they, the essential they, shall have rebirth // Whenever a word of them is spoken." Gilmore, *The Passionate Heart*, 1.

line between enjoying those gifts and participating in the dominant culture's idolatrous distortion of them. This means that discerning the identity of "beastly" idolatry requires potentially more wisdom (13:18) today than it did in the first century—a constant evaluation of what we might best refrain from, and what we can participate in, while maintaining an explicitly different framework and motivation.[48] John's vision of the two beasts encourages us to look beyond what might appear benign on the surface, and realize that worship of anything other than God is idolatrous—a blasphemous rejection of his rightful rule. Refusing to participate in our society's idolatry is an integral part of our attractive difference.

## A tale of two destinies

There's no middle ground in Revelation. John's vision presents his minority with a choice: you're either on Team Jesus or Team Beast. As deSilva observes,

> John articulates a worldview that establishes alternatives and then forces choices between them. This is highly significant in light of the rival agendas among the churches, most notably the agendas of Jezebel and of the Nicolaitans, whose position seems to envision Christians coexisting alongside and within Roman imperialism and its legitimation mechanisms. John doggedly rends asunder what Jezebel would join together.[49]

And the consequences of that choice are starkly and powerfully presented over the remainder of the Apocalypse.

## Team Beast

For Team Beast, grisly images of judgment await: the torment of burning sulfur (14:9–11), trampled in a bloody winepress of God's wrath (14:17–20), and the seven last plagues poured out over *all* the earth (15:1–16:21)—no quarter- or third-measures now, as the time for warnings is over.

For the city of Rome, judgment is coming. Continuing the subversion of Rome's spin doctors, she's not the queen of heaven—merely a cheap, drunk whore who sits atop the beastly empire, which is the source of her power and wealth (17:1–6). *Why would you want to compromise with Rome*

---

48. One example might be the enthusiastic celebration of military memorial services with the self-sacrificial, peace-bringing God in his rightful place at the center.

49. DeSilva, *Seeing Things John's Way*, 114.

*when she's the one exploiting you?* Mother Rome is recast as "mother of prostitutes and of the abominations of the earth" (17:5), who's intoxicated with the blood of the martyrs (17:6). *Why would you want to compromise with Rome when she's the one persecuting you?* She's also nicknamed "Babylon," another spectacularly beautiful ancient city which ruthlessly exploited other nations to build an empire, set up idols and rulers as objects of worship, and mistreated God's people. *Why would you want to compromise with this "Babylon," when you recall the fate of the previous Babylon?* John's vision then describes the eventual destruction of Rome. The nations she exploited will turn against her (17:15–18) and judgment will be swift (18:18). Those who profited from her exploitation will mourn (18:9, 11, 18–19) while God's people will rejoice at their oppressor's defeat (18:20). *Why would you want to compromise with the Eternal City when the only thing eternal about her is the smoke of her destruction (19:3)?*[50]

And for all those who remain opposed to God, judgment is coming. Jesus turns up riding on a white horse, symbolizing victory (19:11), and crowned with many crowns, symbolizing supreme authority (19:12). He "treads the winepress" of God's wrath (19:15), the result of which is a feast for carrion birds (19:17–18)—a gruesome counterpart to the wedding feast to be enjoyed by God's people (19:9). At the end of the great battle, the beast and the false prophet are thrown into the fiery lake of burning sulfur (19:19–21), along with the devil (20:10), showing that the powers opposed to God will be defeated and destroyed. In sum, John's vision sends the message: *why would you choose Team Beast, when its future is incomprehensibly terrifying?*

Before looking at the contrasting future of Team Jesus, we need to address how appropriate this kind of rhetoric is for today—especially the shocking nature of the imagery. Firstly, it needs to be pointed out that this wouldn't have been *as* shocking in the ancient world—or, indeed, in some parts of our world today. Invasion and conquest were facts of life; armies would often do incredibly brutal things to those they conquered, then dishonor their bodies after death as a way of rubbing the defeat in. A lot of the time it was vengeance for what had been done to *their* nation last time *your* nation won. In modern warfare—governed by the Geneva convention and a desire to avoid harming non-combatants—this kind of behavior, while it still can happen, is (rightly) condemned. But Revelation is speaking to a context in which this was common behavior for conquering armies.

Secondly, this wasn't written directly to us, but to a marginalized, often persecuted, and sometimes martyred people, reassuring them that justice

---

50. Beale, *Revelation*, 929.

would eventually be done to the ones who had thus mistreated them. It's sending the message: *stay strong and endure, because one day your oppressors will have the tables turned on them!* And it's not even addressed to those oppressors, but for internal consumption.

Thirdly, these are symbols: the beast and the false prophet are thrown into a fiery lake, symbolizing the destruction of evil powers; even the vulture scene (19:17–18) is simply drawing on earlier imagery (Ezek 39:17) about a great battle. While the images and language are drawn from the realities of warfare in the ancient world, let's not assume they're literal any more than we think that one day we're going to be living in a city that's literally a 1,500 mile-high cube (21:16). The point is: *one day there'll be nothing left which opposes God or his people, so total will his victory be.*

But finally, this *does* talk about judgment and destruction for those who are opposed to God. Let's not shy away from that. But remember that God has been graciously holding off this judgment since Genesis chapter 3, sending plenty of warnings. Even in Revelation, we've seen sets of judgments that caused increasing amounts of destruction (a quarter, then a third), along with his witnesses (the church) to interpret the judgments and implore people to repent. But they still didn't; in fact, they killed the witnesses who were bringing them the message of hope! So at this point, nothing is left except for God, with heavy heart, to enact his final judgment. It reminds John's audience: *although it looks like your oppressors are getting away with it, they won't do so forever.*

## Team Jesus

For Team Jesus, the future is vastly different. In contrast to Team Beast, for whom there's no rest, those who belong to Jesus "will rest from their labor" (14:13). They don't wear Rome's purple and scarlet robes of prostitution, but are dressed in fine white linen (19:7–8) as befitting the bride of Christ.[51] They aren't on the menu at the "great supper of God" but are the guest of honor at the "wedding supper of the Lamb" (19:9). Their future lies not in the lake of burning sulfur, but in the new heavens and new earth.

Throughout the final two chapters of Revelation, the new creation is described using the vocabulary of Genesis, as a symbolic reversal of the curse (22:3). The open gates (21:25) and lack of sea (21:1) promise not just safety from danger, but a world in which nothing can oppose God nor his people. There's no temple needed (21:22), because unlike the distant gods and emperors worshipped by the majority culture, they'll have direct access

---

51. Reddish, *Revelation*, 364.

to God himself. The tour of the holy city is given by the same angel who was the tour guide for Babylon (21:9; cf. 17:1),[52] making the comparison clear: *why compromise with Rome, when you will inherit a far greater city?* And entry to it is a great privilege—greater than that which Rome can bestow—being only for those whose names appear in the Lamb's book of life (21:27). In sum, the vision says: *why would you not stay with Team Jesus, when its future is so unimaginably great?*

## Conclusion

Revelation has been misused in the past, being scoured for signs of our geopolitical future in a way that ignored the relevance to its original audience. This has subsequently made us wary of using it at all. And its unfamiliar genre makes it difficult to understand, and harder still to communicate it in a meaningful way to contemporary audiences. Yet it contains a powerful message that's still supremely relevant today, in how it seeks to subvert the attractiveness of compromise with a majority culture that dares to set itself up in defiance of God and his just rule. Its rhetoric comforts those who suffer ostracism and persecution because of their faithfulness to Jesus; and it challenges those who are tempted to compromise in order to avoid it. As deSilva concludes,

> John seeks to demonstrate that the worship of God and the worship of idols are fundamentally incompatible, and that the person who engages in the latter cannot escape punishment for sharing God's honor with God's enemies. He regards the voices that make room for idolatrous practice in any form as especially great dangers to the churches, and dedicates much of his vision to rendering their position untenable.[53]

Revelation urges us to remain loyal to God and his faithful minority, even if it means being seen as *dis*-loyal to the wider culture. The forces against us may appear imposing and all-encompassing. But in comparison to the rest of the created order *they* are the minority; *they* are the aliens in God's world. If we allow John to take us through the door in the heavens, we'll see things as they really are, and a sovereign God who will soon bring justice for his people.

---

52. Witherington, *Revelation*, 266.
53. DeSilva, *Seeing Things John's Way*, 71.

*Part 3*

# Paul's Epistles

We're not covering *all* of Paul's letters in this book.

THE FIRST REASON IS the obvious one: it would take at least the entire book to do it properly. For each of Paul's letters, his audience's minority status forms an important element of the background. All of his letters deal in some way with the identity of his audience as God's people, and the way in which that identity ought to define their court of reputation, alter their worldview, and be worked out in their behavior. As with the other authors of the New Testament, Paul is writing minority group rhetoric.

The second reason is that in most of Paul's letters, his audience's minority status stays largely in the background. He might be forming and reinforcing the identity of the group, but he's not setting that identity *over against* that of the dominant culture as frequently or explicitly as is the case with 1 Peter or Revelation, for example. Pressure from the majority culture is ever-present, and is often one of the cultural drivers of the issues Paul addresses (like Jew-Gentile relations in the church), but most of the time it's not tackled head-on in the way we've seen in some of the other New Testament writings so far. So a detailed look at all of Paul's writings through the minority group lens wouldn't look much different from a standard, rhetorically-informed commentary—with the phrase "because they were a minority" scattered throughout.

For this reason, we'll look at a sample of four of Paul's letters. These have been selected because the central issue—or proposition, to use the rhetorical terminology of Paul's day[1]—is explicitly related to his audience's

---

1. Paul's letters follow, to a considerable extent, the conventions for speech-writing in the Greco-Roman world outlined in handbooks by the likes of Aristotle, Cicero, and Quintilian. This shouldn't be a surprise, as most people were illiterate and there was no printing press, so his letters had to be "performed" out loud. The proposition of such

status as a minority group that's called to be attractively different from the world around it. In **Philippians**, Paul defines citizenship for Jesus' followers *over against* the way the dominant culture saw it. In **1 Corinthians**, he urges his audience to make judgments about a person's status *over against* worldly judgments. In **1 Thessalonians**, Paul encourages the fledgling church to continue to live out its new identity as children of the light *over against* the darkness of the idolatrous majority. And in **Colossians** he urges a purely Christ-centered worldview *over against* adding elements of the empty "philosophy" found in the surrounding culture. This will provide us with a sufficiently representative sample of the ways in which Paul's rhetoric of minority might be used today.[2]

---

a speech was usually located after the rapport-building introduction and narrative of events that occasioned it, and sets out the thesis statement—the truth of which the rest of the speech would attempt to persuade the audience. My previous book, *Catching the Wave*, is all about how we might preach in light of this, building on the work of e.g., Witherington, *New Testament Rhetoric*; Kennedy, *New Testament Interpretation*.

2. Romans and Galatians are primarily addressed to the problem posed to group identity by the inclusion of both Jews and Gentiles; this may have been driven, in part, by outside pressure, but Paul doesn't primarily concern himself with this dynamic. 2 Corinthians is indeed a sequel, but mainly deals with the relationship between Paul and the Corinthians as a result of the issues tackled in his previous letter. Ephesians is similar to Colossians, but its rhetoric of praise is less explicitly focused on the contrast with the wider world. The Pastoral Epistles deal mainly with in-house matters like leadership and false teachers, although still with an occasional eye to being an attractively different minority (e.g., 1 Tim 2:1–4).

# 8

## Philippians
### Citizens of Heaven

CITIZENSHIP IS IMPORTANT TO all of us. It gives us a sense of belonging to something bigger than just ourselves, our families, or even the collection of everyone we know. In most places it entails a set of rights we have as we interact with our fellow citizens, as well as a set of responsibilities to live up to, whether they be in the form of written laws, or spoken or unspoken values and behaviors. Our citizenship of a city or nation-state gives us a sense of group identity.

Citizenship can cut two ways. It can be inclusive, setting out aspirational ideals and inviting others who are like-minded to join, as well as respecting and celebrating models and instances of citizenship other than our own. Or, as we know too well, it can be exclusive, drawing a tight boundary around "us" and "them," sometimes to the exclusion of some within the group, let alone those outside. In the latter case, citizenship of one group is set *over against* those of other places, and becomes a source of rivalry and tension.

There's also the difficult question of "dual citizenship." My country recently had to deal with this issue when it was discovered that a number of parliamentarians hadn't formally renounced their citizenship of other countries—citizenship that, for some, they didn't even know they had—making them technically ineligible to be an elected representative.[1] The rationale for this rule is that there are times it might be difficult to act in the interests of the citizens who elected you if you're also a citizen of another country. Citizenship can raise interesting questions about loyalty.

---

1. How do you not know you're a citizen of another country? It turns out that some countries, like our neighbor, New Zealand, automatically confer citizenship on a citizen's children regardless of where they were born, and it's something that needs to be deliberately renounced. Thankfully we uncovered New Zealand's plot to infiltrate us just in time!

The citizens of Philippi were proud of their status as a Roman colony and their strong connection with the emperorship: only recently, in 31 BC, Emperor Augustus had named the city after his daughter and granted it citizenship of Rome.[2] And it's to this city that Paul speaks in the language of citizenship and empire, using it to tell the Christian minority there how to live as citizens—*now that they have another, greater citizenship "in heaven."* Talk about playing with fire! Does that mean they need to live like they've renounced their Roman citizenship? Or somehow live as dual citizens, with the inevitable divided loyalties? And is this alternative citizenship going to be *attractively* different, if it's defined *over against* that given by Rome?

This isn't just a problem faced by the Philippians. For the past two millennia, the church has struggled with how to live on earth as citizens of heaven, often lurching between two extremes. On the one hand, the primacy of our "heavenly citizenship" can be stressed to the extent that we neglect to be good neighbors and citizens who take an active role in how our society treats one another and stewards its resources. We can become too busy building our own alternative society to get involved in the affairs of the wider community. On the other hand, embracing the idea of "dual citizenship" can lead to various forms of compromise in which our heavenly allegiance is limited to private matters, while in public matters the state holds sway.[3] Or we identify our heavenly citizenship with simply the good we do as part of our local neighborhood, or among the marginalized.[4] Worse still, God's kingdom and the nation-state can become conflated, so that the church becomes a holy cheer squad for the national interest and provides the appearance of divine endorsement of secular moralities in exchange for a seat at the table.

But Paul's approach is at neither extreme. Let's look at how he uses citizenship language, beginning with the central proposition of his address.

## Citizens worthy of the good news

> Whatever happens, conduct yourselves in a manner (*politeuesthe*) worthy of the good news (*euangelion*) of Christ. (Phil 1:27a)

Most English translations tend to obscure the concept of citizenship that's inescapably tied up with the Greek *politeuesthe*, although it's not hard to

---

2. Fee, *Philippians*, 25–26.
3. Fowl, *Philippians*, 62.
4. See McKnight, *Kingdom Conspiracy*, 1–12, for a balanced critique of this approach.

see the word for "politics" hiding there in plain sight. This is a call for Paul's audience to *live as citizens* in a manner that's consistent with the good news, with all of the citizenship connotations that would have had in a Roman colony like Philippi.

Moreover, their conduct ought to be worthy of the "good news" about Jesus. These days, "good news" is about as Christian a term as you can get. But in the Greco-Roman world—and especially in the imperial colony of Philippi—this would have had strong associations with the Emperor. An inscription written in 9BC from the Provincial Assembly of Asia describes the day of Emperor Augustus's birth as being "for the whole world the beginning of the good news (*euangelion*) concerning him."[5]

So at this point, the Philippians would have been thinking in terms of their Roman citizenship and the emperor who bestowed it. But there's already a twist, isn't there? The good news is not that of the emperor's birth, but the birth *of Christ*. Some argue that here, in the first instance, Paul's talking about how they ought to live out their *Roman* citizenship in a way that's consistent with the gospel—and this then forms a backdrop to the greater, "heavenly" citizenship Paul introduces later in the letter (3:20).[6] But straight afterwards, Paul seems to clarify that he's talking about their conduct *within* the group in the face of outside pressure:

> Then, whether I come and see you or only hear about you in my absence, I will know that you stand firm in the one spirit, striving together as one for the faith of the gospel without being frightened in any way by those who oppose you. (1:27b–28a)

The chief characteristic of the group's civic life is to be an unbreakable unity. This could still be seen as having implications for their Roman citizenship: "their good conduct as citizens in their heavenly colony, the church, will be a brilliant witness in their life as citizens in Philippi, the Roman colony."[7] But here, the rhetoric about unity in the face of opposition seems more directed at the minority as an assurance of vindication than as a witness to those outside:

---

5. Dittenberger, *Orientis Graeci Inscriptiones Selectae* 2.458, cited in Horsley, *Jesus and Empire*, 24.

6. See the discussion in Hansen, *Philippians*, 94–95, along with Winter, *Seek the Welfare of the City*, 85; also Brewer, "The Meaning of *Politeuesthe*," 76–83. Fowl, *Philippians*, 60–62, disagrees, pointing to the similar way in which this word is used in the LXX to refer to a (minority) Jewish way of life over against the (majority) Gentile culture.

7. Hansen, *Philippians*, 95.

> This is a sign to them that they will be destroyed, but that you will be saved—and that by God. (1:28b)

What's more, it was to be a unity that looked strikingly different from that found in the wider culture, rejecting the expected struggle for honor in favor of humility and putting others first:

> Do nothing out of selfish ambition or vain conceit. Rather, in humility value others above yourselves, not looking to your own interests but each of you to the interests of the others. (2:3–4)

In an honor-shame culture, this is radically different—yet at the same time potentially attractive to those on the outside who found themselves losing at the world's status game.

Paul then offers a series of selfless, humble prototypes on which the group was to base their alternative civic life. Jesus is the first and most famous (2:5ff), although we often get distracted by the majestic Christology of the Christ-hymn and forget to apply it the way Paul did: as a pattern for our own selflessness and humility as citizens of living lives worthy of the good news. Timothy is mentioned next, explicitly as an example of someone who lives counter-culturally, not living for his own interests but those of Jesus and his fellow citizens (2:20–21). He's followed by Epaphroditus, who nearly gave his life in the course of exercising his civic duty (2:30). Paul saves his own example for last (3:17) as one for whom his heavenly citizenship is the primary goal (3:14), and he expands it to include all those known to the Philippians who live similarly. As we saw in chapter 1, highlighting prototypical group members is an important strategy in maintaining strong group identity.

In amongst these examples is the message that their counter-cultural unity and other-centeredness has an ambassadorial function in relation to the majority culture. They will be "children of God without fault in a warped and crooked generation" who will "shine *among them* like stars in the sky" (2:15)—a clear call to attractive difference as they live out an alternative kind of citizenship as aliens and exiles.

A little later on, the implicit source of this alternative citizenship is made explicit:

> Their mind is set on earthly things. But our citizenship (*politeuma*) is in heaven. And we eagerly await a savior (*sōtēr*) from there, the Lord Jesus Christ, who, by the power that enables him to bring everything under his control, will transform our body of humiliation so that it will be like his body of glory. (Phil 3:19b–21)

As well as citizenship, this is also an allusion to the Emperor—the same one who granted the Philippians citizenship of the distant city of Rome. The allusion becomes clearer when we read more of that earlier inscription about Augustus, which describes him as a "savior (*sōtēr*) [who] has put an end to war and has set all things in order."[8]

Why is Paul describing Jesus and the believing community in these terms? It's more than just being relatable. He's being subversive: taking the language of the dominant culture in relation to citizenship and emperor, and using it instead to describe membership of the minority group and its leader. Further, this alternative citizenship is depicted as a *greater* one (implied by the contrast between heaven and "earthly things"), as is the savior they're eagerly awaiting. And this greater savior will one day come and make the full measure of their citizenship rights a reality when he turns up and—as part of his bringing all things under his control—he reverses the minority group's shame by allowing them to share in his honor.

## Citizens of heaven today

In making use of Paul's rhetoric of an alternative, heavenly citizenship, three observations will help us avoid the extremes of accommodation and isolation mentioned earlier.

Firstly, notice that Paul doesn't speak of the Philippians' Roman citizenship in a negative way, nor are they told to renounce it in favor of their heavenly citizenship. Instead, he uses the language of earthly citizenship and empire to point to a greater reality. The implied rhetoric is more like: *you think it's good being a colony of Rome; how much better is it being a colony of heaven! If the people around you strive to live a life worthy of Rome and the Emperor, how much more should you strive to live a life worthy of the good news of Jesus Christ!*[9]

It's not difficult to replace "Rome" with our own city or nation, and see how our desire to belong to a community and live by its rules could be presented in the same way, pointing to a greater citizenship. Paul affirms the concept of performing our civic duty; it's just that for Jesus' followers, civic duty is now defined by a different set of values that won't always coincide with those of the surrounding culture. (And that's happening with much greater frequency in the West today, making us increasingly reminded of our minority status.) Yet when those values *do* coincide, Christians should have an even greater reason and ability to live up to them. At least some of

---

8. *Orientis Graeci Inscriptiones Selectae* 2.458, in Horsley, *Jesus and Empire*, 24.
9. Fee, *Philippians*, 379.

the time, our attractive difference can be the spirit and integrity with which we participate in society.

For example, in my own country of Australia, our key aspirational values—with the stress on *aspirational*—would include "mateship" and giving everyone "a fair go." Following Paul's lead, we might suggest that Australian Christians strive to be known as shining examples of these ideals—especially in how we extend that sense of belonging and equality of opportunity to *everyone* (not just those who look like us) in light of God's concern for the marginalized. Within our minority community, we might appropriate the language of "mateship" and "a fair go," redefining it as we go to be based on our commonality in Christ and our desire to follow him in putting others first. That is, we live as good citizens of Australia *whose worldview has been transformed by the good news of Jesus Christ*, because our ultimate citizenship is heavenly.[10]

Secondly, however, Paul subverts the language of citizenship and empire in order to set up a sharply contrasting alternative, namely a heavenly citizenship which is attractively different. And this citizenship must take priority:

> The language of civic responsibility and affiliation 'has been transferred to the corporate life of the church' to make clear that Christ, Christian principles, and Christ's people have a higher and prior claim on their lives.[11]

This is the counterbalance to the first observation, and guards against the conflation of the Christian community and the nation-state. As well as allowing the good aspects of our earthly citizenship to point towards a greater one, we need to follow Paul's lead in painting a picture of how our heavenly citizenship requires counter-cultural living. This means urging our community of believers to live a life shaped by Christ's humility and other-centeredness. It means honoring the stories of those among us who exemplify this way of living in order to make this radical pattern *prototypical* for us, rather than a rarity. And it means pointing out the "warpedness and crookedness" of our generation—not to pass judgment on it, but so that we're crystal clear about the backdrop against which we're called to stand out like shining stars, and to send the message to the world that we're not going to tolerate it if we find it among ourselves—especially among our leaders.

---

10. I'll leave it to other nations to work out their own appropriation of citizenship ideals. But perhaps believers in the land of the free could use e.g., Gal 5:13–15 to transform the idea of "freedom" in light of the good news of Jesus.

11. Witherington, *Friendship and Finances in Philippi*, 99, briefly citing Fowl, *The Story of Christ in the ethics of Paul*, 86.

Too often, however, the impression we give of our heavenly citizenship is like that of a Western tourist visiting an impoverished nation: a condescending air of superiority and the knowledge that the shuttle to the airport is leaving soon. But Paul doesn't allow us to see it that way.

Because thirdly, Paul brings our heavenly citizenship down to earth, as it were. His rhetoric of citizenship needs to be seen in light of its end goal: when the true savior-emperor comes *from heaven* in order to vindicate his people and bring everything under his control (3:21). This isn't an escapist rhetoric, encouraging the Philippian believers to hold onto their heavenly citizenship as a ticket out of here—any more than a citizen of Philippi would expect to end up one day in the city of Rome. Rather, it's about eagerly awaiting the just and peaceful rule of a greater savior-emperor turning up to set things right for all who live in the city. Our status as aliens won't end as a result of our repatriation to heaven, but when heaven one day colonizes earth.

In the meantime, the way in which the Philippian believers live as citizens while they wait is to be a foretaste of that coming reality, both for themselves and for their earthly city. Sometimes that will be by living out, in an exemplary fashion, the highest ideals of the wider society; other times it will be by living in a radical, counter-cultural fashion. Witherington encapsulates the tension in this way:

> Paul's already-and-not-yet eschatology required of his converts an interesting balancing act between: (1) rejection and acceptance of some of the larger cultural values; (2) inclusivity and exclusivity of community, entailing open, yet somewhat clear, ethical and theological boundaries for the community; (3) de-enculturation and yet transformation of the larger culture, at least as one dealt with individuals who were being led to Christ. These are the normal tensions inherent in a missionary religion with an eschatological world view that nonetheless wishes to maintain a clear sense of its identity.[12]

Citizenship rhetoric backfires when it loses its already/not yet tension. When it focuses on the "already," the two cities blur prematurely and our identity as a distinctive minority is lost. When it focuses on the "not yet," our heavenly citizenship turns our gaze inward, away from the world in which we're called to shine like stars. It's only when our distinctive citizenship is seen as an eager anticipation of the coming of a savior—the one who will set all things in order—that it navigates the tension of being both attractive and different.

---

12. *Friendship and Finances in Philippi*, 101–02.

# 9

## 1 Corinthians
## *Are You not Worldly?*

WHILE WRITING THIS BOOK I spent a few weeks travelling in North America. As usual, the first few days were spent bumping into people as I attempted to pass to the left of them on the sidewalk (or footpath, as it should be called; but hey, I can be all things to all people). Of course, I knew that Americans did it differently (or wrongly, as we call it in our minority group Down Under), but a lifetime of instinctively moving left meant that it took about a week to change that ingrained habit. Thankfully for everyone involved, I was better at driving on the right-hand side of the road—having the steering wheel on the left is a helpful reminder.[1] But I remember years ago trying to drive a stick shift in Europe; I ended up with bruised knuckles from hitting the door handle every time I wanted to change gear.

When visiting or joining a new culture (or subculture), we don't just need to unlearn a lifetime of physical habits. We also encounter different ways of thinking, relating, and acting—many of which are less immediately apparent than the side of the road we drive on. And we find some of our basic, previously unquestioned assumptions about what we do and why we do it being challenged in this new setting. Some unlearning is going to have to take place if we're going to fit in.

This was the case with the Corinthian believers Paul addresses in his first letter to them. To put it in the most charitable light, a lifetime of living by the values of Greco-Roman society meant that, for many, it hadn't even occurred to them that some of those values might be incompatible with the new community they'd joined. Although they'd embraced the good news about Jesus, they were bringing *uncritically* the values and behavioral patterns of their culture of origin into the group. The faction-ridden,

---

1. I won't tell you the number of times I got in on the passenger side and was surprised by the absence of the steering wheel.

status-seeking, ultra-competitive culture of the wider world was still playing out in the church—resulting in some of them having more than just bruised knuckles (11:30–31). Paul writes his letter as a response to this problem, urging them to "unlearn" their ingrained habits that were a threat to the minority group's distinctiveness.

## Worldly judgments[2]

After reminding his audience of the status, knowledge, and gifts they *share* because they are *in Christ* (1:3–9 is, with hindsight, a not-too-subtle hint of what's to follow), he gives the central proposition of his address:

> I appeal to you, brothers and sisters, in the name of our Lord Jesus Christ, that all of you agree with one another in what you say and that there be no divisions among you, but that you be perfectly united in mind and thought. (1:10)

This is an appeal to concord: to harmony and unity within the group. It's a common theme for deliberative speeches in the ancient world because its opposite, discord and factionalism, was also common.[3] Paul goes on to quote their cries of support for the different preachers who had passed through Corinth, which took the same form as political slogans of the day:[4]

> What I mean is this: One of you says, "I am of Paul"; another, "I am of Apollos"; another, "I am of Cephas"; still another, "I am of Christ." (1:12)

The important thing to note for our purposes is that in the Greco-Roman world, and especially in a status-chasing, "new money" city like Corinth,[5] *this was perfectly normal behavior.* In the absence of reality TV, public oratory was one of the main sources of entertainment.[6] The speakers themselves would compete for status by entertaining the crowd with their wise and eloquent words. The wealthy who owned large homes would compete for a kind of status-by-association by hosting the best speakers.[7]

---

2. The material in this section summarizes a fuller treatment in my *Preaching the New Testament as Rhetoric*, 212–35.

3. Mitchell, *Rhetoric of Reconciliation*, 182.

4. Welborn, *Politics and Rhetoric*, 16.

5. Fee, *1 Corinthians*, 1–3; Hays, *First Corinthians*, 3.

6. Ciampa and Rosner, *The First Letter to the Corinthians*, 3.

7. Lucian, *Merc. cond.* 25, spoke of the wealthy man's desire to be associated with the best public speakers because "it will make people think him . . . a person of taste in literary matters."

And everyone else picked a favorite and barracked for their heroes in the analogue precursor to a live Twitter feed; see this (disapproving) description from an ancient observer:

> That was the time, too, when one could hear crowds of wretched Sophists [eloquent speakers] around Poseidon's temple shouting and reviling one another, their disciples, as they were called, fighting with one another, many writers reading aloud their stupid works, many poets reciting while others applauded them.[8]

What's more, the kind of oratory that impressed the public was one that placed the emphasis on style over substance; it gave an appearance of wisdom (Greek: *sophia*), leading to them being called *Sophists*.[9] And just as today everyone is invited to "join the conversation" on social media and rate the service they received, it was expected that everyone would weigh in to pass judgment on every instance of public speaking.[10]

The problem Paul faced was that the Corinthian believers were bringing this dynamic into the church. It wasn't just that they were divided around their leaders—as bad as that was—and comparing Paul with the more eloquent Apollos. The deeper issue was that they were competing for status the same way the surrounding culture did, seeking and making judgments according to the world's superficial, style-over-substance criteria. The members of his minority group hadn't yet managed to unlearn their ingrained cultural behavior, constantly hitting their knuckles on the door handle of worldly wisdom and as a consequence remained stuck in first gear:

> Brothers and sisters, I could not address you as people who live by the Spirit but as people who are still worldly—mere infants in Christ. I gave you milk, not solid food, for you were not yet ready for it. Indeed, you are still not ready. You are still worldly. For since there is jealousy and quarrelling among you, are you not worldly? Are you not acting like mere humans? For when one says, "I am of Paul," and another, "I am of Apollos," are you not mere human beings? (3:1–4)

This doesn't simply result in division over Christian orators, but it's the cause of most, if not all of the other problems Paul addresses in the remainder of the letter. For example:

---

8. Dio Chrysostom, 8.9. See also Seneca, *Controversiae* 10.15; Suetonius, *Tiberius* 11.3; Philostratus, *Vitae sophistarum* 1.8.490.

9. Witherington, *Conflict and Community in Corinth*, 41–42; Winter, "Is Paul among the Sophists?," 28–38.

10. Litfin, *St. Paul's Theology of Proclamation*, 86, notes the pervasive culture of critique surrounding public oratory in Corinth.

- Their attitude of permissiveness in sexual behavior was even ahead of the mainstream (5:1–2), and probably involved the same double-standards that applied in the wider society to the heads of wealthy households.[11] Paul sees this as a failure to judge within the group by God's standards (5:3, 12).[12]

- Some were using the legal system the way everyone else did, bringing accusations against one another in order to gain wealth and honor (6:1–11).[13] This was again a failure to judge within the group, with their recourse to secular judges giving the wider society opportunity to judge the group in a negative light.[14]

- The wealthy were behaving at their communal meals the way they would at a dinner party on the Corinthian social scene: giving seating and catering priority to those with status while ignoring the needs of the poor—the day-laborers and slaves, the nature of whose employment meant they could only turn up late (11:17–34).[15]

- Some were using their spiritual gifts as a means to gain status for themselves rather than to build up others (chs. 12–14), which is exactly what the majority culture had taught them to do since birth.

- Finally, some were holding onto the Greek philosophical assumptions of the dominant culture, which saw resurrection as a person's soul ascending to the gods, thus denying the group's teaching about a bodily resurrection (ch. 15).[16]

It's not hard to see how an uncritical adoption of *our* world's values and judgments can impact our distinctiveness as Christians today. They might be similar to those Paul highlights, such as: seeking status-by-association with our favorite preachers, Christian authors, or worship styles; exercising our gifts in the church in order to gain recognition or build self-esteem; and allowing cultural assumptions not only about the afterlife, but about gender, abortion, or sexuality to drive our way of reading Scripture, rather than the other way around.

---

11. Perkins, *First Corinthians*, 86, argues that "since the illicit marriage is something of a cause célèbre and its resolution is not to send the woman packing, it is likely that one or both parties are high-status individuals."

12. Ciampa and Rosner, *The First Letter to the Corinthians*, 193.

13. Perkins, *First Corinthians*, 86; Ciampa and Rosner, *The First Letter to the Corinthians*, 222-23.

14. *The First Letter to the Corinthians*, 193.

15. Fee, *1 Corinthians*, 540-44.

16. Witherington, *Conflict and Community in Corinth*, 306-07.

Further, we might notice some *different* ways in which we adopt the world's value system—particularly in how we construct our public image in an age of glossy brochures and curated Instagram stories. A graphic designer friend once told me about having a high-profile church client, and how the pastor instructed her to replace a particular image in her design with some people who were "more attractive." It's this kind of thinking by which the church becomes just another player in a market that wants to sell us a superficial idea of success.

But the point is to follow Paul's lead. Use 1 Corinthians to help us identify—specifically and critically—the ways in which we're going along with the majority culture *simply because it seems perfectly normal to us*.[17] Because only then will we be able to embrace for ourselves the Paul's counter-cultural rhetoric.

## Foolish wisdom

Paul's primary rhetorical strategy is to take ownership of the dominant culture's language, redefining it in light of the minority group's narrative about what it means to follow Jesus. Three times he uses a phrase, *en sophia logou*[18]—literally, "in the wisdom of speech"—that describes the Sophistic attitude toward public speaking we looked at earlier, favoring stylistic eloquence over substance. And he says, emphatically, that's what he's *not* doing:

> For Christ did not send me to baptize, but to preach the gospel—not with wise-sounding speech, lest the cross of Christ be emptied of its power. (1:17)

> My message and my preaching were not with persuasive, wise-sounding words, but with a demonstration of the Spirit's power, so that your faith might not rest on human wisdom, but on God's power. (2:4–5)

This isn't to say Paul doesn't use rhetoric at all[19]—throughout this and other letters, as well as how Luke presents him in Acts[20] he clearly does; even

---

17. For a more detailed cultural exegesis of the Australian church in light of 1 Corinthians, see my "Preaching Paul's Epistles to Australians," 162–88.

18. 1 Cor 1:17. The two other occurrences have a slight variation in form but with the same idea: "superiority of speech or wisdom" (2:1), and "in persuasive, wise words" (2:4).

19. Contra e.g., Weima, "Aristotle," 465; Winter, "Is Paul among the Sophists?," 35.

20. Witherington, *Acts*, 407, notes that Paul's speeches in Acts follow the form and character of judicial rhetoric, with Luke describing him as taking the pose of an

to claim not to be using rhetoric was a known rhetorical move at the time.[21] Rather, it's a rejection of the Sophistic form of rhetoric that entertained and pandered to the world's superficial judgments.[22] But even more importantly, it's a claim that the wise-sounding words the world thinks to be persuasive are inferior to the power of God. Later on (4:19), he even offers to demonstrate that power when he arrives, in order to put those talking arrogantly against him in their place:

> For the kingdom of God is not a matter of talk but of power. (4:20)

The wider world can speak as wisely and as eloquently as they like, but God's the one who can back it up with action. Power undercuts any human pretension to wisdom.

But if it's *wisdom* you're looking for, then Paul takes ownership of that word, too. God's wisdom is superior to human wisdom (1:20), it's just that humans can't understand it—it appears as foolishness to them:

> For the message of the cross is foolishness to those who are perishing, but to us who are being saved it is the power of God. (1:18)

> For since in the wisdom of God the world through its wisdom did not know him, God was pleased through the foolishness of what was preached to save those who believe. (1:21)

This is classic minority group rhetoric: *those outside are incapable of understanding what we're on about, that's why we can ignore their disapproval and maintain our difference. Why would we want to go chasing their so-called "wisdom" when it hasn't helped them know God?*

By contrast, those in the group have been given special insight in order to understand. Although it was once a mystery, it's now been revealed to those who have the Spirit of God, so that they no longer make judgments according to the world's criteria, but God's, since they have "the mind of Christ" (see 2:6–16 where he takes ownership of the word "judgment" in the process; also 4:1). *We're different because we've been given special insight.*

---

orator, "So Paul motioned with his hand and began his [legal] defense *(apologia)*." He also points out that in Acts 17:2, the Greek words used of Paul's presentations in Thessalonica ("reasoned," "explained," and "proved") were technical terms for rhetorical persuasion (504–05).

21. Quintilian, *Institutio oratoria* 4.1.8–10; Classen, *Rhetorical Criticism*, 44.

22. Resner, *Preacher and Cross*, 4. Many in Paul's era also took a dim view of sophistry: e.g., Aristotle, *Ars rhetorica* 3.3; Quintilian, *Institutio oratoria* 4.1.8–10; see Judge, "Paul's Boasting," 37.

Further, the surrounding culture of wisdom and rhetoric hasn't benefited most of those in Paul's audience, serving merely to reinforce the existing social hierarchy and honor-shame system. In the gospel, God has turned the notion of privilege upside down—so no wonder the educated élite find it "foolish"! Instead, he's offered it first to the weak and marginalized, in order to shame the strong and important:

> Brothers and sisters, think of what you were when you were called. Not many of you were wise by human standards; not many were influential; not many were of noble birth. But God chose the foolish things of the world to shame the wise; God chose the weak things of the world to shame the strong. God chose the lowly things of this world and the despised things—and the things that are not—to nullify the things that are, so that no one may boast before him. (1:26–29)

In other words: *why would you continue to live by the judgments of the world when the world's judgments about you aren't all that favorable? Instead, embrace God's different kind of wisdom that reverses what the world considers honorable and shameful!*

The phrase "so that no one may boast before him" and what follows is crucially important—pun intended—as it sets this reversal of privilege within the group's defining narrative of Christ crucified. It ought to undercut any attempt to take this rhetoric as merely giving another group a source of pride and status over against the majority. In overthrowing the status system of the world it replaces it with a counter-intuitive, counter-cultural message of a crucified savior, an honorable source of shame, and a power displayed most clearly in weakness. The unique identity of this minority group is that its claim to an alternative source of status from a different court of reputation is part of a narrative that subverts the world's idea of status altogether, so that any kind of "status" within the group is as paradoxical as the message of the cross itself.

This nuance is difficult to communicate, and can easily devolve into *we're better than you* on the one hand, or *we're no different from you* on the other. In the former case it's not attractive to outsiders, although genuinely oppressed minorities tend to wear it best; in the latter case it minimizes difference, making it the outfit of choice for those of us who think there's still a chance the world might accept us. To maintain an attitude of *we're different from you only because of an undeserved privilege that you can also have* takes a bit more work, but a regular reminder of Paul's approach here is a good place to start.

There's no space here for a look at all of Paul's arguments in 1 Corinthians through the minority group lens, but we've laid the foundations upon which one could be constructed. As we said before, each of the issues Paul addresses can be seen as the outworking of allowing worldly judgments to continue to operate within the group. But they also provide us ways to counter that dynamic. Here's just a handful of examples:

**Maintaining group boundaries.** The ongoing tolerance of some sins threaten the identity and unity of the group. Paul applies the Old Testament principle, "expel the evil from among you,"[23] in order to maintain group boundaries regarding acceptable behavior. Judgment *within* the group, while painful, was needed, but without passing judgment on those *outside* (5:12). Ironically, today we often find it easier to do the opposite. While it could be argued that excommunication is problematic to enforce in a world with a multitude of denominations and alternatives, there are many other avenues open to us if we're serious about communicating and (to some extent) enforcing group behavior.

**Making boundaries permeable.** Paul's sometimes complicated advice on the eating of idol meat (chs. 8–10) is the application of a rather simple, yet counter-cultural principle. In contrast with the wider world, members of the Christ-following minority shouldn't make judgments based on what might be to their own advantage. Instead, they should follow the example of Paul and Jesus, only making judgments that honor God and are for the benefit of others, both inside and outside the community (10:31–11:1). One important outworking of this is Paul's principle of being "all things to all people" for their ultimate benefit (9:22), in which being attractively different involves minimizing non-essential differences.

**Subverting the language of the dominant culture.** One of my favorite examples of this is Paul's use of the "body" metaphor to describe the believing community (1 Cor 12:12–31). He didn't invent it, with numerous ancient writers using it to quell factions. A famous speech by Menenius Agrippa in 493 BC included a fable in which the various parts of the body thought the stomach wasn't serving any useful purpose, and stopped feeding it. The other parts then became weak, and realized they needed the stomach to survive, after all. Agrippa used it to argue that the lower classes needed the

---

23. 1 Cor 5:13; cf. Deut. 13:5; 17:7; 19:19; 21:21; 22:21, 24; 24:7. Rosner, *Paul, Scripture, and Ethics*, 69–72, argues that Paul's sin list in 5:11 is drawn from those sins in Deuteronomy for which the expulsion formula is invoked, and includes sins which are particularly *community destroying*.

patrician class to survive, and thus to end their walkout.[24] Paul, however, uses it in the opposite way. Instead of getting the lower members of society to keep serving the upper classes, he wants to show that in the church, those who might think themselves superior do, in fact, need *all* the other parts of the body[25]—to whom God has, in his "foolish wisdom," given special honor (12:22–25). And whoever uses their gifts should do so in order to build up the body, not inflate themselves (ch. 14).

While we might not as readily have a metaphor to subvert, the church today should be a place in which the world's judgments about a person's status and usefulness should be upended. The language of secular leadership that is so easily borrowed needs to be redefined—or replaced entirely—using more biblical images of servanthood, nurture, and discipling. And it needs more than just contemporary management-inspired stunts like turning the org chart upside down and proclaiming, "that'll send the message—job done!" It requires forming structures and acquiring new habits that force us to unlearn a lifetime of worldly judgments, bruising our knuckles until we instinctively reach out in the other direction to include the voices and contributions of those the world discards. That's what will make us attractively different.

---

24. Livy, *Ab urbe condita* 2.32.12, during the First Secession of the Plebs. Other uses include Epictetus, *Dissertationes* 2.5.25; Seneca, *Epistulae morales* 2.31.7; Plutarch, *Morales* 797E; Dionysius, *Antiquitates Romanae* 6.86.2.

25. Witherington, *Conflict and Community in Corinth*, 259.

# 10

## 1 Thessalonians
### *How You Turned from Idols*

A GOOD PARENT, THE experts generally tell us, doesn't just reprimand a child when their behavior is wrong, but also praises a child when their behavior is right. In fact, without diminishing the necessity of the former, the latter is increasingly being seen as more effective.[1] But I'm not sure this is understood as well in some of our pulpits, and maybe we have something to learn from both current parenting trends and the Apostle Paul. We'll come back to that thought later.

Because we've just seen Paul appropriately reprimanding the Corinthians for their bad behavior, sending at least one into time out (1 Cor 5:13) and threatening the rest with the "rod of discipline" once their "father in the gospel" gets home (4:15, 21). But in 1 Thessalonians, his approach is the opposite; instead, he highlights what they're doing well as a way of encouraging them in that behavior. In technical terms, it's not a deliberative speech like 1 Corinthians, in which he urges a change in behavior in light of their different identity. The rhetoric of 1 Thessalonians is *epideictic*, a genre which originated at celebrations and festivals. This was the rhetoric of honor and shame, praising behavior and attitudes considered honorable by the group as a way of inspiring them to do that all the more. It's why Paul offers no specific thesis statement which he needs to prove; he simply reminds them of things they *already* know and do, enhancing their understanding and urging them to keep going.[2]

---

1. Witness the current "positive parenting" trend, the extremes of which urge parents to dispense with negative consequences entirely. For the record, I think both are needed, and are supported by both Scripture and clinical research. See, e.g., Larzelere et al., "Critiquing the Evidence for Exclusively 'Positive' Parenting," 24–35.

2. See Witherington, *1 & 2 Thessalonians*, 21–29, for a fuller discussion of the rhetorical genre and form.

This makes sense, considering the setting. We read in Acts (17:1–9) that Paul and Silas briefly founded a small group of believers in the city, but strong opposition from the synagogue—backed up by the city officials—meant they had to move on quickly. So there hadn't been enough time for Paul to forge a strong group identity, and he was concerned about their ability to withstand the inevitable pressure from the majority culture. Although he'd heard some encouraging reports from others in Macedonia and Achaia (1 Thess 1:8–9), it was only when Timothy returned with good news that he could feel confident about their progress and steadfastness (3:6–8). And it's at that point he wrote 1 Thessalonians, praising the encouraging first steps these new converts had taken, as a way of shoring up their ongoing commitment.

### Praise for enduring opposition from the majority

The first thing Paul praises them for is remaining faithful despite experiencing strong opposition. In other words, they've maintained their minority group's identity in the face of pressure from the majority to conform. They've rejected the dominant cultural narrative of pagan gods (idols), and in its place embraced the narrative of the one, true God who promises eternal advantage:

> ...you turned to God from idols to serve the living and true God, and to wait for his Son from heaven, whom he raised from the dead—Jesus, who rescues us from the coming wrath. (1:9–10)

In so doing, they've faithfully copied the prototypical examples of Paul, Silas, and Timothy—as well as Jesus himself—in joyfully embracing the message despite the serious consequences:

> *You became imitators of us* and of the Lord, for you welcomed the message in the midst of severe suffering with the joy given by the Holy Spirit. (1:6)

More than that, in displaying this fundamental group value they became, in turn, prototypical for others:

> *And so you became a model* to all the believers in Macedonia and Achaia. The Lord's message rang out from you not only in Macedonia and Achaia—your faith in God has become known everywhere. Therefore we do not need to say anything about it, for they themselves report what kind of reception you gave us. (1:7–9)

The fact that this is described as a report from others is important, since having a reputation to live up to can be a powerful motivator.[3] The social psychologist we met in chapter 2, Robert Cialdini, says that we all want "to be (and appear) consistent with what we have already done."[4] One of many examples he cites is a simple experiment run at a top Chicago restaurant in 1998. Although it was a popular establishment, one of its biggest problems was the "no-show"—people not turning up when they'd booked a table. So they ran a little test. When they took a booking, they *used* to say: "please call us if you have to cancel." But they decided to say it differently: "if you have to cancel, *will you* please call us?" And then they waited. The customer dutifully answered "yes." And because they'd said it *out loud*, it had an impact on their actions. The rate of no-shows dropped from 30% to 10% immediately.[5] People want to be seen as consistent, whether it be in trivial matters or in issues of supreme importance. This is why making the Thessalonians aware of their developing reputation is a powerful rhetorical strategy.

It can also be a powerful approach for us to embrace, following Paul's lead in highlighting where our community *is* exhibiting prototypical behavior—whether collectively or through particular individuals. Naturally, we have to be careful it doesn't devolve into self-congratulation that encourages us to rest on our laurels; that would be opposite to the intent of epideictic rhetoric. Or worse, we have to make sure that it doesn't foster a sense of status and competition; 1 Corinthians would have something to say about that. Paul's framework of thanksgiving for what God has done in us (1:2) through the power of his Spirit (1:6) guards against this, while allowing what we've done in the past to spur us on to do even more in the future.

As well as talking about their own reputation, Paul also reminds his audience that they're not doing this alone. They stand in solidarity with others who've been in the same situation, struggling against the pressure and persecution from their culture of origin:

> For you, brothers and sisters, became *imitators of God's churches in Judea*, which are in Christ Jesus: You suffered *from your own people* the same things those churches suffered *from the Jews* who killed the Lord Jesus and the prophets and also drove us out. They displease God and are hostile to everyone in their effort to keep us from speaking to the Gentiles so that they may be

---

3. One of Dale Carnegie's principles of influence is, "give the other person a fine reputation to live up to" (Carnegie, *How to Win Friends and Influence People*, principle 7).

4. Cialdini, *Influence*, 43.

5. "The Science of Persuasion," 77–78.

> saved. In this way they always heap up their sins to the limit. The wrath of God has come upon them at last. (2:14–16)

The message is: *you're in good company! The original followers of Jesus were mistreated by their own people. Just as God will deal with their persecutors, you can expect he'll deal with yours, too!* And notice how the motivation for the Jewish opposition was to stop the Gentile mission. The implication is that just as that instance of persecution was unsuccessful in its aim—evidenced by the conversion of Paul's Gentile audience—so, too, will the persecution of the believers in Thessalonica. *Remove the majority culture from your court of reputation: they're opposed to God and ultimately powerless!*

While on the subject of persecution, we again see the rhetorical strategy of predicting opposition as a way of owning the narrative and reassuring the group that everything is still going according to plan (cf. 1 Pet 4:12). Paul reminds them of his prediction and its fulfilment:

> We sent Timothy, who is our brother and co-worker in God's service in spreading the gospel of Christ, to strengthen and encourage you in your faith, so that no one would be unsettled by these trials. For you know quite well that we are destined for them. In fact, when we were with you, we kept telling you that we would be persecuted. And it turned out that way, as you well know. (1 Thess 3:2–4)

In this way, persecution doesn't threaten the group's identity; if anything, it reinforces it, since they were told to expect it from the start.

In recent generations, this has been underemphasized in the Western church—understandably, given the general lack of persecution. But the consequences have been significant. After a series of high-profile Christians publicly renounced their faith, David French made a telling observation in the *National Review*:

> As our culture changes, secularizes, and grows less tolerant of Christian orthodoxy, I'm noticing a pattern in many of the people who fall away . . . They're retreating from faith not because they're ignorant of its key tenets and lack the necessary intellectual, theological depth but rather because the adversity of adherence to increasingly countercultural doctrine grows too great . . . They're afraid to say what they believe, not because they face the kind of persecution that Christians face overseas but because they're simply not prepared for any meaningful adverse consequences in their careers or with their peers.[6]

---

6. French, "Another Pop-Culture Christian Loses His Faith."

In our rediscovery of our minority status, it's important to reclaim a form of this rhetoric, appropriately modulated to the level of threat we face. Our preaching and discipling ought to remind believers that much of the time, people won't find our difference all that attractive. As aliens and exiles, we should expect to be thought of as strange, mocked for our "premodern superstitions," and rejected in our attempts to be valued participants in the wider society. We should tell our teens, in particular, to expect this—if they haven't faced it already—when they turn up to tertiary education or enter the workforce, so that it doesn't come as the faith-questioning shock it can be for so many. Remind everyone: *it's OK, it's part of the plan. Jesus and the New Testament writers told us to expect this; God's still got it all under control.*

In sum, Paul's praise for the Thessalonians' steadfastness under pressure not only expresses his genuine joy at their progress, but is designed to encourage them to continue.

### Praise for prototypical group behavior

The second major area in which Paul praises his audience is for adhering to group norms, which we identified in chapter 1 as being an important function of minority group rhetoric. And he does this in several specific areas.

The first is what should be the most fundamental ethic of any Christ-centered minority group, namely, love for others, both within the group and outside:

> May the Lord make your love increase and overflow for each other and for everyone else, just as ours does for you. (3:12)

The implication is twofold: the ability to love comes from God, and the Thessalonians are already evidencing that love. This made explicit a little later on:

> Now about your love for one another we do not need to write to you, for you yourselves have been taught by God to love each other. And in fact, you do love all of God's family throughout Macedonia. Yet we urge you, brothers and sisters, to do so more and more. (4:9–10)

The reason love for one another is foundational is that it's the most significant characteristic of the group's founder; love for one another is evidence that group members truly belong. But it's also important in a practical way because, to some extent, it mitigates the effects of opposition and rejection by family and the wider world. This is why, despite the encouraging start, Paul sees it important to remind them to do it all the more.

Paul goes on to clarify how they might do this:

> . . . and to make it your ambition to lead a quiet life: You should mind your own business and work with your hands, just as we told you, so that your daily life may win the respect of outsiders and so that you will not be dependent on anybody. (4:11–12)

This seems to be an instruction to reject the usual status-seeking behaviors of the dominant culture, both within the group and without.[7] It isn't just an outworking of the love command, but it's a practical way in which they could demonstrate attractive difference. We won't labor the application of this point to the present day, as we've dealt with it adequately in connection with the previous two epistles.

Although Paul seems genuinely pleased with their progress in love, there's another area that may not be so positive. It's still introduced within a general framework of praise for their behavior:

> As for other matters, brothers and sisters, we instructed you how to live in order to please God, as in fact you are living. Now we ask you and urge you in the Lord Jesus to do this more and more. (4:1)

Yet it seems that, at least in one area, there's room for improvement:

> It is God's will that you should be sanctified: that you should avoid sexual immorality; that each of you should learn to control your own body in a way that is holy and honorable, not in passionate lust like the pagans, who do not know God. (4:3–5)

This was an area in which group norms would have stood in stark contrast to those of the dominant culture. It made it vitally important for the maintenance of the group's distinctive identity, but also very difficult to establish. And the fact that Paul tells them to "learn" this behavior is a strong indicator that their progress in this area isn't up to standard. In fact, this issue receives the strongest words in an essentially positive epistle.

Paul tackles it by defining what their court of reputation ought to be. It shouldn't include the society around them: the "pagans who do not know

---

7. Witherington, *1 & 2 Thessalonians*, 121–22, sees this as referring to honor-seeking behavior which is not only a sell-out to the majority cultural values, but is also a way to attract unnecessary negative attention to the group. He also notes that Winter, *Seek the Welfare of the City*, 42–60, sees a reference to the patronage culture by which some would attach themselves to wealthy benefactors, involving themselves as middle-men in the constant flow of favors and honor, rather than any productive activity.

God" (4:5). Their ignorance of God excludes them as arbiters of right behavior. Instead, he reminds them that God is the one who judges, issuing a stern warning:

> The Lord will punish all those who commit such sins, as we told you and warned you before. For God did not call us to be impure, but to live a holy life. (4:6–7)

God is judge. More than that, God is the one who called them *out* of that culture into a group with a different set of ethical norms. It's his verdict that counts, not the world outside.

Sexual ethics is, once again, an area in which we are starkly at odds with the world around us. The temptation remains for Christians to take our cues from the majority culture rather than God—whether to justify acting on our own desires, or to keep favor with a culture that increasingly sees expressing the Bible's views as not merely antiquated, but acts of verbal violence toward other minorities. We need to remind one another constantly of the truth Paul expresses here: this difference exists *because they don't know God*, which ought to disqualify them from our court of reputation. This shouldn't result in judgmentalism toward outsiders (cf. 1 Cor 5:12); simply a rejection of the world's judgment in favor of God's.

More broadly, Paul gives us one "parental model" for how to inculcate group norms, even when addressing matters in which the group has a long way to go. In this particular setting, with a promising but not-yet-mature church, he chooses positive reinforcement as his primary strategy. Even when he has to address a significant negative, it's in the context of praise for what they've achieved thus far (4:1). He approaches it from the standpoint of *these are our values*, rather than *make these our values*. This stands in contrast with letters like 1 Corinthians, in which he reprimands a church that ought to be more mature than it is (1 Cor 3:1–4); or Galatians, in which he expresses parental exasperation (Gal 4:19–20). The point is not to argue for one over the other; simply that 1 Thessalonians gives us a potentially underutilized mode of forming group identity and behavior that should encourage us to put a sticker chart on the church refrigerator at least once in a while, metaphorically speaking.

## Salience and group identity

While persecution has a way of focusing attention on things that really matter, so, too, do thoughts of death and judgment. In the latter part of Paul's address, he looks at two related topics that speak to the *salience* of group identity: why it's important *right now*.

The first is that of how grief is felt within the minority group, which is explicitly contrasted with that of the majority culture:

> Brothers and sisters, we do not want you to be uninformed about those who sleep in death, so that you do not grieve *like the rest of mankind, who have no hope.* (4:13)

This is another reason to reject the world's narrative and judgments: it offers no hope. This is contrasted with the group narrative of a returning savior and resurrection of the dead (4:16). Although both groups might grieve the death of loved ones, Paul insists that we include the garden in the comparison (see chapter 1). When death happens—quite possibly through persecution, although Paul doesn't say this explicitly[8]—group membership is salient because it's the only source of hope.

Having recently had the privilege of speaking about the hope of resurrection at my mother's funeral after her battle with cancer, I'd suggest the word "salient" isn't quite strong enough to capture both how in-your-face death is, as well as how comprehensively the gospel message transforms it. The different way we grieve may well be the most attractive of our differences. And it's why Paul says to "encourage one another with these words" (4:18).

This talk of resurrection leads, quite naturally, to the timing of Christ's return. What makes this all the more salient is the fact that there will be no warning:

> Now, brothers and sisters, about times and dates we do not need to write to you, for you know very well that the day of the Lord will come like a thief in the night. (5:1–2)

This won't go well for those outside the group:

> While people are saying, "Peace and safety," destruction will come on them suddenly, as labor pains on a pregnant woman, and they will not escape. (5:3)

"Peace and safety" was a political slogan of the empire.[9] Although people put their trust in Rome for their security, the day of the Lord will show how ill-placed that is. Whether they are hoping for "Change we can believe in" or wanting to "Make America Great Again"—or even embracing the

---

8. Furnish, *1 Thessalonians, 2 Thessalonians*, 100.

9. See Witherington, *1 & 2 Thessalonians*, 146–47, for a list of ancient sources extolling the "peace and safety" brought by Rome and her Emperor, esp. Velleius Peterculus 2.103.5; 2.126.3.

bland Australian version, "jobs and growth"—the majority culture in our day has a similarly misplaced hope in human institutions. Instead of buying into one or other of these slogans, followers of Jesus in the first and twenty-first centuries are reminded that their peace and safety comes from elsewhere.[10] Group membership is salient because Christ's return will happen without warning, and at that time those outside will discover their sense of security was a delusion.

Paul's minority group audience will have a different experience because they have a radically different identity; as different as night and day:

> But you, brothers and sisters, are not in darkness so that this day should surprise you like a thief. You are all children of the light and children of the day. We do not belong to the night or to the darkness. (5:4–5)

And it's that identity as "children of the light" that drives their different behavior:

> *So then*, let us not be like others, who are asleep, but let us be awake and sober. For those who sleep, sleep at night, and those who get drunk, get drunk at night. *But since we belong to the day*, let us be sober, putting on faith and love as a breastplate, and the hope of salvation as a helmet. (5:6–8)

Wakefulness and sobriety function as metaphors for behavior that reflects this identity of God's daytime children. But get the rhetorical stance: it's not a case of *be awake and sober* so we can be children of the day; or even *be awake and sober* so we can know we're children of the day. Rather, it's *since we are children of the day* let's act like it. Group identity drives group values, not the other way around. Or to put it in a more familiar fashion, being in Christ leads to good works, not vice versa.

In 1 Thessalonians Paul gives us a helpful reminder of how to encourage strong behavioral boundaries that will help a minority group like ours withstand the pressure to conform to the majority culture: focus primarily on *who we are*, out of which then flows what we do. And we'll hold our group identity as being of first importance the more we are encouraged to see it set against the dark backdrop of a world without hope or the knowledge of God, and in light of our impending death, our future resurrection, and Christ's return.

---

10. This isn't a critique of either "side" of politics against the other, nor is it a suggestion that Christians ought not to be involved. See chapter 8 on Philippians for being good citizens who live as a foretaste of a different regime. But our ultimate trust is in God to put things right, not our own political manœuvring with the inevitable compromises that entails.

# 11

## Colossians
## *Let No One Take You Captive*

WHILE 1 CORINTHIANS DEALS with the problem of the majority culture's social behaviors and values influencing the way members of the minority group interacted with one another, Colossians addresses the issue of the majority culture's religious and philosophical beliefs and practices being added to the Christian message. That is, it guards against the temptation to religious syncretism, blurring the boundaries of the group.

Colossians can be helpful for us in two important ways. Firstly, it gives us a lens by which we can identify similar elements in our own surrounding culture and identify why we might be attracted to them, and why we might want to add them to our way of following Jesus. Secondly, it shows us that the antidote lies in presenting Jesus as the real answer to the questions the majority culture is asking, and the alternative answers it offers are simply "a shadow of the things that were to come" (2:17). The example sermon[1] presented below shows some of the ways in which we might use Colossians in the former task, and sets us up for the latter.

∽ ∽ ∽

### True Followers of Jesus

Real coffee lovers drink it black. The rest of you just like hot milk or sugar or flavored syrup—and are using coffee as an excuse. Sure, you can kid

---

1. It's a little denser than the average sermon, and could well provide the framework for three sermons (with space in each to show how Jesus is superior to the cultural alternatives). Here, it does the job of illustrating how Scripture can be used to do cultural exegesis.

yourself by having it made by an "artisan" with pants that don't cover his ankles, sprinkle it with hipster beard scrapings or whatever, then sit around drinking it on upturned milk crates. But when it comes down to it, you're not a real coffee lover if you add anything else to it. Real coffee lovers take their coffee straight up.

Now, of course, you're free to disagree with me about coffee. Or, as I see it, you're free to be wrong. But in today's reading from Colossians chapter 2, Paul talks about something even more important than coffee. (I know, this must be serious, so let's pay attention.) He tells us that true Christians take their Jesus straight up, without any additives. No milk. No sugar. And certainly no pumpkin spice. Let's take a look.

Firstly, he tells them to keep on making coffee the way they'd been taught:

> So then, just as you received Christ Jesus as Lord, *continue to live your lives in him*, rooted and built up in him, strengthened in the faith as you were taught, and overflowing with thankfulness. (2:6–7)

Your way of life should be based on Jesus as your Lord, flowing out of what he's done for you. What's more, don't think you have to add anything to it to make it more palatable. Because that's what the influences of our world, the influences of the wider culture will try and tell you.

> See to it [watch out!] that no one takes you captive through hollow and deceptive philosophy, which depends on human tradition and the elemental [spiritual?] forces of this world rather than on Christ. (2:8)

Don't let other people, don't let cultural forces deceive you into thinking Jesus is somehow insufficient. That you have to add anything else, if you want to have all the fullness of a tasty caffeinated beverage; if you want to experience all the fullness of life the way God intended it to be. Don't mix in elements of other worldviews that come from human beings—or worse, if the NIV translation is correct in seeing these as spiritual forces.[2]

---

2. The forces may not be spiritual; the Greek word *stoicheia* could refer to the elements of Jewish teaching; the elements of the material world (earth, water, air, fire); or elemental spiritual beings (e.g., angels and demons).

## What are the potential additives?

So what did Paul mean by "hollow and deceptive philosophy"? Or "decaf" as I translate it? What was this alternative philosophy the Colossians were tempted to add to their faith in Jesus, to make it a bit tastier?

First off, we need to understand that "philosophy" in the ancient world was a bit different from how we often use the term. It was more than just a set of beliefs or principles. Philosophy referred to a way of life that resulted from a particular worldview. So when Paul said back in verse 6, "live your lives in him," he's telling them to live out a philosophy based on Jesus, rather than one based on the ideas of the culture around. Make sure your whole lifestyle flows from a Christian worldview, rather than how the world wants us to see things.

But what was this competing "philosophy"? This tempting alternative? What were the Colossians wanting to add to Jesus? This has been debated by Bible scholars for centuries. (They've got to have something to do.) And that's because the clues in Paul's letter point in different directions. Some of the clues in the letter make it look like the alternative philosophy was Jewish—leading some to see the whole controversy being about Judaism. But other clues look a bit more like the pagan, mystic religions common in Asia Minor at the time. And still others make good sense against the background of certain schools of Greek philosophy. The problem is, it's hard to reconstruct a single, plausible philosophy that existed in the first century with all of these elements.[3]

To be honest, I'm not really sure it was one coherent alternative; more a bunch of cultural tendencies that were around in Colossian society at the time.[4] Things that Paul is worried will be added to the way of life of Jesus' followers in Colossae. So today, I'm going to take us through each of these elements, one by one. To see whether we, too, might be tempted to add the twenty-first-century equivalents to our coffee; add them to our own way of life in following Jesus.

---

3. See Talbert, *Ephesians and Colossians*, 206–09, for a summary.

4. For this view, see Copenhaver, *Reconstructing the Historical Background of Paul's Rhetoric in the Letter to the Colossians*, 235–37. The application given here isn't dependent on this, as we get to essentially the same place if it refers to a syncretistic version of Judaism or another coherent philosophy which contains all of the elements discussed. The only position it doesn't work as well with is e.g., Wright, *Colossians and Philemon*, 24–25, who sees Paul critiquing synagogue Judaism by portraying it simply as another pagan religion.

## Religious practices

Firstly, let's look at Judaism. As I said, one set of clues in the passage suggests that the Colossians were being influenced by Jewish religious practices:

> Therefore do not let anyone judge you by what you eat or drink, or with regard to a religious festival, a New Moon celebration or a Sabbath day. (2:16)

This is a pretty clear reference to the Jewish food laws and holy days. A lot of the first converts in Colossae would have been Jewish,[5] so many people in the church would already have been observing them, and continued to do so. It was part of their culture, and there's nothing wrong with that. It only becomes a problem if those religious practices are imposed on others. Why is that a problem? Because, says Paul, they've now been superseded by Jesus.

> These are a shadow of the things that were to come; the reality, however, is found in Christ. (2:17)

So, what does that mean for us? It's hard for most Westerners to apply this directly, because we're not normally tempted to observe Jewish regulations about food and holy days. We like our bacon, and we're here on a Sunday. All good.

But if we think about the pattern for a minute, we might see something there for us. After all, what was the reason for those practices in the first place; what made those regulations attractive to the Colossians? I think there's at least a couple of factors involved:

Firstly, the Jewish laws and rituals prescribed a way of life that, in the past, was pleasing to God. And it's not as though it suddenly became displeasing to him. The point was simply that they were no longer needed, because God had provided a better way. No longer was it about the letter of the law; it's now about the power of the resurrected Christ in us, helping us from within to live a life that pleases God. But still, for some followers of Jesus, going back to rules and regulations might have seemed appealing: a bit simpler and clearer than this fuzzy idea about "living by the Spirit" Paul kept talking about. Adding rules makes things clearer. Adding rules gives us a list we can check off to reassure ourselves we're doing it right. Adding rules makes it more palatable to our desire to be self-reliant.

*I'll have Jesus, but can you just add some religious milk and sugar?*

Secondly, the food laws and festivals acted as an outward marker of belonging to the people of God. More than that, they were handed down

---

5. There had been a significant Jewish settlement in the Lycus valley since at least the third century BC. See Bruce, *Colossians, Philemon, and Ephesians*, 8–13.

from the people who'd been the people of God for a lot longer. So those who'd arrived more recently might be tempted to follow them—to fit in, and to avoid being judged by the old guard. In turn, the old guard might have been tempted to use these practices as a way protecting their status as the ones who run the show. Sure you can join us! Just do things the way we've been doing them. (Sound familiar?)

*I'll have Jesus, but I'd better add some religious milk and sugar, 'cause it's the way everyone else here seems to drink it.*

I don't think it'd take you long to spot that dynamic occurring in many social groups, including churches: service styles, Bible translations, evangelism strategies, leadership structures, bible teaching methods, dress codes, music styles, and discipleship disciplines—just to name a few. Things that worked well in a previous era can become fossilized as the only way it can be done; or at the very least, the only way it *should* be done if you want to fit in with us; if you want to be accepted here.

But Paul reminds us that no matter how helpful a human-created guideline, or resource, or way of doing things might have been in the past—and might continue to be for you—it can't be imposed on others in different times and contexts. The risen Christ and the power of his indwelling Spirit are central. Anything else, however helpful, shouldn't be a source of pride or judgment or division; nor should it ever replace humble, Spirit-dependence as a means of living a life that's pleasing to God. By all means, if something helps you follow Jesus more faithfully, then do it! But don't think you—or anyone else—has to add any human religious practice to what you already have in Christ.

## Emotional or spiritual experiences

The second influence from Colossian society came from the local mystic religions:

> Do not let anyone who delights in false humility and the worship of angels disqualify you. Such a person also goes into great detail about what they have seen; they are puffed up with idle notions by their unspiritual mind. (2:18)

Again, the precise meaning of what's going on in Colossae is debated, but the general vibe is pretty clear. A lot of the local religions in Asia Minor had this mystical element. Often involving ecstatic states and out of body experiences. People were seeking emotional, spiritual experiences in order to get a sense of connection with the divine. So it's not surprising that the Colossian Christians were influenced in this direction. Followers of Jesus might be tempted to chase this sort of thing, too, to get the "full experience" of worshipping God. And the motivation is significant: they were seeking the experience so they could boast about it and gain status by telling everyone else.

Paul's response? It's a distraction which can disqualify you. That is, it can draw you away from the true worship of God. They think they're being spiritual, but they're not. They're doing it for reasons of status, just like we saw in the previous two verses with Jewish laws and rituals. They've made it all about themselves. About their experiences and their public image. And in so doing, they've disconnected themselves from Christ and his body, the people of God:

> They have lost connection with the head, from whom the whole body, supported and held together by its ligaments and sinews, grows as God causes it to grow. (2:19)

Now we're not being misled by mystic religious practices from Asia Minor (I'm guessing). But there are plenty of religions in our world that have similar elements: some quite exotic, such as the whirling dervishes of the Sufi branch of Islam who spin themselves into ecstatic trances. Or the narco-cults of the Caribbean which add traditional drugs into the mix. Others are more common, like New Age spiritualities and Occult practices that seek a feeling of connection with the natural environment or the spirit world. Or perhaps some meditative rituals that come from Eastern religions. This common human desire for a religious experience can influence the way in which followers of Jesus practise their faith. We see this in the various Christian groups which prioritize the experiential aspect of faith over the cognitive and behavioral.

For us, are we influenced by this desire for an altered state or an emotional experience of the divine? Are there experiences we seek out because they emotionally convince us that we're more connected to God? Or they give us a sense of importance among others in the church? Here are some questions we might want to ask ourselves:

- Do we attend church services primarily for the feeling it gives us? (And then, sometimes, get disappointed and feel spiritually disconnected when that feeling doesn't turn up when it's supposed to?)
- Do we make sure we look like we're having an emotional or spiritual experience in public worship, with an eye to how other people perceive us?

- Do we place undue pressure on others to have the same kind of emotional or spiritual experience we have in worship, when God may just have wired them differently? (And then judge them when they don't look like they are?)
- Are there particular events or conferences or other Christian gatherings we go to just because we want a particular feeling?
- Do we chase supernatural experiences (such as exorcism, prophecy, tongue speaking) because we need them to sustain our relationship with God? Or because we need them to feel important and useful to him? (Here, our motivation is what I'm talking about, not those practices in themselves, which are perfectly biblical.)

In other words, have we sometimes made spiritual experiences into an idol? Have we disconnected ourselves from our Head in search of feelings and experiences which continually need "topping up" in order to sustain our faith?

*I'll have Jesus, but can you just mix in a little pumpkin spice mysticism to go with it?*

Now hear me correctly: I'm not suggesting, in any way, that experiences and emotions and the supernatural have no place in our relationship with God. Of course they do! But it's God himself whom we are to seek. Not the rush of emotions that may or may not come with that, from time to time. And not the experience of supernatural phenomena themselves. Like the difference between being in love with your partner, and being in love with the feeling of being in love. They're subtly different.

## Man-made self-help strategies

The third influence seems to be connected to a common element in Greek philosophy:

> Since you died with Christ to the elemental spiritual forces of this world, why, as though you still belonged to the world, do you submit to its rules: "Do not handle! Do not taste! Do not touch!"? These rules, which have to do with things that are all destined to perish with use, are based on merely human commands and teachings. Such regulations indeed have an appearance of wisdom, with their self-imposed worship, their false humility and their harsh treatment of the body, but they lack any value in restraining sensual indulgence. (2:20–23)

In the first century, the dominant schools of Greek philosophy promoted a lifestyle based on reason alone; on rational thought, rather than being swayed by their passions and desires. This goes back a few centuries to a philosopher named Plato, who saw our passions and emotions as belonging to our inferior, bodily existence—in contrast with reason, which belonged to the superior, spiritual dimension.

The goal, then, was to suppress our passions and desires, and achieve perfect "self-mastery." And each of the philosophical schools offered different ways of doing this. The description in these verses of self-denial and harsh treatment of the body best fits a group called the Neo-Pythagoreans—named after Pythagoras, whom you might remember from Mathematics. The Neo-Pythagoreans punished their bodies in order to purge their desires—possibly using the pointy bits of right-angled triangles. Although I may have made that last part up.[6]

The point is, they were human-devised strategies to achieve this ideal of self-mastery; of controlling your bodily desires. And they were highly popular in the surrounding culture, among those seeking honor and virtue.

We have our own versions of them, don't we? Self-help gurus like Tony Robbins and Oprah encourage us to impose lifestyle disciplines or recite affirmations as a way to become a better, more successful version of ourselves. The health and fitness industry promises life-transformation though adopting a paleo diet or taking up triathlons during our mid-life crisis. Everyone's selling a new self-help strategy to happiness and success.

The danger is that Christians can overlay this self-help approach to life onto how we follow Jesus. You can see how that might have been attractive to Paul's readers in Colossae. After all, we're called to live a life that doesn't give in to our sinful desires and passions. And to be transformed by the renewing of our mind. So if that's the goal, why not give a bit of Greek philosophy a go? Self-denial; self-mastery. It can't hurt, right?

The problems, however, should be obvious. Firstly, the diagnosis provided by Greek philosophy is a bit off-target: passions and desires aren't all sinful! God gave us good passions and desires, and he created this material, embodied existence to which Plato thought they belonged—and said that *it was good!* Desires aren't all bad.

Secondly, the prescribed treatment plan is all about self: *self*-denial, *self*-abasement, *self*-mastery. It's striving for something good by human effort rather than by the power of the resurrected Jesus. It's a human-devised self-help strategy to solve a human-defined problem.

---

6. Apologies for that tangent.

If we're not careful, we can do this today, taking the self-help strategies of our culture, and overlaying them onto the way we follow Jesus. Often very subtly. Christian books can sometimes contribute to this, if unintentionally, along with the preaching that's often based on them. Particularly the way in which they tend to look like their secular counterparts: seven steps to this, five habits of highly effective that. The danger is that they reduce discipleship to a set of human-devised rules and strategies.

Or, more subtly, they give perfectly good biblical teaching on spiritual transformation in a packaging that makes it look like just another self-help offering in the marketplace. So that when it doesn't seem to "work" straight away, we throw it in the bin along with the latest fad diet, rather than persist with the slow, unpredictable work of the Holy Spirit within us.

*I'll have Jesus, but can you just add some self-help syrup as well?*

But not only do self-help techniques not work. If we're not careful, they slowly start to redefine the problem in human terms. Our goals become more here-and-now; more self-focused. Jesus is the one who gives me physical health and financial well-being. Or Jesus is the one who makes me feel better about myself. Jesus is the one who fixes my broken relationships.

In 2005, a couple of social scientists[7] set out to research what young Americans actually believed about God: what their idea of a divine being was, and how we live in light of that. Essentially, they ask what their religious philosophy was—their worldview that guided their way of life. And the findings were fascinating.

Because—regardless of what religion they notionally thought of themselves as—for the majority of American youth, their beliefs and practices were quite similar. Their religious philosophy was the same. And the researchers coined a new term to describe it: "Moralistic Therapeutic Deism." So what do they mean by that? Let's break it down.

- It was moralistic: they believed that living a good, moral life in terms of how we treated others was the most important thing. Note that nothing is said about how we treat God.
- It was therapeutic: the goal of this moral life was happiness and fulfilment; it made them feel better about themselves. Note that it's all about self, and all about this life.
- And it was deistic: that is, their conception of God was remote and impersonal—not particularly relational. God's role is simply to be our trouble-shooter when life isn't going right. He's there to fix problems

---

7. Smith and Denton, *Soul Searching*.

and make us feel better about ourselves. To be our "divine butler and cosmic therapist," as the researchers put it.[8]

Moralistic Therapeutic Deism is, in essence, what Western culture increasingly believes about God—for those who haven't rejected the idea of God altogether. It's the "hollow and deceptive philosophy" of our own age.

Have we been taken captive by it? Have we, perhaps subconsciously, incorporated any of its assumptions into how we follow Jesus? Do we come to him to have our problems fixed, and to feel better about ourselves, rather than because of who he is? Is Christ an end in himself—or just a means to a happy, fulfilled life as we or our world would want to define happiness and fulfilment?

*I'll have Jesus, if it gets me that temporary sugar high the rest of the world is satisfied with.*

## Jesus doesn't need any additives

But Paul says: don't add anything to your Jesus. He doesn't need sweetening or watering down or spicing up. The pure Jesus already has everything we could possibly want.

> See to it that no one takes you captive through hollow and deceptive philosophy . . . (2:8a)

Why? He gives us the essence of the answer in the next verse:

> For in Christ all the fullness of the Deity lives in bodily form, and in Christ you have been brought to fullness. He is the head over every power and authority. (2:9–10)

Jesus is all the fullness of God. That's it. Nothing else is needed.

He's in *bodily form*: he's not distant and unreachable. He's stepped into our world to become one of us. We don't need out-of-body mystical experiences to relate to the divine, precisely because Jesus had an into-body experience two thousand years ago.

What's more we've been *brought into that fullness*. We don't need any of those man-made religions or experiences or self-help philosophies to have life to the full. To live a moral, meaningful, virtuous life. Because through his death and resurrection Jesus made it possible for us to experience all the fullness of God: forgiveness of sins, and the power to live a life of obedience.

---

8. *Soul Searching*, 165.

We don't need to go adding any other source of help, looking to any other power, obeying any other authority—because Jesus is the head over every power and authority.

The biggest threat to Christianity in the twenty-first century is not atheism. Just like in first-century Colossae, the biggest threat doesn't come from those who oppose belief. It comes from followers of Jesus being taken captive by the hollow and deceptive philosophies of the world around us, watering down what we have in Jesus with man-made additives of religious rules, experiences, and self-help strategies. If you want to add stuff to your coffee, well, go ahead, that's your loss. But don't add stuff to your Jesus. Instead, "continue to live your lives in him, rooted and built up in him, strengthened in the faith as you were taught, and overflowing with thankfulness."

Now that sermon was long on diagnosis, but short on cure. Ideally, we'd follow up the next week by preaching from the Christ hymn in Colossians chapter 1. It gives a *tour de force* of all that makes Jesus superior to the empty philosophies of the world.

> The Son is the image of the invisible God, the firstborn over all creation. (1:15)

Jews worshipped the invisible God in whose image they were created; Jesus is the image of the invisible God made visible. Jewish writings personified wisdom as God's firstborn son by which God created and sustains his world (Prov. 8:22–30; Wis. Sol. 1:7, 14; 7:26); Jesus is the firstborn over all creation—not an abstract concept but wisdom-made-flesh, in whom all God's fullness dwelt.

> For in him all things were created: things in heaven and on earth, visible and invisible, whether thrones or powers or rulers or authorities; all things have been created through him and for him. (1:16)

To those seeking an experience of angels or the invisible spirit world, he *created* that world.

> Once you were alienated from God and were enemies in your minds because of your evil behavior. But now he has reconciled you by Christ's physical body through death to present you holy in his sight, without blemish and free from accusation—if you continue in your faith, established and firm, and do not move from the hope held out in the gospel. (1:21–23)

To those seeking self-mastery in order to live a life acceptable to God, Jesus has already dealt with that.

> He is before all things, and in him all things hold together. And he is the head of the body, the church; he is the beginning and the firstborn from among the dead, so that in everything he might have the supremacy. (1:17–18)

And to those wanting a sense of belonging to the majority culture, again we see Paul subverting the rhetoric of empire. Although the emperor was hailed as "equal to the beginning of all things,"[9] Paul says that Jesus *is* the beginning; for he is *before all things*. Contrary to Rome's public relations department, the emperor isn't the "head" of the body politic, *Jesus* is. And the body isn't the empire, but the tiny minority group called *the church*.[10]

What's more, this tiny minority group has the privilege, along with Paul, of knowing and declaring this previously-hidden mystery (the language of scarcity, from chapter 2):

> I have become its servant by the commission God gave me to present to you the word of God in its fullness—the mystery that has been kept hidden for ages and generations, but is now disclosed to the Lord's people. (1:25–26)

In short, no matter how the majority culture dresses up their competing philosophies, *how could you ever want to add to that?*

The overall effect of Paul's response is to create a clear distinction between those who are in the group, and those who are on the outside. This paves the way for him to speak more positively in the second half of the letter, describing the values and behaviors that should characterize those on the inside (3:1–17), and stand in contrast to those outside (3:18–4:1).[11] Adam Copenhaver aptly describes this attractive difference:

> In summary, Paul's argument to the Colossians is that because of the new life they have received in union with Christ, they have been brought out of the world and into the body of Christ. Therefore, they are to live in newness and cohesiveness as a body within the world, *distancing themselves* from the practices and dogmas of the world, exchanging the old virtues of the world for the new virtues of life in Christ, and conducting themselves

---

9. Dittenberger, *Orientis Graeci Inscriptiones Selectae*, 2.405.

10. See Walsh and Keesmaat, *Colossians Remixed*, 82–95, for how the Christ-hymn in Colossians subverts the rhetoric of the Roman Empire.

11. Copenhaver, *Reconstructing the Historical Background*, 127.

within the world in a manner that pleases Christ and is *attractive to outsiders.*[12]

But this attractive difference will only be maintained if group members resist the temptation to add elements from the surrounding culture to their group identity and practices. If they remember their new status as aliens and exiles.

---

12. *Reconstructing the Historical Background*, 140.

*Part 4*

---

# The Gospels

EACH OF THE FOUR Gospels was compiled in the first century for use by a Jesus-following minority. Two of them—**Matthew** and **John**—appear to be especially conscious of their audiences' minority status not just as part of the assumed background, but as an important issue to be addressed through their presentation of the Jesus story. We'll look at each of these in turn over the next two chapters.

Following that, we'll turn our attention to the two-volume history, **Luke–Acts**. It also contains themes related to the minority status of the early church, seeking to provide (among other things) a rational apologetic for its existence and legitimacy in order to commend it to those, like Theophilus, who were from the educated classes. It also sought to allay fears that the church was a dangerous group that posed a threat to civil society.

Before we get to that, however, we need to point out two complications that arise when reading the Gospels as minority group rhetoric. The first is the existence of two distinct audiences: (a) the original audience *in* the narrative, who heard Jesus' words and witnessed his deeds; and (b) the later audience *of* the narrative, for whom the Gospels were compiled. And it's this second audience that's the marginalized minority, so we need to pay attention to what the Gospel author is trying to say to it by the way in which he presents the narrative.[1] This isn't to say—as some allege—that the Gospel writers *made up stories and sayings* of Jesus to speak into their own community's situation.[2] Rather, they selected and told the stories

---

1. There is the possibility of a given story or saying functioning one way in its original historical context, and in a slightly different way for the audience of the written Gospel. For example, John the Baptist's word of *judgment* on the Jewish leaders (Matt 3:7–10) may also function as a word of *vindication* for a later audience being mistreated by synagogue Judaism.

2. See e.g., Goulder, *Midrash and Lection in Matthew*, 33, who states that at times

in such a way as to bring out the particular relevance for their audience. And often, this related to how they ought to respond to their marginalized status as followers of Jesus.

The second complication is that the Gospels are *narrative* rhetoric. There will be some stories and sayings that appear to have relevance for the audience as a minority group, but they could just as easily be a recount of what was said or what happened without the Gospel author's intending to make such a point. How can we tell?[3] At times we might gain clues from the surrounding context or, in the case of Matthew, the changes he makes to Mark's account. Other times we'll have to live with some ambiguity. But for the most part, the observations in the following chapters will focus on the more obvious applications for the Gospel audiences—and there are plenty of those!

---

"Matthew makes stories up." This approach is often accompanied by elaborate reconstructions of a hypothetical audience—usually a small and idiosyncratic Christian community—who created the Gospels in this way for their own unique purposes. For a rebuttal of this sectarian view, see Bauckham, *The Gospels for All Christians*.

3. Stanton, *A Gospel for a New People*, 45.

# 12

## Matthew's Gospel
### *Here Are My Mother and My Brothers*

A MAN WHOSE PARENTS refused to attend his wedding, because he was marrying a Christian. A late teen whose car keys were hidden by her father each Sunday so she couldn't go to church. A woman cut off from her family for deserting the Orthodox church in which she was raised. These are just three examples of people for whom the idea of the believing community *as family* holds special significance because of how their family of origin has treated them. And they are just three of many that came to mind from my decade as a pastor in an average, middle-class suburb of Sydney, Australia—an environment not known for being particularly hostile to Christians.

Of course, in many parts of the world and throughout history, the physical, social, and economic consequences of being rejected by family are much more severe—particularly in more collectivist societies in which the group is primary. And this was the case with first-century Jews who chose to align themselves with Jesus as the Messiah, once it became clear that the majority wasn't going to embrace the idea. However, "leaving" Judaism wasn't all that straightforward. It wasn't like changing denominations today, but "involved the painful severing not only of family and cultic ties but being cut off from the whole life of a community upon which one was socially and economically dependent."[1] It made the pressure *not* to leave intense, encouraging at least outward conformity to avoid the life-altering consequences of being cut off from family and synagogue.

Matthew's Gospel was compiled for a community (or communities) of Jewish followers of Jesus.[2] Where that audience was in its relationship

---

1. Davies and Allison, *Matthew 1–7*, 1, 695.

2. This doesn't preclude some Gentiles being part of the community. Keener, *Matthew*, 40, provides a summary of the evidence for the Gospel's Jewish character, and lists a raft of scholarly support.

with synagogue Judaism is difficult to pinpoint.[3] Some see them as still trying to be a part of the synagogue community,[4] while the majority thinks that by this point a decisive break had been made with the parent group.[5] For our purposes, it's sufficient to see the audience as a distinct group that was in conflict with majority Judaism (particularly Pharisaism[6]), and had been in some way ostracized and alienated by their community. Stanton describes their self-perception as being "under threat of persecution . . . a somewhat beleaguered minority at odds with the parent body, and to a certain extent, with the Gentile world."[7] This—it should come as no surprise—led to the minority group rhetoric found in Matthew's Gospel. It's well-summarized by Reddish in this way:

> The rhetoric of Matthew's Gospel is that of a minority group (the Christian community) that is alienated from the dominant group (mainstream Judaism) and is trying to establish its own worldview as the correct one. Both groups claim to be the true heirs of Judaism. The church's claim that Jesus was the Messiah and the authoritative teacher of the law was a major point of contention between the two groups. Matthew's church was trying to understand the rejection of Jesus by the rest of Judaism. The church was moving beyond its Jewish roots and embracing a gentile mission. This, too, added to the tension.[8]

This was compounded by the shameful nature of their Messiah's death: crucifixion. Those who followed him faced strong social pressure from the rest to conform, or be cut off from the community altogether.

Matthew's Gospel, then, was composed in part to bolster the resolve of his audience to stand firm in the face of shame and rejection. It speaks of an alternative community in which they are honored and those who persist in rejecting them will ultimately be dishonored. Loyalty to this new "family" is to take priority over old family ties. In this way, Matthew offers not just a word of comfort, but a *reorientation* for all of Jesus' followers who have experienced rejection on account of him—especially those who've been mistreated or shunned by their own families.

---

3. Hagner, *Matthew 1–13*, 1, lxviii–lxxi.
4. Keener argues for this view in Keener, *Matthew*, 49.
5. Stanton, *A Gospel for a New People*, 124–31.
6. Keener, *Matthew*, 46.
7. Stanton, *A Gospel for a New People*, 94.
8. Reddish, *An Introduction to the Gospels*, 119.

## Redefining the court of reputation

Matthew's primary strategy is one which is by now familiar: a redefinition of the audience's court of reputation, with God at the center and those who oppose him (including family) removed from it. Famously, when Jesus' own family is described as "standing outside" (which is no mere physical detail), he gives this response:

> Pointing to his disciples, he said, "Here are my mother and my brothers. For whoever does the will of my Father in heaven is my brother and sister and mother." (12:49–50)

He also repositions the debate to take into account eternal consequences. There's no point in gaining honor in the court of public opinion only to lose it in the one jurisdiction that counts:

> Do not be afraid of those who kill the body but cannot kill the soul. Rather, be afraid of the One who can destroy both soul and body in hell. (10:28)

> What good will it be for someone to gain the whole world, yet forfeit their soul? (16:26)

But perhaps Matthew's most distinctive contribution is found in the Sermon on the Mount, in which an alternative community is described. It's not merely a replacement kinship group for those rejected by their family of origin, but a rival court of reputation in which the "rules" of the honor game are redefined, often in quite counter-cultural ways.

## An alternative community of honor

In Matthew's setting of the sermon he notes that Jesus sees the crowds, who are present throughout the sermon and are amazed at his teachings (7:28). Yet he addresses the sermon in the first instance to *his disciples* (5:1–2), calling them "blessed" whenever they are insulted and persecuted because of Jesus (5:11–12). Already, Matthew's audience is being invited to see itself as belonging to this inner group.[9] And it's about this group that the "blessings" of the Beatitudes are spoken.

> *"Great,"* says Matthew's minority group, *"we're blessed!"*

But not quite. Because the English translations of "blessing" or "happy" miss the honor-shame context of the Greek word *makarios* (and

9. White, "Grid and Group in Matthew's Community," 81.

its negative counterpoint, *ouai*, usually rendered "woe"). As Hanson has shown, these don't function as pronouncements of blessings and curses, so much as publicly proclaimed value judgments about the honor or shamefulness of the subject. A better translation would therefore be, "How honorable are those . . . !"[10] If we look at the Beatitudes in this light, we see how Jesus is taking what's been disvalued and shamed by the wider culture and declaring it to be *honorable* in the alternative community he's creating,[11] the kingdom of heaven.[12]

> "OK," says Matthew's minority group, "we're honorable!"

Correct. But if we look more specifically at what Jesus is calling honorable, we see that they are "the very opposite characteristics" of those outside the group,[13] and constitute a refusal to play along with the honor games of the wider culture:

- They are powerless, being poor and in mourning (5:3–4). Yet their focus is on storing up treasure in heaven in order to be honored by God, rather than treasure on earth so they can be honored before people (6:19–21). They don't worry about their daily provision like the wider world—which doesn't know God—but trust his fatherly care (6:32–33). Neither do they display their mournful fasting to gain honor in public (6:16–18).[14]

- They are meek and merciful (5:5, 7). They turn the other cheek when dishonored and leave it to God to defend their honor (5:38–39).[15] They don't seek revenge, but instead pursue reconciliation (5:23–26) and forgiveness (6:14)—considered a sign of weakness in the ancient world.[16]

- They hunger and thirst for righteousness (5:6). This is the kind of righteousness that exceeds that of the Pharisees and teachers of the law

---

10. Hanson, "How Honorable! How Shameful!," 81–111. The "woes" ought to be rendered, "How Shameful are . . . !" or even, "Shame on . . . !"

11. Neyrey, *Honor and Shame*, 167.

12. White, "Grid and Group in Matthew's Community," 83, concludes that the kingdom of heaven "is presented in the beatitudes as an alternate world, another forum in which the righteousness of the disciples is recognized, and thus becomes a fact. There the honor of the community is established before God."

13. Esler, "Group Norms and Prototypes in Matthew 5.3–12," 162.

14. "Group Norms and Prototypes," 162.

15. Keener, *Matthew*, 197. The blow to the right cheek would be with the back of the hand; it's not so much an act of violence as an act of dishonoring.

16. Neyrey, *Honor and Shame*, 194–95.

(5:20) because it's done in secret, and will be honored in God's court rather than the court of public opinion (6:1–8).[17]

- They are pure in heart (5:8). They don't use their eyes to look lustfully at a woman, committing adultery with her in their heart (5:28), thereby dishonoring her and her husband.[18] Instead, their eyes will "see God."

- They are peacemakers (5:9). They show they belong to God's family by exhibiting his family values, imitating his love for their enemies and persecutors (5:44–45).

> "Right," says Matthew's minority group, "we get it. We've been dishonored and rejected by our family and community because we've stopped playing their game. But that's precisely what makes us winners in God's eyes, according to his standards about what's honorable behavior."

Exactly. So don't continue to play the world's honor games and judge others by its standards, or you'll be judged by those very same standards (7:1–2).

The final two Beatitudes then make the applicability to Matthew's audience more explicit, referring to *persecution*—or perhaps more accurately in this context, *ostracism* from the community[19]—for the sake of Jesus:

> How honorable are those who are persecuted/shunned because of righteousness, for theirs is the kingdom of heaven. How honorable are you when people insult you, persecute/exclude you and falsely say all kinds of evil against you because of me. Rejoice and be glad, because great is your reward in heaven, for in the same way they persecuted/rejected the prophets who were before you. (5:10–12)

Members of Matthew's minority group are called "honorable" whenever they are rejected by the wider community because it's a sign they've stopped playing by its rules. In fact, they've left the game altogether. In light of this, they should rejoice because eventually they'll be vindicated by God and share in the blessings promised to their persecutors.

> "Rejoice, indeed!" says Matthew's minority group, "Because although we've lost our family and our inheritance, we've become

---

17. Neyrey, *Honor and Shame*, 221, describes this as a call to "vacate the playing field" where honor games are played out.
18. Neyrey, *Honor and Shame*, 196–97.
19. Neyrey, *Honor and Shame*, 185.

> 'sons of God' who will be the ones to 'inherit the land' promised to God's people. And we'll share in our heavenly reward, together with all of the prophets who were mistreated just like we are."

This leads us to ask a difficult question: does the Western church today still function as this kind of alternative community, with a counter-cultural set of attitudes and behaviors it holds to be honorable? And if not, why not?

Part of the answer may lie in the fact that Jesus' teachings have influenced, to a degree, Western culture, so that traits like forgiveness, mercy, and peacemaking are less counter-cultural—at least in an aspirational sense. But some of the answer may have more to do with the fact that most of us haven't had to lose all that much to follow Jesus. Discipleship hasn't been anywhere near as costly for us as it was for Matthew's audience. Although it's hardly something to complain about, it can mean we don't sense as acutely the need for an alternative court of honor; after all, some of the world's honor is still available to us! And since we're still getting some love from the world, it's harder for us to give up its game completely. So we try to play both games, like James warns against. Or we bring the world's game with us into the church, like the Corinthians did.

But just like Matthew's community, Jesus' followers today should be known for not playing the game at all. It might help if we look at the opposition we face—usually in the form of mockery and exclusion—in the same way Jesus did. That is, we view it as something to be celebrated rather than an inconvenience to be endured; as evidence we've vacated the world's playing field.

In other words, our church communities should be set up to honor that which they were designed to honor: those who have "lost out" in the eyes of the wider culture because they've opted out of its value system to embrace Jesus' value system. Too often in our churches we honor the same things the world honors, and get a little embarrassed by those whose allegiance to Jesus has brought them shame in the world's eyes. But the church should be a place where all that gets turned upside-down. It shouldn't just be a *refuge* for those who have most suffered the consequences of living God's way—although it is, particularly for those who've been rejected by their family. It should also be an alternative court that judges them worthy of *extra* honor. (Possibly Paul was hinting at something like that in 1 Cor 12:23?)

Moreover, the result of such an alternative community of honor is not just for the benefit of group members, helping them to see their difference as honorable; it's also what makes that difference attractive. And it's no coincidence that right after the final Beatitude about persecution comes this:

> You are the salt of the earth ... You are the light of the world. A town built on a hill cannot be hidden. Neither do people light a lamp and put it under a bowl. Instead they put it on its stand, and it gives light to everyone in the house. In the same way, let your light shine before others, *that they may see your good deeds and glorify your Father in heaven.* (5:13–16)

## Membership requires loyalty

This new community with an alternative system of honor is also the one which demands the primary loyalty of its members—even those who might still be part of their family of origin. After warning of persecution and promising God's providential care in spite of it (10:17–31), Jesus makes the call to loyalty clear:

> Whoever acknowledges me before others, I will also acknowledge before my Father in heaven. But whoever disowns me before others, I will disown before my Father in heaven. (10:32–33)

The only real threat to group members is not persecution or marginalization, but of leaving the group, publicly denying their association with Jesus and his followers. Their disloyalty dishonors the one who has offered them honor; it rejects God's patronage, sending the message that they've chosen the approval of the outside world instead.

This loyalty could prove costly, as Jesus' kingdom is divisive. It may require group members to choose Jesus over their family, if their family has rejected Jesus:

> Do not suppose that I have come to bring peace to the earth. I did not come to bring peace, but a sword. For I have come to turn 'a man against his father, a daughter against her mother, a daughter-in-law against her mother-in-law—a man's enemies will be the members of his own household. (10:34–36)

The allusion to Micah 7:6 reminds Matthew's audience of the original context. Micah is lamenting his minority status of one who "watches in hope for Yahweh" while the rest of his community continues to live in a state of rebellion against God and, just as significantly, in disloyalty and dishonor to one another.[20] Jesus continues:

---

20. Waltke, *Micah*, 428–29.

> "Anyone who loves their father or mother more than me is not worthy of me; anyone who loves their son or daughter more than me is not worthy of me. Whoever does not take up their cross and follow me is not worthy of me. Whoever finds their life will lose it, and whoever loses their life for my sake will find it." (10:37–39)

This is a call to put loyalty to Jesus and his community ahead of everything, including one's family, one's public honor (metaphorically carrying the shame of the cross), and even one's own life. Failure to do so is dishonorable, being judged "not worthy" of him.

Elsewhere, Jesus expands this call to loyalty to include prioritizing him over family obligations. And he does it in a rather startling response to what sounds to us like a perfectly reasonable request:

> Another disciple said to him, "Lord, first let me go and bury my father." But Jesus told him, "Follow me, and let the dead bury their own dead." (8:21–22)

Scholars are divided as to what's going on here. It may be intended as a shocking overstatement, trying to show how following Jesus comes before *everything*—even something as significant as grieving for family; even something that was required by the Law (Ex 20:12; Lev 21:11; Num 6:6–7).[21]

Or it may be that the man's father wasn't actually dead yet. *First, let me go and bury my father. It'll take some time, as I'm still in the interview phase for a suitable hit man.* No, not like that. But it may refer to his obligation to look after his aging parents until their death. Once he's free from all of his family obligations, *then* he'll leave everything and follow Jesus.[22] To which Jesus says, "Follow me, and let the dead bury their own dead." That is, leave those who are spiritually dead to worry about earthly matters.[23] *This* is more important, taking priority over even the most significant of human relationships. It can't wait until the end of your priority list, once you've done everything else.

Either way we take it, this speaks loudly to us today. Our culture pressures us to put family first, and to put them first in the way that everyone else does. As Christians, we can still buy into the idea that we owe our children a certain level of opportunity, a certain standard in education, music

---

21. Witherington, *Matthew*, 188.
22. Keener, *Matthew*, 275–76.
23. Davies and Allison, *Matthew 8–18*, 2, 56. It could also refer to the practice of reburying his father's bones in an ossuary one year later.

lessons, clothing, holidays, birthday parties, and smartphones. And so we work even harder to provide all this for them.

Then there's the school involvement. For a while there, when people asked me what I did for a living, I told them that I worked as part of a two-person support team for my children's educational and social experiences—and lectured in the New Testament on the side when I had some free time. It seemed a full-time job to keep track of all the assignments, field trip permission notes, party invitations, and oddly-scheduled sports practices. Our culture can make our children our idols, if we're not careful.

Now of course, Christian parents *need* to be involved in their children's lives, being interested, engaged, supportive, and empowering. But Christian parents *also* need to show their children that they're not the center of their universe; God is.

I've seen the opposite happen to people slowly over time: those whose lives were all about serving God in their school and university years get their first job, and it starts to tail off a bit, quite understandably. Then the children come along, and life as they knew it ends. Again, it's understandable. But the problem is when it never starts up again. *I'll follow you, but first, let me get my kids through school and college, and married off. Then I'll follow you.* Twenty years or so later, they've forgotten what it's even like to put Jesus and his family first.

While most of us in the Western world aren't in the position of facing a stark choice between identifying with Jesus and his family, and identifying with our biological family, we face a series of smaller choices about priorities every day. Do we follow the world in prioritizing our family, or do we show how attractively different it is when we model a family that puts Jesus and his kingdom first?

## Members are few, yet honored

Not many will be prepared to make this commitment. This means that Matthew's minority group is small, which presents a threat to its survival. *How can this be God's chosen community if most of our relatives and friends have rejected it?* To counter this, the Gospel uses the strategy of "scarcity" which we discussed in chapter 2. Although participation in Jesus' community—the kingdom of heaven—is of supreme value, entry is via a narrow gate that few will find (7:13-14). This not only highlights the enormous privilege of entry into the kingdom, but also goads his audience into rising to the challenge of finding it. Additionally, although the community may be small, there are promises of it having an influence on a global scale.

Matthew 13 contains the greatest concentration of this theme, beginning with the parable of the sower. Although three of the four types of soil failed to produce a crop, the good soil yielded a superabundance (13:23). It makes a similar point to the parables of the mustard seed and the yeast (13:31–33) concerning the disproportionate influence the faithful minority will end up having. Further, two of the soil types which failed did so because of pressure to conform to the majority culture: persecution (13:21) and the competing priorities of life (13:22). And the crops that *did* grow are described as honorable (*makarios*) because they understood and responded, as well as privileged because they'd been allowed to see what "prophets and righteous people longed to see" in the past (13:16–17). In contrast with those outside, the "secrets of the kingdom of heaven" have been given to them (13:11–12).

The parables of the weeds (13:24–30) and the net (13:47–50) address the present coexistence of those who belong to the community and those who don't. The weeds (and bad fish) will eventually be removed, but not until the proper time so that their removal doesn't also affect the wheat (and good fish). Vindication is coming, at the end of the age (13:39, 42).

The parables of the hidden treasure and the pearl (13:44–46) again contain the motif of scarcity, in that the object of supreme value is difficult to find. But they also emphasize the prudence of selling everything they had in order to possess it. This is something not everyone was capable of doing, as we see in the story of the rich young man who went away sad because he couldn't prioritize Jesus ahead of his wealth (19:21–26). Indeed, the response of Jesus' disciples in that story—"Who then can be saved?"—highlights the impossibility of the challenge. Jesus reminds them—and Matthew's community—that God is the one who makes it possible, both as a word of reassurance, and in case those who *did* rise to the challenge thought it was something to boast about. Many may have been invited, but few are chosen (22:14). For those who've given up everything to gain the kingdom Jesus promises great reward, while again stressing that "many" won't do so:

> Jesus said to them, "Truly I tell you, at the renewal of all things, when the Son of Man sits on his glorious throne, you who have followed me will also sit on twelve thrones, judging the twelve tribes of Israel. And everyone who has left houses or brothers or sisters or father or mother or wife or children or fields for my sake will receive a hundred times as much and will inherit eternal life. *But many who are first will be last*, and many who are last will be first. (19:28–30)

This theme in Matthew's Gospel is a timely reminder that the smaller we might become—or feel like we've become—in comparison to the rest of the world, it doesn't mean our influence in the world will decrease or that the eventual outcome has been placed in doubt. A faithful minority has been part of God's plan from the start.

Moreover, it encourages us as preachers to inspire our own audiences to rise to the challenge of a difficult, even impossible task, knowing that God is the one who can do the impossible. Rather than presenting Jesus' call to give up everything for the sake of the kingdom as a negative but necessary requirement, we can recast it as something an honorable and wise person would do—and do so *joyfully* (13:44) in anticipation of what they stand to gain.[24] If we truly find our joy in what makes us different, it'll go a long way to making it attractive.

## Dealing with shame from the majority

As well as the positive task of convening an alternative court of reputation, Matthew's Gospel also goes about its opposite: excluding the rival court and insulating the group from its opposition.

### Expect opposition to happen

Multiple times throughout the Gospel, Jesus stresses the inevitability of persecution and hatred, nowhere more strongly than in chapter 10:

> "I am sending you out like sheep among wolves. Therefore be as shrewd as snakes and as innocent as doves. Be on your guard; you will be handed over to the local councils and be flogged in the synagogues. On my account you will be brought before governors and kings as witnesses to them and to the Gentiles. But when they arrest you, do not worry about what to say or how to say it. At that time you will be given what to say, for it will not be you speaking, but the Spirit of your Father speaking through you. Brother will betray brother to death, and a father his child; children will rebel against their parents and have them put to death. You will be hated by everyone because of me, but the one who stands firm to the end will be saved. When you are persecuted in one place, flee to another. Truly I tell you, you will not finish going through the towns of Israel before the Son of Man comes." (10:16–23)

---

24. Piper, *Desiring God*, 70.

Poignantly for Matthew's audience, Jesus predicts rejection by family and synagogue communities, as well as governing authorities; they will become the "repugnant cultural other." The result of this is that when opposition eventuates, not only should Matthew's minority not be surprised, but it serves to reinforce Jesus' message and the group's narrative (see chapter 2). *Look, it's happening, just like he told us!* In fact, those who deny the inevitability of persecution find themselves in the position of Peter, when he rebuked Jesus for predicting his own persecution. Jesus' response was not only to ascribe that attitude to the Enemy of God's people, but to see in it Peter's allegiance to the "human concerns" of the wider society (16:22–23).

Perhaps the most significant effect of Jesus' warning on the group is the reminder that when opposition arises, God is still very much in control. So they should trust in him for the outcome, rather than thinking it depends on them. For a start, this means relying on God to defend their honor when they find themselves rhetorically out of their depth before the educated élite; just as they should *expect* persecution, so they should also *expect* divine enabling (10:19–20). It also means not taking matters into their own hands physically, following Jesus example; although he had the power to order a military solution, he told his disciple, "put your sword back in its place," and to trust in God's counter-cultural plan of non-violence and suffering (26:52–54). Doing it God's way is not easy; Jesus' own soul was "overwhelmed with sorrow to the point of death," and he prayed that the cup of suffering might be taken from him, yet he still submitted to the Father's will (26:38–39).

There's a further lesson to be drawn both from being forewarned about persecution, and from knowing that God is in control of it: they can be "shrewd as snakes" (10:16), not seeking out opposition for the sake of it, and even beating a strategic withdrawal if given the opportunity (10:23). This is exemplified numerous times throughout Jesus' life, each time using the same word for "withdraw" (*anachōreō*) to describe the avoidance of unnecessary persecution:

- The magi *withdrew* by another route to avoid Herod (2:12).
- Joseph *withdrew* to Egypt (2:14) and then Galilee (2:22) after being warned of danger.
- When Jesus heard that John the Baptist had been imprisoned, he *withdrew* to Galilee (4:12).
- The Pharisees were plotting to kill him (12:14), and Matthew notes that Jesus became "aware of this" and *withdrew* (12:15); this is significant,

since Jesus' awareness is an editorial addition by Matthew (cf. Mark 3:6–7).

- When Jesus heard about John the Baptist's beheading, he *withdrew* to a solitary place (14:13); again the linking of the two is an editorial addition (cf. Mark 6:29–32).
- Immediately after challenging the food laws in the hearing of the Pharisees, Jesus *withdrew* (15:21).

This may well be drawing on one or more instances of strategic withdrawal in Israel's history, associated with the same Greek word: Moses' withdrawal from Pharaoh to Midian (Ex 2:15, LXX); and an incident during the Maccabean Revolution in which Judas Maccabeus and ten of his followers withdrew to the wilderness to hide, before coming back and defeating the army of Antiochus (2 Macc 5:27). In both cases, strategic withdrawal led to God's people being rescued and their enemies being defeated. Alternatively, or additionally, it could be using the motif of personified "Wisdom" withdrawing back to God's side after encountering opposition and rejection on earth (e.g., Prov 1:24–25; Baruch 3:12; Enoch 42:2),[25] functioning as an act of rejection on those who themselves have rejected God.[26] In any case, Jesus' own withdrawals from hostility exemplify his instruction to flee persecution (10:23).[27] It's not cowardice, but shrewdness (or Wisdom), relying on God to act and vindicate according to his plan.

Jesus offers two other interesting examples of shrewdness in avoiding unnecessary opposition. While their exegetical complexity can make drawing lessons from the details problematic, their wider intent is clear enough. The first is the story of the coin in the fish's mouth, in which Jesus responds to an earlier question about whether he pays the two drachma tax:

> "What do you think, Simon?" he asked. "From whom do the kings of the earth collect duty and taxes—from their own sons or from others?" "From others," Peter answered. "Then the sons are exempt," Jesus said to him. "*But so that we may not cause offense*, go to the lake and throw out your line. Take the first fish you catch; open its mouth and you will find a four-drachma coin. Take it and give it to them for my tax and yours." (17:25–27)

---

25. See all three possibilities outlined in Good, "The Verb Ἀναχωρεω in Matthew's Gospel," 6–10.
26. Osborne and Arnold, *Matthew*, 597.
27. Gundry, *Matthew*, 59; contra Stanton, *A Gospel for a New People*, 201.

While there is debate about whether the tax in Jesus' day was for the Temple or Rome, for Matthew's post-70AD audience the temple tax had been appropriated by the Empire anyway.[28] And in broad terms, the story speaks to a situation in which the demands of the majority are in conflict with the worldview of the minority: payment of tax to the Temple or Empire acknowledges their sovereignty, but Jesus' followers view God as the true sovereign, meaning they as his "sons" should be exempt.[29] Here, Jesus appears to be advocating accommodation to the conventions of the majority to avoid unnecessary conflict; but he does it in a way that reframes the payment as an acknowledgement of *God's* sovereignty, since he's the one who provides payment for the tax.[30]

> "OK," says Matthew's minority group. "We pay the tax, but do so out of what God provides for us as an acknowledgement that everything belongs to him, not any human authorities."

Similarly, when Jesus is challenged by the Herodians about whether to pay tax to Caesar (22:15–22), Jesus issues a counter-challenge to show him the coin with which the tax is paid, and which bore Caesar's image. When one is produced, it exposes their hypocrisy: despite the fact that they objected to Caesar's image being in Jerusalem, they themselves carried such a coin.[31] Remember that earlier, Jesus himself didn't have one, but sent Peter to shake down a passing fish to pay theirs.[32] Jesus then utters his famous pronouncement, "So give back to Caesar what is Caesar's, and to God what is God's." In contrast to a previous revolutionary who refused (Judas the Galilean, in AD 6),[33] Jesus suggested this wise avoidance of conflict—again, with the reframing that everything ultimately belongs to God anyway.

> "Got it," says Matthew's minority group. "We give Caesar back the coins that bear his image; but we give ourselves back to God, with whose image we are stamped."[34]

Except it *may* be even cleverer than that. N.T. Wright makes the intriguing suggestion that Jesus is alluding to the last words of Mattathias during the Maccabean revolution. To the end, he refused to compromise, calling his

---

28. Keener, *Matthew*, 444. Cf. Dio Cassius, *Historiae romanae* 65.7.2.
29. Witherington, *Matthew*, 333.
30. The fish is symbolic in Matthew's Gospel for God's provision: 7:10; 14:13–21; 15:36. See Carter, "Paying the Tax," 27–29.
31. Keener, *Matthew*, 524–26.
32. Carter, "Toll and Trouble," 427.
33. Josephus, *Wars*, 2.118.
34. Gundry, *Matthew*, 443.

followers to rebel against foreign rulers and obey God. Mattathias said, "Pay back (*antapodote*) the Gentiles in full, and obey the commands of the law" (1 Macc. 2:68). So when Jesus says, "Give back (*apodote*) to Caesar the things of Caesar, and to God the things of God," he may be engaged in a kind of Gentile dog-whistling. That way he has plausible deniability before Pilate, but keeps the crowds on side (who are duly amazed, in verse 22).[35]

> "Understood," says Matthew's minority group. "We can avoid unnecessary conflict and participate in things like taxation, but we reframe it, so that among ourselves we understand what we're doing in decidedly different terms."

In the Western church, we've grown accustomed to relatively benign conditions for Jesus' followers, to the point that we've started to be surprised on the occasions we're met with opposition, exclusion, and hatred. Jesus' words to his disciples, via Matthew's minority group audience, should remind us that this was always going to be the case; Jesus foresaw it, which is evidence that God still has everything under control. We don't need to worry that the plan has gone off track! What's more, the plan's success isn't up to us. *God* is the one whose power works through us; he's the one who will bring in his kingdom on earth.

Matthew's Gospel should also remind us to be wise in how we go about our interactions with the dominant culture. If we start to think persecution is a sign things have gone wrong, we can be tempted to try to manipulate our way back into favor with the majority. At that point we may find ourselves, along with Peter, doing the work of Satan in selling out to "human concerns."

On the other hand, we're not called to walk around with unnecessary targets on our backs seeking out conflict. Wisdom sometimes calls for a strategic withdrawal, not having to win every battle with the dominant culture—or even fight *every* fight. This is particularly the case when the fight is something of symbolic significance (as was the case with paying tax to secular authorities in the first century) but may serve to distract outsiders from the core message of the gospel. Or there may be a moral issue on which we've taken our stand, over which hostility grows to the point that we prudently withdraw from public debate, leaving a rebellious world to the consequences of its choices.

Whichever we choose, wisdom rather than fear should drive our approach.

---

35. Wright, *Jesus and the Victory of God*, 2, 504–06. I'm almost persuaded.

### Those who oppose you are on the losing side

In any case, Matthew's minority group can take comfort in the fact that their persecutors will ultimately be on the losing side. That's the rhetorical stance Matthew's Gospel takes toward the Jewish leaders who opposed Jesus and, by extension, the leaders in the post-70AD synagogue communities who opposed Matthew's audience. If God's at the center of their redefined court of reputation, the shaming that comes from those outside can safely be ignored because they don't belong to God.

The Gospel famously portrays the Jewish leaders in negative terms. John the Baptist calls them a "brood of vipers" who might look like they're seeking God, but don't produce fruit appropriate to repentance—the axe will soon fall on them (3:7–10). Jesus calls them "old wineskins" whose minds can't be stretched to accommodate the new thing God is doing (9:17). They're described inconsistent, so that even if someone tries to please them, they can't win (11:18–19). Although they tried to dishonor Jesus at every turn, every time he turned the tables on them with his responses, to the point that they eventually had to admit defeat (22:46).

The scribes and Pharisees come in for the harshest criticism, being labelled "hypocrites" who don't do what they preach, and are a hindrance to those wanting to enter the kingdom (Matt 23). Jesus predicts that they would persecute his followers and reject their message, as they did the prophets in previous generations (23:33–36). So, just like his followers were to shake the dust off their feet and leave those who don't welcome them (10:12–14), Jesus says he'll leave them to it. In a great reversal, it's *their* house that will be left desolate (10:38), as the glory of God in the person of Jesus goes out from the temple once more and settles on the Mount of Olives to pronounce its destruction (24:1–3; cf. Ezek 11:23).[36] That generation of Israel will receive the harshest judgment (23:36) for their persecution of Jesus' followers and for putting to death Jesus himself—with the crowd famously accepting responsibility for the latter (27:25).

> "Too right," says Matthew's minority group. "Our oppressors will be judged by God for what they've done to us."

We're in uncomfortable territory here, due both to the subsequent treatment of Jews by those claiming to follow Jesus, as well as Western

---

36. Davies and Allison, *Matthew 19–28*, 3, 334–36. Note, too, that in the next verse (10:39), Jesus quotes Psalm 118, "Blessed is he who comes in the name of the Lord"; this psalm contains the rejected-stone-becomes-cornerstone imagery of reversal and vindication.

culture's (aspirational) move away from vilifying opponents as an acceptable rhetorical move. So we need to say something here.

Firstly, it's not anti-Semitic. And it's tragic that people have used it that way at various times in history. To view it as such misses some important and obvious details. Firstly, not only was Jesus himself Jewish, so was Matthew and his audience. Secondly, it's directed against a particular generation of God's people for rejecting his messenger, standing in continuity with the numerous times God has promised and enacted judgment on his people throughout Israel's Scriptures. Jesus sees their persecution of his followers as not being out of ignorance (as might be the case with Gentiles), but from a willful rejection of their Messiah. Thirdly, at the time Matthew's Gospel was compiled, there wasn't a sharp break between "Christianity" and "Judaism" as we now know it, making this still an internal debate among Jews; Jewish followers of Jesus were, as Johnson notes, "part of a much larger debate in Judaism, a debate with many parties, concerning the right way to read Torah, the text that shaped the people."[37] Fourthly, although this type of invective is considered to be out of place in civilized debate today, it was typical of how rival groups spoke of each other in the ancient world, among both Jews and Greeks.[38] In fact, in some places *not* to speak like this would be a sign you weren't all that serious. Finally, it wasn't being spoken from a position of power or security, but by a powerless, persecuted minority about their persecutors.

Apart from obviously ruling out anti-Semitism, this should also cause us to think very carefully before we engage in a similar style of rhetoric about those who oppose us. I would argue that each of the above points rules out using that kind of rhetorical stance in the Western church. Granted, there might come a time in which some of us become a powerless, persecuted minority, and it may be the case that the cultural acceptability of invective is an inverse function of the level of oppression experienced. But still, the high ground is still to be found in less combative rhetoric, particularly if we want our difference to remain attractive. Perhaps in such a case we might entertain an internal rhetoric that simply reassures the persecuted faithful that there's a time coming when, willingly or not, every knee will bow and every tongue confess.

---

37. Johnson, "The New Testament's Anti-Jewish Slander," 428.

38. Witherington, *Matthew*, 429. There's still plenty of uncivilized debate today; the difference is that *ad hominem* arguments are, aspirationally at least, discouraged rather than positively encouraged. See a fuller discussion in chapter 5, in our look at 1 John.

## God will vindicate you

That promise of eventual vindication at the end of the age, in the form of a divine reversal, is found particularly in the latter part Matthew's Gospel. In contrast with the fate of the wicked, "the righteous will shine like the sun in the kingdom of their Father" (13:43). Those who've lost family and inheritance for the sake of Jesus will receive a hundred-fold in return, and inherit eternal life (11:29), with those who are first changing places with those who are last (11:30). The wicked tenants who rebel against the landowner's servants and kill his son will be removed, and other tenants brought in; Jesus cites Psalm 118, in which the psalmist is surrounded and outnumbered by his enemies, yet is delivered by God, so that "the stone the builders rejected has become the cornerstone." Similarly, when Jesus cries out from the cross, "My God, my God, why have you forsaken me?" (27:46), he invokes Psalm 22, in which David is a persecuted minority surrounded by his enemies, yet still trusts that God will bring about a reversal (Ps 22:22–31).[39]

> "That's us," says Matthew's minority group. "We're the ones who feel forsaken by God, yet still trust him. We're the rejected stones out of which God has built a new people. We're the last who will be first. We're the ones who will inherit our Father's kingdom."

The prophetic parable of the sheep and goats also appears to speak of vindication, in which the king judges the sheep on the basis of how they've treated "the least of these brothers of mine." If "brothers" means what it has meant throughout Matthew's Gospel, it refers to Jesus' followers,[40] and Matthew's audience is neither the sheep nor the goats. It thus functions as a promise of vindication for the Jesus-following minority which has been mistreated by those outside, as well as a word of inclusion for those who welcome Jesus' followers and their message. This doesn't stop the parable reminding those of us who are relatively well-off to care for the poor and oppressed, it's just that the story began life having a different function:

> It was a story told by oppressed, poor, minority Christians. It was their assertive and even arrogant way of insisting that their cause was God's cause. The story may therefore serve as a reminder to those of us who are white, male, comfortable, and Christian. It may remind us that the claim of poor people, or minorities, or women that their cause is God's cause is very much like the claim which our fathers and mothers in the faith

---

39. Keener, *Matthew*, 683; Witherington, *Matthew*, 519–20.

40. See e.g., 12:50; 28:10. So e.g., Keener, *Matthew*, 605–06; Gundry, *Matthew*, 511–14; Witherington, *Matthew*, 466.

once made. This story may function in our community as the stories of slavery in Egypt functioned for a people comfortably established in the Promised Land . . . So we read this story of judgment in Matthew 25:31–46 and remember that our fathers and mothers were once poor and oppressed.[41]

*"That makes sense," says Matthew's minority group. "If we're persecuted, God will judge our oppressors. And if we see others being similarly mistreated, we should stand in solidarity with them because we know what it's like."*

Being part of a divine reversal isn't merely passive. It's not enough to trust God to turn the tables on those who mistreat us because we're followers of Jesus; while we wait for God's reversal, we turn tables for others when in a position to do so. A minority group that fights for the rights and survival other minority groups—even those which might be opposed to it—is not only attractively different, but is evidence that we are indeed children of our Father in heaven (5:45).

---

41. Bartlett, "An Exegesis of Matthew 25:31–36," 212–13.

# 13

## John's Gospel
### *If the World Hates You . . .*

I BELONG TO A Facebook group for Australian fans of American football. Frequently, new members who are just getting into the sport will ask for recommendations on which team to follow. This might seem an odd way to go about it, but most of us have no family or geographical ties to any of the teams or cities. (I started following the Green Bay Packers due to a fascination with both Brett Favre's quarterback play and a fan base committed enough to wear Styrofoam cheeses on their heads.[1]) Invariably, discussion turns to the merits of following the New England Patriots: more often than not you'll be on the winning side, but you'll also face hostility from fans of the other thirty one teams. It's an invitation to a victorious yet hated minority existence.

Similarly, John's Gospel is a call to join (and remain in[2]) the minority group which follows Jesus in order to experience life both now and into the postseason (20:31). But it gives a sobering warning to those who do so that although they will ultimately be victorious, they will face hatred and alienation from the outside world:

> "If the world hates you, keep in mind that it hated me first. If
> you belonged to the world, it would love you as its own. As it is,

---

1. I also find some scriptural support in "Blessed are the cheesemakers," admittedly in a poorly-attested and very late manuscript.

2. Space precludes entry into the debate over whether the primary purpose of John's Gospel is to bring non-believers to faith or to encourage believers to continue in faith, as well as the related textual issue of the tense of the verb "believe" in 20:31. Here, we will follow e.g., Carson, *John*, 87–95, and Witherington, *John's Wisdom*, 32, in seeing the Gospel as written primarily for believers to use in evangelizing outsiders, without denying that at many points (esp. ch. 13–17) it addresses how to *remain* in the community of Jesus' followers. Indeed, the debate at times perpetuates the false dichotomy between conversion and discipleship.

you do not belong to the world, but I have chosen you out of the world. That is why the world hates you ... If they persecuted me, they will persecute you also." (15:18–20)

"In this world you will have trouble. But take heart! I have overcome the world." (16:33)

This warning typifies the Gospel's rhetorical stance toward the outside world in two significant ways: highlighting both the *conflict* experienced and the stark *contrast* that exists between the group and the outside world.

## Conflict and contrast

Firstly, the Gospel brings to the foreground the conflict between Jesus and the Jewish leaders throughout his ministry, beginning with his cleansing of the temple (ch. 2), continuing through various accusations and counter-accusations (ch. 5, 7–8), and culminating in the decision to put him to death (ch. 12). In Jesus' farewell speech, this is explicitly linked with the later experience of Jesus' followers, warning them that they'll face similar hostility and conflict at the hands of the synagogue community (15:18–16:3). As we noted in chapter 1, this prediction of persecution serves to inoculate group members against its effects, so that when it happens, it doesn't take them by surprise but actually reinforces the group's narrative and therefore its leader's authority:

"All this I have told you so that you will not fall away ... I have told you this, so that when their time comes you will remember that I warned you about them." (16:1, 4)

We also observed that heightening the group's perception of conflict can have a positive effect on group unity, encouraging them to unite against a common threat and rely on one another. It's no accident that these warnings are preceded by Jesus' instruction that mutual love be the defining group characteristic, and that they're to remain in the vine if they want to bear fruit (15:1–17). The warnings are then followed by Jesus' prayer for the unity of his followers (ch. 17).

However, the rhetoric isn't entirely insular. The purpose of their mutual love is so that outsiders will see (13:35). They're to remain connected to Jesus in order to "bear much fruit" (15:8). And the unity for which Jesus prays is because they've been sent into the world (17:18) so that others might believe through their message (17:20) and know of God's love (17:23). As Witherington notes,

> One of the essential stresses of the prayer in John 17 is to make clear to the disciples their mission and obligation to carry on Jesus' work and witness in the world.[3]

Even the arguments Jesus has with the Jewish leaders are carefully narrated to show that as a result of the conflict, some believed (e.g., 7:41) and some were moved to investigate further (e.g., 7:50–51; 10:21). Conflict itself is portrayed as an opportunity to win over outsiders.[4]

As well as warning of conflict, John's Gospel depicts a stark contrast between Jesus (and his followers) and the "world" outside. He famously uses pairs of opposites to heighten the sense of contrast between those in the group and those outside. For example:

- **Light and dark:** Jesus is the light sent into the darkness, which is unable to "grasp" the light (1:5). Darkness symbolizes unbelief and ignorance (12:25; cf. Judas's betrayal and Nicodemus's questioning which were both done "at night"), while light stands for truth. Jesus proclaimed himself to be the "light of the world" which leads to life (8:12), and those who walk in his light become "sons of light" (12:36).

- **Life and death:** Jesus is the source and embodiment of life (1:4), and has authority to raise the dead and give them life (5:21). Jesus' followers have "already crossed over from death to life" (5:24) and experience "life to the full" (10:10). Jesus is "the resurrection and the life" so that those who belong to him "will live even though they die" (11:25). Those in darkness are opposed to the light because they "fear that their deeds will be exposed" (3:20).

- **Above and below:** Jesus famously tells Nicodemus that he must be born again "from above" (3:3). While Jesus is "from above," his opponents are "from below" (8:23), and are thus incapable of accepting his message.

- **Of this world and not of this world:** Similarly, Jesus' opponents are "of this world" (8:23). In John's Gospel, the "world" refers to that which is ignorant of and hostile to Jesus (1:10) and is ruled by Satan (12:31). It's also that which Jesus was sent to save (3:16) and out of which he will return to the Father (13:1). The world will also be hostile to his followers (16:33), whom he's called out of the world (15:19; 17:6) in order

---

3. Witherington, *John's Wisdom*, 32.

4. See our discussion on conflict in chapter 2; Coser, *The Functions of Social Conflict*, 121–23.

that they, like Jesus himself, might not be of the world (17:14; 18:36) yet be sent back into the world (17:17).

The effect of this pervasive language of contrast is to sharpen the boundary between the group and the wider world. As we saw in chapter 1, the more group members focus on the similarities they share with each other over against the outside world, the more cohesive the group becomes.[5] In turn, they internalize these similarities which become characteristic of the group as a whole.[6] John's Gospel creates a clearly delineated group which perceives itself as not belonging to the same "world" everyone else does.

Again, however, this isn't purely for the sake of insulation. The language of opposites noted above is clearly set within the framework of the Father's sending of the Son into the world in order to save it (3:16), that those in the dark might embrace the light (12:36), and those in the world might receive it and become children of God (1:12). Just as light stands out in the midst of the darkness, Jesus' followers are to be *attractively different*.

It's clear from this focus on conflict and contrast that the audience of John's Gospel was not just a minority, but one under active threat of persecution—in particular, from the synagogue (cf. 9:22; 12:42; 16:2).[7] This should make us cautious before we unthinkingly appropriate the rhetoric of conflict and contrast for the Western church today, as Keener warns:

> Western Christendom has sometimes appropriated rhetoric originally conceived from the perspective of an oppressed minority to express an oppressive triumphalism . . . But a triumphalist interpretation is an illegitimate appropriation of the text,

---

5. Turner et al., *Rediscovering the Social Group*, 51.
6. Esler, "Social Identity Theory," 24.
7. There is ongoing scholarly debate as to the precise nature of the audience for which this Gospel is written. The spectrum ranges from "everyone" (e.g., Bauckham, *The Gospels for All Christians*) to Martyn's reconstruction of a narrow, sectarian community for which the stories about Jesus function as allegorical references to internal disputes (Martyn, *History and Theology in the Fourth Gospel*; similarly, Brown, *The Community of the Beloved Disciple*). Hakola, "The Burden of Ambiguity," 448, rightly sees the truth as lying somewhere in the middle, with the Gospels being generally applicable but mirroring, "at least to some extent, the experiences and needs of those particular communities where they were produced." For our purposes, we need only identify the intended (initial) audience as being Jesus-followers who were experiencing persecution and ostracism mainly at the hands of synagogue Judaism, and were "sectarian" only in the sense that they were a minority in the Greco-Roman world, but not necessarily to other groups of Jesus followers (Michaels, *The Gospel of John*, 38). For a fuller discussion, see Keener, *The Gospel of John*, 149–52; Esler, "Community and Gospel," 235–48; Oropeza, *In the Footsteps of Judas and Other Defectors*, 163–64.

> a counterreading that ignores the ideal audience, a marginalized minority community.[8]

However, Keener also goes on to suggest that we might begin to adopt such rhetoric—cautiously and proportionally—to the extent that our experience of marginalization increases.[9] Michaels muses similarly, but perhaps a little too hopefully:

> As Christians in America become a smaller and smaller minority, not only in self-perception but in actual fact, there is the possibility that the Gospel of John may draw them closer to each other and, at the same time, separate them more and more from the prevailing values of the culture.[10]

This will require what Kysar describes as appropriating "the best of that sectarian strain" without also giving in to its excesses:

> Can we find empowerment for a mission to the world—a mission that subverts the powers of injustice and oppression, on the one hand, and refuses, on the other, to be seduced by a hostility and hatred toward others? . . . Will the Johannine witness to the Creator's love of *the kosmos* sufficiently qualify the Gospel's sectarian strains?[11]

The hope is that John's rhetoric will help to make our difference from the world the *right kind* of difference, displayed in love for one another which can't help but spill over into love for the world—a world which may be hostile to us and ignorant of Jesus, but is still the place out of which we've been called in order to be sent back into it, bearing the message of Jesus' attractively different love.

## Narrative characterization

Conveniently borrowing John's language, the Fourth Gospel's minority group rhetoric does many other things as well; if every one of them were written down, I suppose that even this whole book would not have room for the chapters that would be written. Given this, the focus of the remainder of this chapter will be on one of John's distinctive features: how it communicates

---

8. Keener, *The Gospel of John*, 151.
9. *The Gospel of John*, 152.
10. Michaels, "The Gospel of John as a Kinder, Gentler Apocalypse," 197.
11. Kysar, "Coming Hermeneutical Earthquake," 186.

through its presentation of the various characters in the story as *prototypical* for the Gospel's audience, whether positively or negatively.[12]

## Come and see

We see this right from the start when it comes to individual testimony, with John the Baptist functioning as the prototypical witness to Jesus (1:6). John points out Jesus to two of his disciples, who then start following him. Jesus encourages them to "come and see" (1:39) if they want their questions answered—an Old Testament phrase with overtones of God at work in the world (cf. Isa 66:18; Ps 46:8) that also seems to address the Gospel audience directly.[13]

Shortly afterwards, Andrew tells his brother, Simon Peter, that he's found the Messiah and brings him to Jesus (1:41–42). The next day, Philip follows Jesus and gives a Nathanael the same message, using the phrase "come and see" (1:46); despite his skepticism, he does so, functioning as a "type" for those in Israel who are initially dubious, but are prepared to investigate, making his testimony all the more compelling.[14] The Samaritan woman similarly urges her whole village to "come and see" whether Jesus was indeed the Messiah, despite her own (at this point) hesitant faith (4:28).

This theme is transformed in Jesus' high priestly prayer to include those who will believe through the testimony of others who have seen (17:20), and explicitly commends those who believe eyewitnesses without needing to "see" for themselves—in contrast with Thomas (20:29). As Keener notes, "the witnesses in the Fourth Gospel, from John the Baptist to the disciples to the Samaritan woman, thus become a bridge to, *as well as a paradigm for*, the faith of John's audience" (emphasis added).[15] John's use of these characters, then, highlights two important prototypical behaviors for John's minority: inviting others into the group to "come and see" who Jesus is, and trusting in the testimony of the group that he is the Messiah (cf. 20:31; 21:24).

---

12. Suggit, "Nicodemus," 90–91, observes, "though they are historical characters, they are presented by the evangelist in such a way that they are seen not simply as persons of past history, but as embodying the different responses which men and women can make to the person of Jesus at any age." Koester, *Symbolism in the Fourth Gospel*, 33–78, provides an excellent systematic treatment of how John uses the real, historical characters as "representative figures" in the narrative which spoke to the audience for which his Gospel was composed.

13. Carson, *John*, 154–55; Bultmann, *John*, 100.
14. Witherington, *John's Wisdom*, 71.
15. Keener, *The Gospel of John*, 1061.

Although it's probably stating the obvious, this pushes back against an evangelistic approach focused merely on winning people over to the truth about Jesus, without also inviting them to "come and see" an attractively different community characterized by Jesus' love (13:35). My experience as a pastor, anecdotal though it is, has convinced me that being drawn into the "orbit" of a faith community is frequently a more effective form of witness than carefully laid out rational or historical argument (as important as that is). What's more, sometimes those who are drawn into the periphery of the group can be the most prolific at issuing further invitations to "come and see," even though they're still on the journey to faith themselves—much like the Samaritan woman. John's Gospel reminds us that not only is the minority group the custodian of the objective testimony *about* Jesus; in one sense it *is* the testimony.

## Nicodemus

Nicodemus is another "type" encountered both by Jesus and by John's audience: like Nathanael, he represents an educated Jew who was nevertheless open to the possibility that Jesus was, at the very least, "from God" (3:2). He's the kind of person who had seen the signs Jesus had been performing, but didn't (yet) have adequate faith (2:23-25).[16] A the start, he's depicted as still being in the dark, both literally and metaphorically, as he comes to Jesus "by night." His confusion at Jesus' statements about being "born again/from above" (3:3) and being "born of the spirit" (3:8) bears this out. The quick shift from singular to plural "you" in his response (3:11) shows us that Nicodemus is indeed functioning in the Gospel as a representative of not-yet-believing Jews.[17]

The next time Nicodemus occurs in the narrative is in the context of division over who Jesus is (7:43). It seems that while some in the crowd are entertaining the idea that he's the Messiah (7:41), the leadership views it as a position only those who don't know the law could hold (7:48-49). But it's precisely at that point that Nicodemus, whom John stresses was "one of their own number," cites the law as a reason at least to investigate with an open mind:

---

16. The chapter break and some English translations obscure the fact that Nicodemus is introduced as a "man" of the kind the narrator had just described: Jesus "did not need any testimony concerning man; for he knew what was in man. Now (a) man of the Pharisees, named Nicodemus . . ."

17. Keener, *The Gospel of John*, 558-59.

"Does our law condemn a man without first hearing him to find out what he has been doing?" (7:51)

At this point, Nicodemus serves as a paradigm for those, either among John's community or being evangelized by them, who have some kind of education and authority within the synagogue—perhaps other "teachers of Israel" (3:10)—and who therefore have much to lose in terms of status in the majority culture. His example tacitly acknowledges this, and provides a pattern they could follow, taking steps to investigate while still being *one of their own number*. Nicodemus encourages such a person to view giving the Jesus movement a fair hearing as the right and honorable thing to do,[18] similarly to how the figure of Gamaliel functions in Luke's narrative (Acts 5:33–40).[19] Conversely, to reject the group's claims without even a hearing is closed-minded and an act of willful ignorance, just like the Pharisees in the story. They hadn't bothered to check where Jesus is "from" even in an earthly sense, assuming incorrectly that his birthplace was Galilee (7:52); how could they be expected to evaluate whether he was from God or not?[20] This episode depicts the struggle of Nicodemus—shared by later prospective or tentative followers of Jesus from among the synagogue community—in trying to belong to both groups, and makes it clear that at some point he will have to choose sides.

Nicodemus appears again at the end of John's Gospel, joining Joseph of Arimathea in burying Jesus' body (19:39). There's been much discussion about whether Nicodemus truly became a follower of Jesus, or whether his story is left intentionally ambiguous.[21] The fact that Joseph is named as a "disciple" despite doing it in secrecy for "fear of the Jews" (19:38) points toward the probability that Nicodemus is also, by now, a secret disciple. He's also described as having previously come to Jesus at night, suggesting that now he might well be taking his first steps into the literal (it's before sunset [10:42]) and metaphorical light, since by burying him he risks being identified with Jesus. We're not told what happened to Nicodemus after Jesus' resurrection, but John's narrative gives us a glimpse of a small yet probably decisive step in aligning himself with Jesus. "Nicodemus's movement toward the light is gradual."[22]

---

18. Suggit, "Nicodemus," 99, describes this as "the next stage in the process of coming to faith—the openness of mind and freedom from prejudice, without which the truth cannot be perceived nor the light seen."

19. Hakola, "'Friendly' Pharisees and Social Identity in the Book of Acts," 181–200.

20. Keener, *The Gospel of John*, 735.

21. Hakola, "The Burden of Ambiguity," 438–55; Bassler, "Mixed Signals," 635.

22. Brant, *John*, 79. She concludes (255–56) that Nicodemus is at the very least

At the very least, Nicodemus represents someone from the outgroup who is open and positive toward Jesus, even if he hasn't fully grasped what it all means by the end of the Gospel. Hakola argues,

> it is especially in his role as an outsider that Nicodemus can give a boost to the social identity of the Johannine group. The mere presence of a Pharisee who does not consistently sustain the rejection of Jesus and his message serves to contest the principles the Pharisees represent in the Gospel.[23]

It sends the emboldening message: *even some from among our opponents aren't entirely opposed to us. Indeed, some of them may even now be on a journey toward the light.* This is becoming more significant for us today, when the Western world's narrative is that Christianity is a dying religion, with its supposedly primitive superstitions inevitably giving way to secular reasoning and social progress. Aside from the often neglected fact that Christianity is thriving in many parts of the majority world, even in the West it's a reminder that there may be far more sympathy for us than the media might have us think. More than that: God is still at work drawing people to himself.

Further, regardless of whether Nicodemus himself ended up a fully-fledged disciple of Jesus, he still functions in the Gospel as an exemplar, issuing a challenge to those among John's audience who are, at present, "secret" disciples. "John invites them to go public with their confession of faith in Jesus."[24] In fact, according to Bassler, his ambiguity may well be central to his function:

> The figure of Nicodemus works powerfully on the reader precisely *because* it is ambiguous. Since the text provides no definitive closure to the figure, the reader must bring closure beyond the text, but this is not an easy process. Nicodemus creates a cognitive 'gap' in the text that the reader must fill, and in the process of filling this gap the reader is confronted with some serious questions (emphasis original).[25]

In other words, some among John's audience are invited to place themselves in Nicodemus's shoes and ask themselves whether they're prepared to risk

---

"heading in the right direction." Hoskyns and Davey, *The Fourth Gospel*, 536, also note the excessive amount of myrrh, appropriate for a royal burial, which points toward Nicodemus's understanding of Jesus at this point.

23. Hakola, "The Burden of Ambiguity," 455.
24. Keener, *The Gospel of John*, 1162.
25. Bassler, "Mixed Signals," 644.

their status and acceptance among the wider group; are they prepared to step, along with him, into the light? This is the same now as it was then.

Finally, the slow progress (the Nicodemus story spans almost the entire Gospel) is a reminder to John's minority group that transitioning from darkness to light—or from secrecy to openness in group membership—can take time.[26] For those in my pastoral experience who decided to "come and see," it was frequently up to a year for them to clearly identify with Jesus. But they've also tended to be the ones who, years later, have gone the distance.

## Two men healed

John introduces us to an unnamed character in chapter 5. He'd been unable to walk for 38 years, so Jesus heals him, telling him to "pick up his mat and walk" (5:8). John then reveals a key narrative detail: the healing had occurred on the Sabbath (5:9). This sparks a legal challenge to Jesus (5:16), providing him with the opportunity to give a legal defense (*apologia* [5:17]) for his actions.[27] In the process, blasphemy is added to the indictment (5:18) because he claimed his breaking of the Sabbath was a case of following in his father's footsteps (5:17); he was continuing to work in the "family business" of giving life and judging the world (5:19–23). In his defense, he cites the testimonies of John the Baptist, Moses (through the Scriptures), and God himself, evidenced by the miracles he was performing (5:31–40). His accusers thus stand condemned by Moses himself (5:45–47).

By extension, this functions as a defense not only for Jesus but also for the minority group which has aligned itself with him and, in so doing, has made the same enemies.[28] It provides a paradigm for dealing with conflict with synagogue Judaism, not only pointing to the miraculous works of Jesus (to which we could later add his own resurrection), but also appropriating Moses and the law as being on the side of Jesus and his followers.

However, in between the healing and Jesus' defense speech is an intriguing narrative detail. The Jewish leadership challenges his actions of carrying his mat on the Sabbath, to which the healed man gives the "I was only following orders" defense:

> But he replied, "The man who made me well said to me, 'Pick up your mat and walk.'" (5:11)

---

26. Farrelly, "An Unexpected Ally," 42.
27. For the trial motif, see Harvey, *Jesus on Trial*.
28. Oropeza, *In the Footsteps of Judas and Other Defectors*, 198–99.

When asked who made him well, he doesn't know. Later, however, Jesus finds him and challenges him to repent (5:14). Now that he knows Jesus' identity, he's faced with conflicting loyalties: does he show gratitude to his new benefactor, as patronage conventions would expect, and risk being identified with a "lawbreaker"? Or does he throw Jesus under the bus to save his own skin, acting out of loyalty to the established community leaders? He ends up choosing the latter:

> The man went away and told the Jewish leaders that it was Jesus who had made him well. (5:15)

What's intriguing about this is that it sets up a contrast for another unnamed man we meet later on, in chapter 9. Blind from birth, he, too, is healed by Jesus (9:1, 7), also in connection with a pool (9:6). And again, John holds back the key detail until after the healing: that it took place on the Sabbath (9:14). So the man is brought before the Pharisees to "help them with their enquiries," and initially gives a similar response to the man in chapter 5: he doesn't know who Jesus is. We're meant to read these stories in parallel.[29]

The contrast comes when the Pharisees press him to make a choice for or against Jesus (9:17). He moves from simple testimony about what had happened (9:15) to speculating that he's a prophet (9:17). The Pharisees then call his parents in for questioning, but they refuse to be drawn.[30] John provides the reason:

> His parents said this because they were afraid of the Jewish leaders, who already had decided that anyone who acknowledged that Jesus was the Messiah would be *put out of the synagogue.* That was why his parents said, "He is of age; ask him." (9:22–23)

The Greek more strongly reflects the risk to a person's identity, using the noun to describe their resultant state: they'd be labelled a "synagogue outcast," *persona non grata*, excluded from the social group connected with the synagogue, without support and status in the community.[31] Their fear is alienation from the majority community, a fear shared by many in John's audience as they weighed up where their loyalties lay; it's also evident among others later in the Gospel:

---

29. A list of parallels is supplied in Culpepper, *Anatomy of the Fourth Gospel*, 139. Notably, both stories also allude to the (non-straightforward) relationship between sin and sickness.

30. Keener, *The Gospel of John*, 788–89, sees this as speaking to those whose families have rejected them because of their belief in Jesus.

31. Brant, *John*, 168.

> Yet at the same time many even among the leaders believed in him. But because of the Pharisees they would not openly acknowledge their faith for fear they would be put out of the synagogue; for they loved human praise more than praise from God. (12:42–43)

However, this fear doesn't stop the man Jesus healed. He's questioned again, and this time he defends Jesus as being from God (9:25, 33) and aligns himself with Jesus (9:27). This results in his being "thrown out" (9:34); hearing of this, Jesus goes to meet him (9:35). The man asks for more revelation so he can believe (9:36), Jesus obliges, and the man responds in worship (9:38). Jesus then comments on the man's response, making a pronouncement of divine reversal:

> "For judgment I have come into this world, so that the blind will see and those who see will become blind." (9:39)

The man is thus a positive paradigm for those in the synagogue who wish to follow Jesus. The honorable course of action is to identify with Jesus even if it means being excluded from the majority.[32] (This stands in stark contrast with the man healed in chapter 5 who acts dishonorably in betraying Jesus, thereby functioning as a negative paradigm for those in John's audience tempted to place loyalty to family and community ahead of loyalty to Jesus.[33]) Coming out of the synagogue (cf. Heb 13:13) is where a person is "found" by Jesus (9:35), and results in worshipping him as the divine Son of Man. Those who claim to see but reject Jesus are spiritually blind (9:41), but those who embrace Jesus—and the minority existence he calls them to—will see.

We, too, increasingly face moments in which aligning ourselves with Jesus will mean going against the majority culture's expectations, risking our status and acceptance among it. The two stories of men healed by Jesus show the two options open to us: we can display loyalty to our world and throw Jesus under the bus by remaining silent when we should speak up for him, denying or avoiding association when we should boldly identify with him, and compromising our behavior to avoid being "thrown out" by our world. Or we can display loyalty to Jesus, defending his honor at the cost of our own, testifying to what he's done for us despite what might be done to us, and worshipping him as an increasingly alienated minority. Only one of those choices will be honored in the only court of reputation that counts.

---

32. Koester, *Symbolism in the Fourth Gospel*, 64.
33. Keener, *The Gospel of John*, 644; Koester, *Symbolism in the Fourth Gospel*, 53–54.

## Peter

Simon Peter provides at least two important and contrasting paradigms for John's marginalized minority. The first is in chapter 6, in which Jesus starts with a large crowd of followers; by the end, however, it's been whittled down to a small minority group of twelve, with Peter as their spokesperson. The process by which this happens is instructive.

Initially, the crowds are positive toward Jesus, responding to his ministry of healing (6:2), the feeding of the five thousand (6:14, 26), and subsequent miraculous water-crossing (6:25). They understand that these signs point to his identity as the Moses-like prophet who was to come into the world (Deut 18:15-18). However, their understanding is limited, which is why they try to make him king (6:15):

> The crowds want an earthly deliverer like Moses to supply food and bring political freedom. Jesus seeks to turn their attention from the physical food they seek to the spiritual food he is. Thus he is not merely, like Moses, the mediator of God's gift; rather he himself is God's gift.[34]

From this point in the chapter, it appears that Jesus begins to discourage those who are following him for the wrong reasons.[35] He does this using metaphor—similar to the way his parables function in the Synoptics (cf. Mark 4:10-12; 33-34)—dividing his audience into outsiders who take them literally, and insiders who understand the spiritual meaning. In response his claim to being "the bread of life" (6:35) and the "bread from heaven" (6:41), the crowd "grumbles" just as they did with Moses in the desert (6:41, 43; cf. Ex. 16:2, 8-9). Jesus explains that outsiders are unable to accept it unless drawn by God (6:44), then doubles down on his imagery by making it far more shocking:

> "Whoever eats my flesh and drinks my blood remains in me, and I in them ... This is the bread that came down from heaven. Your ancestors ate manna and died, but whoever feeds on this bread will live forever." (6:56, 58)

For John's minority group audience, this not only takes ownership of the parent group's narrative world of Moses, manna, and the Red Sea crossing, but also places those who reject Jesus—both in the text and in his audience—among the grumbling Israelites who died in the desert (6:49, 58). Pointedly, John again holds back a key narrative detail until now: this

---

34. Keener, *The Gospel of John*, 675.
35. *The Gospel of John*, 696.

occurred while teaching *in the synagogue* (6:59), drawing attention to its relevance for his own community.

> Thus it becomes, for this story and for much of John's own audience, the occasion for misunderstanding Jesus, and deciding between stumbling and perseverance.[36]

At this point, many of those who were following him complain that Jesus' teaching is "hard" (6:60)—not just to understand, but to accept[37]—and for this reason they stop following him (6:66). Jesus then asks his inner circle whether they, too, want to leave, to which Peter famously responds:

> "Lord, to whom shall we go? You have the words of eternal life. We have come to believe and to know that you are the Holy One of God." (6:68–69)

In this way, Peter functions as an exemplar for those in John's community who found holding to Jesus' teachings similarly "hard." At this point in the narrative Peter didn't understand the full implications of those "words of eternal life" (as his actions later show), yet based on what he does know of Jesus, he perseveres in loyalty. He might not have all the answers, but he knows the one in whom the answers are found.

Jesus' teaching can be similarly hard to accept today. For a start, the exclusive claims he makes in John 6 are just as offensive to our pluralistic world now as they were in the first century. Further, most believers would confess to struggling at some point with the implications of this chapter for our free will and God's fairness (6:44). And if we consider Jesus' teaching more generally, some of it—particularly as it relates to sexuality, gender, and the beginning and ending of life—is increasingly difficult for the dominant culture to accept, being in some places labelled "hate speech." This chapter presents us with a similar choice to the one faced by John's audience: turn back and no longer follow Jesus because his teaching makes us or our society uncomfortable; or follow Peter's example, trusting in Jesus as the source of life, whatever the consequences.

Peter's example is also set in contrast with that of Judas (6:64, 70–71), who represents something worse than simply conforming to the majority culture; he actively betrays Jesus, despite being one of their number. John probably highlights this because it speaks to later events among his own

---

36. *The Gospel of John*, 693.
37. Hunter, *John*, 76.

community, who had to come to terms with significant defections and betrayals (cf. 1 John 2:19).[38] As Grene suggests,

> This characterisation of Judas as a devil and false believer from the start might also serve as a theological explanation for the existence of apostasy and schisms within John's community. This is a way of acknowledging the reality of these problems without damaging the Johannine community's sense of close-knit unity and mutual loyalty . . . [and] may be intended to cause John's hearers to reflect on their own status within the movement. Are they beloved or are they betrayers?[39]

Notice, however, that while Peter doesn't betray Jesus to the authorities like Judas does, he still goes on to deny having any association with Jesus (18:17, 25–27), and shows by his act of violent resistance (18:10–11) that his understanding isn't all that different from the crowds (6:15).[40] This is the second way in which Peter functions as a paradigm for John's audience: what happens when someone fails a test of loyalty? Can they be readmitted to the group, and under what circumstances? This was a pressing question for the postapostolic fathers of the second and third centuries,[41] and given John's emphasis on opposition and loyalty throughout his Gospel, it's probably an issue for his audience as well.

Peter's act of disloyalty isn't swept under the carpet, but neither is it irredeemable. In the final chapter of the Gospel, Peter is introduced to Jesus all over again. Around a charcoal fire—also the scene of his denial—he's given the opportunity to pledge his loyalty again: three times, mirroring his three earlier denials and serving as a "painful reminder" of what he had done.[42] He's then commissioned for service, not only in shepherding Jesus' followers, but ultimately in martyrdom.

The inclusion of this story doesn't just provide closure to the story of Peter; it shows John's minority group that even someone who had gone on to pay the ultimate price for following Jesus could give in to the fear of persecution and be disloyal. Without disregarding the gravity of their apostasy, it encourages the community to offer a second chance.[43]

---

38. Keener, *The Gospel of John*, 698; Oropeza, *In the Footsteps of Judas and Other Defectors*, 183–84, 209–10.

39. Grene, *Cowardice, Betrayal and Discipleship*, 285–86.

40. Perkins, *Peter*, 99.

41. E.g., Shepherd of Hermas, *Vis.* 2.2.7–8; *Sim.* 9.26.307; Clement of Alexandria, *Stromateis* 2.13; Tertullian, *De Paenitentia*; Cyprian, *De Lapsi*.

42. Bennema, *Encountering Jesus*, 121.

43. Grene, *Cowardice, Betrayal and Discipleship*, 290, sees this as a feature of Mark's

For churches suffering severe persecution, readmitting those who've succumbed to outside pressure by defection or betrayal will often involve costly forgiveness—something Jesus nevertheless calls his followers to do in imitation of him. However, for most Western churches the opposite lesson may need to be drawn, as our temptation can be to take acts of disloyalty too lightly. Forgiveness and reconciliation is still the goal, but those who've chosen, for a time, to deny association with Jesus need to be confronted with the significance of their actions (just like Peter was) in the process of being gently and pastorally restored. Ironically, the less severe the consequences are for denying Jesus, the more casual we can be in doing so.

## Jesus

To cover all the ways in which Jesus is prototypical for John's minority group would again take many books; he is *the* prototype for the group, after all. So we'll simply draw attention to two well-known and important ways in which Jesus functions in relation to John's minority audience.

The first is in chapter 10, where Jesus calls himself the "gate" for the sheep (10:7), and the "good shepherd" (10:11) who lays down his life for the sheep (10:14). The imagery in this passage paints the Pharisees, with whom John's audience would associate synagogue Judaism, as "thieves and robbers" (10:1, 8), or at best, "hired hands" who don't care for the sheep (10:12–13). Jesus' followers are right not to listen to them (10:5), because they have a different court of reputation.

Jesus, on the other hand, is the gate who controls access to the sheep pen—that is, membership of his flock (10:9), which significantly for the Gospel audience includes more than just Jewish sheep (10:16).[44] Belonging to the people of God—thereby gaining access to the gift of life given by God—is only through following Jesus, and doesn't come through the synagogue. Trying to retain membership of the majority culture has no eternal benefit.

More than that, Jesus is the good shepherd who knows his sheep by name and gives up his own life for the sheep (10:3, 14). This is in direct contrast with the "bad shepherds" of Israel who were in it for their own gain and didn't care for the sheep (cf. Ezek 34:1–10; Zech 11:17). It's this kind of self-sacrificial love which is to be prototypical for Jesus' followers, and of which Jesus is explicitly the example to be imitated:

---

portrait of Peter's restoration; I see no reason to reject its functioning in a similar way in John's Gospel.

44. Witherington, *John's Wisdom*, 189.

> "I am the good shepherd. The good shepherd lays down his life for the sheep." (10:11)

> "My command is this: Love each other as I have loved you. Greater love has no one than this: to lay down one's life for one's friends." (15:12–13)

The second way in which Jesus functions for John's audience is strongly connected with the first: Jesus' unity with the Father is to be the paradigm for the unity of his followers. This is a key theme of his "high priestly prayer" in chapter 17:

> "My prayer is not for them alone. I pray also for those who will believe in me through their message, that all of them may be one, just as you, Father, are in me and I am in you, may they also be in us so that the world may believe that you have sent me. I have given them the glory that you gave me, that they may be one as we are one—I in them and you in me—so that they may be brought to complete unity." (17:20–23)

John's minority group is addressed almost directly here, with two important and complementary ideas: the unity that exists within the Godhead is to be reflected in the unity of believers *both* with Father and Son *and* with one another.[45] Unity within the group can't be achieved without the group also being united with Jesus and his Father, precluding a forced unity with those not truly united with Jesus. Yet unity with God must be reflected in intra-group unity, ruling out a sectarian attitude towards other believers.[46] This will be the defining characteristic and visible testimony—the attractive difference—of the Jesus-following minority. In a first-century world characterized by rivalry and disunity,[47] the group should stand out in how it exhibits mutual love and unity.

---

45. There's debate about the punctuation of verse 21: is there a period after "I am in you" (so NIV) so that the unity of believers is to be *just as* the Father mutually indwells the Son? Or is there a period after "that all of them may be one" (so NRSV) making the mutual indwelling of Father and Son *just as* the indwelling of believers in the Godhead? The former idea (unity with fellow believers) is clearly stated in subsequent verses, so I lean toward the latter (unity with Father and Son), especially because the same preposition (*en*) is used in both clauses. In the text provide I have used commas, following UBS5/ESV, leaving it ambiguous.

46. Witherington, *John's Wisdom*, 270–71, notes that this would have been pertinent for the Johannine community given the disunity and defections evident in the epistles, especially 2 John.

47. Keener, *The Gospel of John*, 1061–62, describes the factious landscape of the first-century Mediterranean world in terms that ought not to be unfamiliar to our own.

It's the understatement of the millennium to say that we haven't done particularly well with this. While there are undoubtedly many examples of individual faith communities which are loving and united—and many examples which are the opposite, or somewhere in between—it's mostly at the macro level that the wider world assesses us. And the assessment, by any measure, would not be good. To some extent we're deserving of the contempt we often receive because of this.

Now it's beyond the scope of this (or any) book to try to solve this discrepancy between group ideals and group practice—most obviously because such a unity can't come about by human effort but flows from unity with God. But a couple of application suggestions are in order, that might help each of us contribute to our attractive difference.

Firstly, no one person or group can "fix" the entire Christian world, but we can contribute to creating a loving, united community where God has placed us. While the "world" as a collective may look the vast array of denominations and religious wars and condemn us for our disunity, individual members of that world will see individual believers in their local faith communities and also make judgments on that basis. If even just one home bible study group, or one small church, shows unity and a selfless love for one another and their neighborhood, individuals can see and be impacted as Jesus intended (13:35; 17:23). The power of one encounter with one or a few representatives of a group can't be underestimated as a means of changing outsider perception of the group as a whole.

Secondly, we can choose not to contribute to the culture of critique and tribalism that's been adopted from the world (similar to the issues in the Corinthian church) and amplified by social media. While we might be on our best behavior when debating with outsiders—remembering Peter's instruction to do so with "gentleness and respect"—we can often let our guard down when debating internally. Under the guise of "tough love," "being a prophetic voice," or "calling out" behavior we deem to be at odds with group norms, we can allow our in-house arguments to become something far from gentle and respectful. And if that's done on social media, those disagreements aren't entirely in-house. Here are two examples of how this can quickly undo our witness.

Recently, I went down the rabbit hole of the comments section on a Facebook advertisement for automated synthesizer "pad" sounds for Christian worship music. It quickly devolved into a heated and not very charitable argument between—as far as I could tell—people who were pro automated synths in church and people who were against. Then others started to weigh in with their quite justifiable observations that this is exactly why they left or never joined the church, if Christians can fight with one another about *that* sort of thing!

It pales into insignificance, however, when compared with the heated argument a few years ago played out publicly (yet mercifully deep in the comments section) of a Christian website about whether the band at a Christian conference ought to have included the omitted final verse of *Amazing Grace* (the one that starts "When we've been there ten thousand years . . ."), whether the rebel audience members at the conference were right in singing it *a cappella* in protest anyway, and whether those who "shushed" them were right to respond to the rebel uprising in the way they did. Not our finest hour.

Of course, this isn't to say that Christians shouldn't ever disagree. But it should give us pause to think about *how* we disagree, as well as the sorts of things it's worth disagreeing about. And let's face it, whether on social media or in person, like me, we've all had some times where we know we've spoken without gentleness and respect towards each other, and probably countless others where we haven't realized it. This shouldn't be a finger-pointing exercise, except that we point the finger right back at ourselves. Because until I hold myself accountable for what I say online—taking the chat log out of my own eye—I can't see clearly to influence others.

In public spaces like social media, no matter what the context, if we're a Christian then we're always representing Jesus and our often maligned minority group. Let's speak to one another like the world is always listening to us—all the while knowing that whether it's listening or not shouldn't make a difference. It's both what Jesus commanded us to do, and the example he laid down for us.[48]

---

48. See the appeal for the church to inhabit a space "beyond enemies" laid out in Fitch, *The Church of Us vs. Them.*

# 14

## Luke–Acts
### *Most Excellent Theophilus*

A SCIENTIST FRIEND SHARES with me her fear that being open about her Christian faith will harm her career as an academic. A friend in the military recounts the journey of how he's tried to reconcile his allegiance to Jesus with his allegiance to commander and country. A prospective politician despairs of the seemingly inevitable compromises to his values that would come with joining a mainstream party. They're all wrestling with the same basic question: with such a vast difference in worldviews, is it possible for a member of a marginalized minority to hold with integrity that kind of position—or indeed *any* position—in the wider society?

So far in our survey of the minority group rhetoric of the New Testament, the recurring theme has been one of attractive difference. For the most part, the initial emphasis has been on the *difference*, drawing clear boundaries in terms of belief and behavior. The purpose of these boundaries is so that the group might continue in its role of living out the values of Jesus' kingdom, rather than assimilating to the majority culture. This is understandable, since the cultural pressure on such a minority would otherwise ensure that movement toward assimilation is the default.[1] The secondary (but equally significant) thrust has been to make these boundaries *transparent*, so that outsiders can see the attractiveness of that difference, and *permeable*, so that barriers to joining the group are minimized.

While the minority group rhetoric of Luke–Acts still contains both of these elements, its distinctive contribution is to this issue of *permeability*. It doesn't shrink from demanding total allegiance (Luke 14:26–27; 17:33;

---

1. As we've seen in the previous two chapters on Matthew and John, this emphasis becomes more appropriate in situations of significant persecution and social ostracism; although persecution and rejection still loom in the background, Acts tends to highlight where faith in Jesus was gaining both acceptance and toleration.

18:22), but shows that this doesn't have to be incompatible with participation in the wider society. In the absence of thoroughgoing persecution, loyal believers can occupy a social position which allows a foot to be placed either side of the group's boundary lines. In this way they can act as a mitigating influence against an insular sectarianism, and provide an entry point to the group. Acts, in particular, speaks to the role members of this minority can have in the majority culture.[2]

## Luke's audience

Luke-Acts is explicitly addressed to a man named Theophilus (Luke 1:3; Acts 1:1). This was a common enough practice for history writers in antiquity: to acknowledge their patron, who may well have commissioned the work, paying for their general upkeep, writing supplies, and travel expenses, and perhaps even furnishing them with introductions to others in their social network.[3] The intended audience, then, is clearly not limited to this one individual. However, the fact that Theophilus was a person of significant status—evidenced by the use of the honorific, *kratiste* ("most excellent")[4]—does give us some idea of the kind of reader for whom Luke was consciously shaping his material.

For a start, he would have been well-educated, which we see borne out in how Luke uses the conventions of Greek rhetoric and historiography.[5] Further, Luke writes as though Theophilus was well-acquainted with the Greek translation of the Hebrew Scriptures; not only does he assume it to be authoritative, he makes frequent allusions to it, crafts implicit parallels with it,[6] and even imitates its language and writing style. This suggests

---

2. The emphasis of this chapter will be weighted toward Acts, both because we've already looked at two Gospels, and because the more distinctive material relating to believers as a minority is found in Luke's second volume.

3. On patronage of historical and scientific works in antiquity, see Alexander, *The Preface to Luke's Gospel*, 190-200. The suggestion that Luke is addressing a generic reader, since the name "Theophilus" means "one who loves God" (e.g., Johnson and Harrington, *The Gospel of Luke*, 28), neglects this convention of dedicating works to patrons or other important persons. It could, however, be an alias, if naming him would put him at risk (Garland, *Luke*, 56).

4. Witherington, *Acts*, 64. Further evidence, discussed below, is found in how Luke frequently highlights where those of high status respond favorably to the gospel (e.g., Acts 13:7, 12; 17:4, 11-12), as well as the Gospel's obvious emphasis on God's concern for the poor and the obligation of the rich to be generous.

5. Witherington, *Acts*, 65.

6. For example, the story of Ananias and Sapphira in Acts 5 has parallels with that of Achan in Joshua 7.

Theophilus may have already been a synagogue adherent, although probably not to the point of becoming a full proselyte, given his social status.[7] That is, he was someone already familiar with having a foot in two worlds. Finally, the explicit purpose Luke gives for writing (Luke 1:4) suggests that Theophilus was a relatively recent convert who may have needed some reassurance about the legitimacy of the message he has received.[8]

While this sketch of Theophilus may or may not reflect the full range of Luke's intended audience,[9] it suggests that Luke had in mind, at least some of the time, a Gentile reader who was an upper class, educated synagogue adherent who had recently embraced the message of Jesus as Messiah.[10] Such a person had a lot to lose in terms of status, compared with poorer converts, and by aligning himself with the Jesus-following minority group he was putting that at risk. The reassurance he needed would have involved answers to questions such as these:

- **Rational basis:** Are there other educated people like me who have become followers of Jesus? In other words, is there a rational basis for belief in Jesus, or is this just another passing fad among the lower classes?

- **Ancient heritage:** If the message of Jesus is indeed the answer to the Jewish hope, and the church its faithful remnant, why have so many Jews rejected it?[11] Can Christianity truly claim to be the fulfilment of an ancient religion, or is it a novelty?[12]

- **Perceived threat:** If our minority group is being persecuted and viewed as subversive by the Roman Empire, can it still be considered honorable? Does it have a legitimate place in the empire or is it a threat to social stability?[13] And on a related note, can I remain in my position of status as a citizen of that empire while also being a loyal follower of Jesus?

---

7. Witherington, *Acts*, 64.

8. *Acts*, 63.

9. Scholarship is divided over whether Luke was writing for a Gentile audience, a mixed audience, or possibly even a Jewish minority within a largely Gentile setting. See Esler, *Community and Gospel in Luke-Acts*, 31.

10. For similar conclusions, see Creamer, *God as Creator in Acts 17:24*, 18–25.

11. Witherington, *Acts*, 74.

12. Aune, *Literary Environment*, 137, notes the prevailing sentiment that "no religious movement or philosophical sect could be credible unless it was rooted in antiquity."

13. Witherington, *Acts*, 74.

These questions all relate to the *legitimacy* of the minority group to which Theophilus now belonged:[14] whether it had a rational basis, could boast a venerable heritage, and posed no direct threat to civic authorities. Among many other concerns (which are less connected with the group's minority status), Luke's narrative seeks to address each of these questions. And so will we.

## Rational basis

In the first instance, a reader like Theophilus would have wanted assurance that there was a rational basis for the claims of the minority group he has recently joined.[15] This was a particular concern of the educated classes for at least two reasons. Firstly, rational thought—reason—was the superior form of motivation for Plato and the influential schools of Greek philosophy which followed him; it belonged to the abstract rather than the material realm, which was the (inferior) domain of emotions and desires. For an educated person in the ancient world, any belief system needed to make *rational* sense.[16] Secondly, the adoption of new religions, particularly from the East, was more prevalent among the lower classes, who were seen by the educated as being more open to "superstitions."[17] They tended to be cults that had a personal and supernatural element—as opposed to the rituals and festivals of the civic religions—characterized by initiations into mysteries and ecstatic experiences. Since Christianity had initial success among the lower classes, initiated converts through baptism into the name of a divine being, and experienced supernatural phenomena such as prophecy and speaking in tongues, there was a very real danger that it would be viewed by the educated as just another cult for superstitious peasants. It's against this background that Luke writes his "carefully investigated" and "orderly account," informed by eyewitness testimony, so that Theophilus "may know the certainty" of what he had already been taught (Luke 1:1-4). This goes beyond simply proving that certain events

---

14. Esler, *Community and Gospel in Luke–Acts*, 16.

15. The inclusion of Theophilus in the phrase "fulfilled among *us*" (Luke 1:1), among other things, marks him out as already being a member of the group. This isn't primarily an apologetic for outsiders (although it could be used that way) but a reassurance for (recent) insiders. See Witherington, *Acts*, 63.

16. The Stoic philosopher, Seneca, advocates "doing nothing without the approval of reason" (*Epistulae morales* 84.11), because "reason is not a slave to the senses, but a ruler over them" (*Epistulae morales* 66.32).

17. See Turcan, *The Cults of the Roman Empire*, 10–18. The religions were often brought by returning soldiers and sailors, who didn't belong to the educated élite.

occurred, also arguing that the Christian interpretation of the significance of those events is the correct one.[18]

Luke lays out the evidence throughout his two volumes, beginning with accounts of angelic announcements and confirming prophecies, before recounting the miraculous deeds and inspiring words of Jesus. The most crucial evidence is, of course, that of Jesus' resurrection. He details several post-resurrection appearances (Acts 1:3), including a post-ascension appearance to Saul (Acts 9:1–19). Significantly, the resurrection is the single common element in all of the evangelistic speeches in Acts,[19] and is usually presented as the linchpin of the argument (e.g., Acts 2:32; 3:15; 7:56; 17:31; 26:23). Luke then chronicles the spread of the gospel throughout the known world, before concluding with the triumphant paradox of Paul freely proclaiming the message of the kingdom to the Gentiles while under house arrest at the heart of the Empire (28:28–31). In other words, the entirety of Luke–Acts *is* a rational defense of the beliefs and practices of the Christian minority which Theophilus has joined.

Perhaps less obvious, but equally pertinent to a reader like Theophilus, is a significant thread which runs through Acts. Numerous times, Luke appears to be highlighting instances in which a rational case is made for the apostles' message, with educated people responding to it favorably:

- On Cyprus, the proconsul is introduced as "an intelligent man" who summoned Barnabas and Saul "because he wanted to hear the word of God"(13:7). A Jewish sorcerer who attempted to dissuade the proconsul was sent blind by Paul. Although it was seeing the evidence of God's power at work that caused the proconsul to believe, Luke is careful to add the supporting reason, "for he was amazed *at the teaching* about the Lord" (13:12). An intelligent person of high status is persuaded by signs of power and rational explanation; *take note, Theophilus!*

- In the synagogue in Thessalonica, Paul is described by Luke as "reasoning" (*dialegomai*) with them from the Scriptures, "explaining" (*dianoigō*) and "proving" (*paratithēmi*) that the Messiah had to suffer (17:2–3).[20] The Greek words used belong to the technical vocabulary of logical and rhetorical argument. As a result, some were "persuaded" (*peithō*), which is the desired outcome of rhetorical proof,[21] and this

---

18. Green, "Internal Repetition in Luke–Acts," 288.
19. Clifford and Johnson, *The Cross Is Not Enough*, 20–21.
20. Kemmler, *Faith and Human Reason*, 35–39.
21. Witherington, *Acts*, 505, argues that Paul is depicted as "engaging in an act of persuasion or rhetoric in the synagogue," and suggests that 17:2–3 forms a rhetorical syllogism (*enthymeme*) which epitomizes the logic of his argument.

included Jews, "many" Greeks, and "quite a few prominent women." However, Paul did experience opposition: because they were "jealous" (an emotional, not a rational motive), some Jews rounded up the day laborers who were loitering in the agora and formed a mob in order to lynch Paul and Silas (17:5). Educated people were being persuaded by rational argument, whereas opposition came from an ignorant mob incited by jealous rivals; *does that reassure you, Theophilus?*

- Having been driven out of Thessalonica, Paul arrived in Berea. Although he followed the same approach, the Berean Jews were more receptive, eagerly receiving Paul's message and then critically "examining" (*anakrinō*) the Scriptures "every day" to evaluate its truthfulness; Luke comments that this is evidence of their "more noble character" than those in Thessalonica (17:11). The result is that "many" of the Jews believed, as well as a number of "prominent Greek women," along with "many" Greek men (17:12). Again, we have an emphasis not only on the high social status of some of those who were persuaded, but also that they were women.[22] If there's more to this than Luke's theme of recording the role of women in the story of the church, it may hint that Theophilus's wife was converted first, in an era in which household members were expected to follow the religion of the male head;[23] *it's OK, Theophilus, you're not the only man this has happened to!*

- Later in Acts, in his appearance before Festus and Agrippa, Paul mounted a legal defense (*apologia*), motioning with his hand the way an orator would begin such a speech (26:1–2). At the end, he responded to Festus's accusation of insanity by asserting that what he was saying was "true and *reasonable*" (26:25). He appealed to Agrippa, who Paul says was "familiar with these things," significantly adding the reason that "it was not done in a corner" (26:26). Agrippa then responded in an enigmatic fashion, "Do you think that in such a short time you can *persuade* me to be a Christian?" (26:28), implicitly acknowledging that Paul had been engaging in a rational argument. While neither Festus nor Agrippa was completely persuaded about the truth of the Gospel, they agreed that Paul was innocent of the charges (26:31–32). Even a high-ranking Gentile (*such as yourself, Theophilus*) evaluates Paul's

---

22. It was possible a little easier for a high status, unmarried female to become a member of the Jesus-following minority since she would have been under less public scrutiny than a high status male. Only females of high status would have had both the education and free time to be able to engage with the rational arguments given by Paul.

23. We're in the realm of speculation here. But interesting speculation, nonetheless!

rational defense not unfavorably; what's more, the events in question were done publicly and are thus open to rational proof or refutation.

- In the final chapter, Paul is in Rome, again trying to "persuade" (*peithō*) the Jews about Jesus, convincing some but not others (28:23–24). Luke depicts this rejection by some as a fulfilment of Isaiah's prophecy about their hardened hearts (28:26–27), which then opens the way for Gentiles (*like you, Theophilus*) to receive the message, which is being met with a more favorable response (28:28).

This theme is pervasive and, Luke hopes, persuasive to Theophilus and others like him. The Christian minority of which he is a part has a rational basis. Educated people throughout the Empire are embracing it, too.

## Reassuring Theophilus today

Atheists have long mocked our belief in an "invisible sky god" as being a relic of a premodern worldview which is now incompatible with the scientific rationalism of our age. But in recent times, attacks have increased in frequency and intensity as the focus has shifted onto the *outworking* of this belief in what are perceived to be primitive and regressive views on gender and sexuality. In the West, both the basis and practices of traditional Christian belief are being dismissed and ridiculed more than ever before. Our churches are full of Theophiloi[24]—educated, articulate believers—who need to be similarly reassured that there is a rational basis for that belief.[25] Our preaching of Acts, then, ought to draw out this theme of how the gospel message not only withstands but even *invites* rational scrutiny.

Without in any way detracting from Luke's emphasis on the kingdom being good news for the poor and downtrodden (which should, of course, be an integral part of our attractive difference), we can follow Luke's lead in highlighting where the message of Jesus is being accepted and defended by some of the finest minds in the world. I think if Luke were writing the story of the church today, he'd casually mention the likes of literary giant C. S. Lewis and how he was persuaded, against his will, of the historical evidence for belief in Jesus;[26] or John Lennox, professor of mathematics at

---

24. I've gone with the Greek plural, since Theophili preferences Latin for no good reason and Theophiluses sounds silly.

25. The perception that Christianity was "anti-science," "anti-intellectual," and gave "simplistic" answers was one of six major factors in young people abandoning their faith, according to Kinnaman and Hawkins, *You Lost Me*.

26. Lewis and Hooper, *The Collected Letters of C.S. Lewis*, 1, 976–77; Lewis, "Myth Became Fact," 63–67.

Oxford University, who argues for the rational basis for God's existence;[27] or even noted atheist Antony Flew, who late in life was persuaded to reverse his opposition to the existence of an intelligent creator, without embracing the Christian God of the Bible[28] (as a kind of Festus/Agrippa character). In line with our principle of social validation from chapter 2,[29] Luke would want to remind us today: *there are still plenty of smart, educated people who believe in God for rational reasons, and have been persuaded by the historical evidence. You can be a Christian and a scientist—or historian, or philosopher, or academic—these things are in no way incompatible!*

As was the case with Theophilus, this isn't simply an apologetic for external use; it's needed *within* our minority group as a means of insulating members from the relentless ridicule that comes from sections of the majority culture. It's particularly important for how churches prepare their teenagers to be confident in their faith in an increasingly antagonistic world; this is especially the case for those educated in faith-based schools who are sometimes more susceptible to the sudden shock of entering tertiary education or workplace environments. Millennials also tend to have weaker ties to faith communities, making it easier for them to leave when they experience doubt, rather than work through it with the help of others.[30] Hopefully this is stating the obvious: we need to encourage our younger believers to look into the historical evidence and rational basis for faith in Jesus, without prejudging the outcome. We need to equip them with answers that aren't naïve or simplistic, even if some of them might make us a bit uncomfortable. And we need to model for them a robust faith that welcomes genuine questioning from the "noble Bereans" of our own day, rather than running in fear from rational debate.

## Ancient heritage

As well as presenting the rational basis for group membership, Luke seeks to legitimize the group by presenting it as the true form of an ancient religion. This is for two main reasons. Firstly, in the Greco-Roman world, novelty was treated with suspicion and greater credence was given to religions with a long history.[31] Esler notes that this is a general tendency for pre-industrial

---

27. E.g., Lennox, *God and Stephen Hawking: Whose Design Is It Anyway?*
28. See Flew and Varghese, *There Is a God*. Note that the book's co-author included a chapter on the evidence for Jesus' resurrection, which Flew did not endorse.
29. See above, pages 31–32.
30. https://www.barna.com/research/two-thirds-christians-face-doubt/
31. For a summary of the evidence that this was Rome's attitude toward the antiquity

societies; they valued the old and traditional, which meant that any new movements would seek to depict themselves as "reassertions of pristine beliefs and practices long dormant."[32] This is one significant motivating factor in Luke's portrayal of the Christian story as belonging to the much older story of the Jewish religion. Although its monotheistic belief set it apart from the surrounding polytheism, its long history meant that it received some level of respect in the Gentile world. In effect, Luke is sending the message, "Christianity is not Judaism, but you may respect it for much the same reasons as you do Judaism."[33]

The second reason Luke stresses continuity with Judaism is more complex, and results from the fraught relationship between the church and synagogue. If Luke's minority group was correct in claiming that it was the fulfilment of the Jewish hope, there needed to be an explanation for why so many Jews had rejected it—not to mention why group members were being persecuted by and excluded from the synagogue, something which may have been part of Theophilus's own experience. At the heart of the issue is the question of authoritative interpretation: "Who interprets the Scriptures faithfully? . . . Whose interpretation . . . receives divine legitimation?"[34]

This is a persistent theme throughout the Gospel, the opening scene of which is pointedly set in the temple, consisting of an angelic announcement to a priest that the next chapter of Israel's history was set to unfold. Luke frames Jesus' entire ministry as the fulfilment of Jewish expectations from the book of Isaiah (4:16–21), and his Gospel concludes with the claim that Jesus' death and resurrection were both the fulfilment of the Hebrew Scriptures (24:27, 44–47) and the validation of Jesus' *interpretation* of them (24:6–8).

Acts continues this theme. This is seen most obviously in key speeches which interpret the Scriptures in light of Jesus and claim validation of that interpretation in his resurrection (e.g., 2:22–24; 3:15; 26:23). We also see it in the motif of conflict with the temple authorities which dominates the first third of the book. In this conflict, the Jewish leadership tries to assert its traditional authority as God's mouthpiece (4:18; 5:40) but is repeatedly thwarted by the power of God, which is decidedly on the side of the Jesus-following minority. This is manifest in numerous healings (3:6–10; 5:12–16),

---

of a religion see Esler, *Community and Gospel in Luke-Acts*, 214–16. Esler also provides evidence that Luke was keen to avoid the charge of novelty, pointing to his redaction of Mark 1:27 which removes the reference to newness: "What is this? A new teaching . . ." becomes "What is this word . . . ?" (Luke 4:36).

32. *Community and Gospel in Luke-Acts*, 20.
33. *Community and Gospel in Luke-Acts*, 214.
34. Green, *Luke*, 23.

boldness in speech despite their lack of education (4:8), earthquakes in response to prayer (4:31), and automatic doors (5:19). At that point, Gamaliel wisely counsels the leadership to stop trying to suppress the message:

> "For if their purpose or activity is of human origin, it will fail.
> But if it is from God, you will not be able to stop these men; you
> will only find yourselves fighting against God." (5:38–39)

The unchecked spread of the Gospel which follows in Luke's narrative thus becomes, in itself, another proof that the church's interpretation of Scripture is the one which has the authority and approval of God. The message is: *God now speaks through us, not through the Jewish leadership; the success of our message shows that he's on our side.*

Luke's presentation of Jesus as the fulfilment of the Jewish hope also provides a theological foundation for full acceptance of Jews who *were* in his minority group, despite ongoing hostility from the synagogue[35] (#notalljews). This lies behind much of Luke's careful portrayal of the Jesus movement as being in continuity with Israel's prophets in two important ways: they're both the legitimate bearers of God's word, *and* consistently rejected by a "stiff-necked people" who always oppose God's purposes (Acts 7:51–53).

For examples of this, we again need only to look at the opening of his Gospel, which emphasizes the devoutness of the Jewish characters in the narrative: Jesus' parents are described as diligently following Jewish customs regarding circumcision and purification offerings (1:21–24), which leads to Jesus being prayed for by two faithful, elderly Jews who had been "waiting for the consolation of Israel" (2:25) and the "redemption of Jerusalem" (2:38).[36] By contrast, those who oppose and subsequently arrest Jesus are described as having dishonorable motives (e.g., 20:19–20; 22:2; 23:2)—a theme which continues throughout Acts as they oppose the apostles (e.g., 4:16; 7:54; 17:5). The implicit message is: *devout Jews who've been waiting on God's rescue are with us, but those who oppose us are simply afraid of losing their power and position.*

Finally, Luke also addresses the question of the increasingly Gentile make-up of the church. The conversion of Cornelius and other Gentiles (*are you still with me, Theophilus?*) is legitimized both by the power of God seen in the manifestation of the Spirit (Acts 11:15–18) and the Jerusalem

---

35. Esler, *Community and Gospel in Luke–Acts*, 67.

36. *Community and Gospel in Luke–Acts*, 19. We see this echoed in the presentation of Paul as one who was zealous for the ancestral traditions (22:3; 24:14; 28:17), even participating in a purification ritual in order to show that he is not opposed to continuing Jewish customs (21:20–26); see *Community and Gospel in Luke–Acts*, 68.

Council's interpretation of Scripture (15:15–18, citing Amos 9:11–12). By contrast, the resistance of Jews to the message is presented in Luke's final scene as a fulfilment of Isaiah's prophecy about hardened hearts (Acts 28:25–28, citing Isaiah 6:9–10). In other words: *the ingathering of the Gentiles was part of God's plan all along.*

## An ancient religion today

At face value, this aspect of Luke's minority group rhetoric isn't directly applicable to Gentile believers in the Western church today, unless we happen to have strong ties with local Jewish communities. For the most part, while the relationship between church and synagogue might be important theologically, it has little day-to-day impact. Even Luke's more universal appeal to Christianity's long heritage seems less relevant in a culture which increasingly sees ancient belief systems variously as superstitious, unscientific, patriarchal, regressive, and oppressive.

However, Christianity's ancient origins may still have something of a countercultural attraction for a mobile and individualistic society in which people can experience intense loneliness, isolation, and disconnection from a sense of place. Historiography, such as we find in Luke, has been shown to have a role in the forming of a collective identity,[37] connecting us "with a peculiar form of temporal continuity . . . which runs from predecessors to successors,"[38] and allowing our "sense of self to be projected (potentially infinitely) across time."[39] Luke's insistence in grounding the story of his marginalized minority within a much bigger story encourages us to find connection not only in our present community, but also in sharing a storied past and a common, cosmos-encompassing future.[40] It reminds us, too, of the value of rituals, liturgies, and songs that—when used thoughtfully—can connect us with this multi-generational story in a way that's attractively different to a disconnected world.

Additionally, we echo here Tom Wright's call for us to tell Israel's story when announcing the good news about Jesus. The death and resurrection of Jesus on behalf of his people only makes *complete* sense when set within the much longer story of God and his people throughout history. When that framing is omitted, the *good news* of what happened in history risks being truncated into an abstraction which consists merely of *good advice* on how

37. Condor, "Social Identity and Time," 305.
38. Carr, *Time, Narrative, and History*, 113.
39. Condor, "Social Identity and Time," 306.
40. Esler, *Community and Gospel in Luke–Acts*, 19.

to be right with God, the sacrifice of Jesus risks being reduced to a pagan caricature of itself, and our future hope risks becoming the rescue of our soul rather than transformed bodies in a renewed heaven and earth.[41] This not only impacts the theology of our minority group, but the way in which it interacts with the wider world.

Finally, our marginalized minority still needs to answer the same question Luke addresses in Acts: *who speaks for God today?* Out of all of the belief systems in our world, what backs up our claim to exclusive truth that "there is no other name under heaven given to mankind by which we must be saved" (Acts 4:12)? As well as the rational proofs concerning the resurrection (discussed in the previous section), Luke's chronicling the story of the unstoppable gospel backed up by displays of supernatural power provides further evidence of divine approval.

## Perceived threat

The third way in which Luke seeks to legitimize his minority group is in response to the perception that it was a threat to the social order. As we noted in chapter 1, the refusal of Christians to participate in civic religion was seen as an act of subversion, putting at risk both the favor of the gods and the Roman peace. The fact that Rome had, at various times and for various reasons, persecuted Christians validated this perception.[42] Group members like Theophilus needed reassurance that they could retain their position in Roman society while being faithful members of the Jesus-following minority—at least while Rome maintained its present, mostly neutral stance toward it. In fact, Luke provides material suitable not only to reassure group members, but to argue for its toleration by civic authorities.

Firstly, Luke includes stories of Roman administrators and military officers showing a favorable attitude towards Paul and his gospel, despite not becoming believers themselves. This includes some of the officials in Ephesus who tried to protect Paul (Acts 19:31); the Roman tribune, Lysias,

---

41. For the simplest presentation of his argument, see Wright, *Simply Good News*. Having said this, I think that Wright often overplays the prevalence of the caricature, at least from my own experience in evangelical churches. Further, this isn't an argument that Israel's story *must be told* in each and every Gospel proclamation; simply that the substance of our proclamation needs to be shaped by our knowledge of the bigger story, which then ought to be told at some point early in the process of making disciples.

42. Luke is writing prior to the empire-wide persecution under the likes of e.g., Domitian and Diocletian, evidenced by his generally positive stance toward it; compare this with the anti-empire rhetoric of Revelation, most likely dated during the persecution of Domitian.

and an unnamed centurion who acted similarly in Jerusalem (21:32, 40; 22:30; 23:10; 12–35); as well as Julius, the centurion who guarded Paul while traveling to Rome, allowing him to have visitors (27:3) and saving him from being thrown overboard (27:42–43).[43]

Secondly, Luke provides examples of Romans who became believers themselves. The centurion in Capernaum is acknowledged as having "great faith" in Jesus (Luke 7:9); only in Luke's account is he described as a patron of the Jews who built their synagogue (7:5), making his inclusion quite pertinent to the former Gentile synagogue adherents in his audience. We can add to this the centurion who, having witnessed Jesus' death, "praised God" and affirmed Jesus as a "righteous man" (23:47); the proconsul, Sergius Paulus, who believed Paul's message (Acts 13:12); and most notably, a centurion named Cornelius, whose conversion becomes the gateway episode for the inclusion of the Gentiles (Acts 10–11).[44]

Thirdly, a constant theme in Luke's narrative is how Gentile courts consistently find Jesus and his followers to be no threat to Rome. Before Pilate, the three accusations that might interest Rome—subverting the nation, opposing the payment of taxes to Caesar, and claiming to be a rival king (Luke 23:2)—are portrayed as false; three times Pilate proclaimed Jesus' innocence (23:4, 14, 22) and only agreed to execute him because of pressure from the Jewish leadership. In Acts, when the Jews brought Paul and Silas before the city officials of Thessalonica accusing him of defying Caesar by proclaiming another king (Acts 17:7), the officials' response was merely to let them post bail and leave (17:9). In Corinth, the proconsul, Gallio, dismissed charges brought against Paul by the Jews as being an internal matter: nothing that needed to concern Rome (18:14–17). In the multiple trial narratives of Acts 23–26, Paul defended himself before three officials, and each time no-one could find him guilty of breaking Roman law (23:29; 25:18–25; 26:32). The only reasons for Paul's continued imprisonment were corruption (Felix hoped for a bribe [24:6]), and the Roman officials' desire to keep favor with the Jews (24:27; 25:9).[45] At no point had any Roman court found the Christian movement to be in breach of Roman law, declaring them innocent every time.

Fourthly, Paul's own actions show him to be a model citizen. In Philippi, he stayed in jail despite having the opportunity to escape (16:28). His conduct

---

43. Esler, *Community and Gospel in Luke–Acts*, 202.

44. *Community and Gospel in Luke–Acts*, 202. Esler also points out how Jesus refers to Naaman the Syrian, in Luke 4:27, who provides precedent for someone who continues to occupy an important rank in a Gentile society while also following the one true God (218).

45. *Community and Gospel in Luke–Acts*, 203–4.

during the shipwreck (Acts 27) was exemplary, at each point working for the common good by warning of danger, promising rescue at God's hand, preventing the crew from abandoning ship, caring for all on board, and preparing the ship to run aground. The safe arrival of everyone on Malta confirmed that God's hand was with him, further evidenced by his survival of a snake-bite, and how he was able to heal the Roman official's father (28:1–10). Luke wants to affirm that members of his minority group can still be good citizens, exemplified by Paul's own conduct; indeed, God even used his Roman citizenship to further his gospel (27:24; 28:17–20, 30–31).[46]

In sum, Luke's concern is to "present Christian history in such a way as to demonstrate that faith in Jesus Christ and allegiance to Rome were not mutually inconsistent."[47] His minority group wasn't a destabilizing force which threatened the social order—or at least, not in the way Rome might have feared—but it was a responsible movement which had a positive impact on those who had come in contact with it. It might have challenged the values of the majority culture in the way it lived out its beliefs, but it wasn't planning a violent revolution.

## A threat to today's world

As noted in the introductory chapter, Christianity is increasingly seen as dangerous and subversive—a threat to the *Pax Tolerantia* because of its claims to exclusive truth and "regressive" teachings in areas such as sexuality and gender. More and more, the majority culture is seeking to curb our influence in secular spaces like schools and politics, citing the harm that could be done by allowing our allegedly intolerant views to be heard by the young and vulnerable. A modern day Theophilus might have similar questions to those of their first-century counterpart. Firstly, is traditional Christianity now a threat to social progress and harmony? (That is, has the present day critique called into question its legitimacy?) And secondly, in the current environment, is it possible to occupy a respected, influential position in the majority culture while being a loyal follower of Jesus?

For a start, we need to acknowledge that our previous position of privilege within society is coming to an end. Let's not lament that fact too loudly, as much of the time that position closer to the centers of power made us more amenable to compromise—often without realizing it. Further, people had grown to resent what they perceived as telling them what to do from our lofty position—and failing to live up to it ourselves, often in spectacular fashion.

---

46. Green, *Luke*, 73.
47. Esler, *Community and Gospel in Luke-Acts*, 204.

Far from enabling us to "Christianize" the world, it mostly secularized the church. So let's not cling on to that position, daring the world to pry it out of our cold, dead hands. Rather, let's embrace the new reality, which looks a lot like the old reality to which Luke writes in the book of Acts.

In the first instance, this involves acknowledging our errors of the past—especially where we *have* acted in ways that caused pain and damage—apologizing and, where possible, making amends. Some of the world's critique of us *is* perfectly legitimate; frequently, we haven't come across as the Paul-like model citizens to which we might aspire. As a result, the world has rightly become suspicious of our beliefs, if they produce the kind of behavior that's been exposed among us in recent times. The burden of proof now rests on the present generation of Jesus-followers to overturn that impression.

Secondly—both in logic *and* sequence—we can point out, with great humility, where the church has worked for the benefit of society as a whole, both now and throughout history. The kingdom "on earth as it is in heaven" has been glimpsed in our longstanding commitment to the common good, including the abolition of slavery, the provision of education and health care for all, and the eradication of poverty. (A good starting point is the documentary series, *For the Love of God: How the Church Is Better and Worse Than You Ever Imagined*, which models this dual approach.[48]) In doing so, we can also note the many committed believers who have occupied Theophilus-like positions in the wider world, such as bringing social change through politics (like William Wilberforce), and making advances in the fields of medicine (Alexander Fleming) and science (Isaac Newton). Christians can make outstanding world citizens!

On a smaller scale, we can work to ensure that the friendships, families, and marriages within our faith communities are a true reflection of Jesus' values, becoming in themselves a persuasive argument for the legitimacy of our minority group. Following Luke's lead, we can seek to legitimize Christianity as a movement that's not just on God's side, but on the side of humanity—declaring not only in words but in our actions that God is *for us*.

Yes, the church *is* a subversive minority group. But not in the way Rome thought it was, nor in the way our own world perceives it to be. Our subversion is not one of violent overthrow, but self-sacrifice. It doesn't grasp for power but radically submits to one another. And it doesn't legislate an agenda, but wins over outsiders by its attractive difference. That's the kind of minority group Luke's history seeks to shape, both in the first century and in our own.

---

48. This was released as a feature film and documentary series in 2018, produced by the Centre for Public Christianity, www.publicchristianity.org/fortheloveofgod/.

*Part 5*

# Final Words

# 15

## Wisdom from African-American Preachers
### *It's Gonna Be Hard for Y'all*

THIS CHAPTER HAS THE potential to be tokenistic and presumptuous, but it's necessary. It's necessary so that those of us who are white, Western Christians, don't fall into the trap of thinking that we've "rediscovered" the notion of being a marginalized minority for the sake of Christ; it's been going on for two millennia, and still today there are countless Christ-confessing minorities who suffer far more persecution that we even dare imagine. And it's also necessary so that we don't fall into the further trap of thinking that it's entirely up to us to "reinvent" how to survive as a marginalized minority, when we can draw upon the wisdom and experience of our brothers and sisters for whom this has long been their reality.

It could, however, be seen as tokenistic, as it comes near the end of the book and engages with only one such minority group. The reason for this is that our primary focus has been a hermeneutical one, seeking to learn from the rhetoric of the New Testament itself in how it formed and nurtured its original minority group audience. Learning from how other groups have done this in subsequent eras is the next logical task, and just as important. So important, in fact, that it's beyond the scope of both this book and this author. In a sense, this chapter is a call for those who possess the requisite experience to look more fully at how various Christian minorities have negotiated questions of identity and mission—and how they've used the models provided by the New Testament in the process.

It may also be seen as presumptuous or even colonial: an attempt by a white author to speak for a marginalized minority. This is especially the case when the minority in question is as storied and diverse as the African American church, about which much has already been written. So in this chapter I simply present the results of several conversations in which I asked some African American church leaders what advice they would give as we enter what is, for us, new and unfamiliar territory. One conversation was with a friend, Dr. Robert Smith Jr., who teaches preaching at Beeson Divinity School; and two were with new friends to whom he introduced me, Dr. Galen Jones, who lectures in Christian Ministry at Samford, and Dr. Reginald Calvert, pastor of the New Jerusalem Missionary Baptist Church in Bessemer, Alabama. What follows is my attempt to relate their wisdom as faithfully as I could.

It should also be stressed that this in no way equates the horrific experiences of African Americans over the past few hundred years with what are presently minor inconveniences felt by the Western church. Nor does it overlook the difference between being mistreated for following Jesus with being mistreated because of the color of one's skin (sometimes by those claiming to be followers of Jesus). But it recognizes that there is much we can learn from how they have used Scripture to shape their identity and strengthen their endurance in response to their marginalized status.

## Identification with God's people

In all three conversations, common themes emerged, beginning with a desire to affirm the common experience of all believers in the West today, regardless of ethnic background. We are facing the same problem of being opposed by an increasingly secular culture because of what we believe and teach. And that opposition isn't consistent: just as there are places in which Anglo churches still have power and acceptance, so there are situations in which the African American churches are "powerful and strong."[1] But when we *are* opposed, both groups can experience pain and distress[2]—something which has the potential to be an impetus toward unity and mutual understanding.

However, all three also agreed that marginalized minorities like the African American church can far more easily identify with the marginalized minorities in Scripture. There's no need of a book like this one when the connection is so intuitive and obvious! The preacher's task is much more straightforward because people of color have, as Jones put it, "a greater sense of emotional and experiential connection with the text." The hermeneutical

---

1. Calvert.

2. Jones noted that African American preachers have helped whites understand their pain; they can also help African Americans understand that "whites feel pain, too" in the struggles and traumas common to us all.

steps outlined in this book might still be *logically* necessary,³ but not always *homiletically*, as most of the time, congregations will perceive it themselves.

Calvert said that the African American church instinctively sees itself in Israel's story, as another generation of God's people being delivered from oppression. They, too, were an enslaved and exiled people who were sent a Moses-like deliverer (Dr. King) to lead them to freedom. Yet still they struggle to possess fully the promised inheritance, living in the land but under foreign rule, as it were. While individual texts might resonate with their experience, the primary connection is with the big story of the Exodus as it unfolds throughout Scripture.⁴ Smith saw this as vitally important to a sense of identity: having been ripped from their ancestral roots in Africa, they find their place in the much bigger story of God and his people.

Jones expanded this to include other marginalized minorities in the US today, including Native Americans. He also suggested that the economic refugees from South and Central America presently being vilified by the majority culture would have a "reading of the text and sense of life from the text [which is] probably much closer to that of the Jewish believers" than African Americans.

As well as identifying with Israel, African Americans also readily identify with the story of Jesus, both in the outcasts he welcomed as well as his own experience of rejection and suffering. Calvert said, "whenever you talk about the crucifixion of Jesus, African Americans can see their ancestors hanging from trees." They see themselves in Jesus' shoes, mistreated and falsely accused,⁵ and resonate with Jesus as the innocent sufferer, despised and rejected: "We find our identity at that place called Calvary ... We never figured out what we did wrong to deserve the type of rejection we've received as a people, and then we see Jesus ... [crucified for something] he didn't deserve to die for."⁶

And as we've seen in earlier chapters, by identifying with Jesus' innocent suffering, they also identify with the promise of resurrection and vindication. They celebrate, because of "what happened Sunday morning. If Friday was the end of the story, it would be devastating for the African American community. But it's because of the resurrection that we find our identity with that crucifixion."⁷

3. Calvert.
4. Jones.
5. Smith.
6. Calvert.
7. Calvert.

## Experiencing the text

Much African American preaching, then, is an encouragement to experience the text from within. Jones' observation is telling: "White evangelicals tend to operate more cerebrally in approaching the text. People of color, particularly African Americans, and people who have been oppressed approach the Scripture from an emotional standpoint, but that doesn't mean it's less intellectual." To some extent, this is similar to the distinction we see between the ways in which the ancient rhetoricians sought to evoke pathos; Aristotle would make a rational case that the audience ought to feel a particular emotion,[8] whereas later, Latin orators such as Cicero and Quintilian would try to produce the emotion in their hearers by the use of emotive language and by exhibiting that emotion as they spoke.[9] The New Testament writers show evidence of both approaches; Paul, in particular, more frequently favored the latter.[10]

Jones stressed that both approaches are important, and it only becomes problematic when one group thinks their approach to the text is "higher, better, more along what God intended." He offered E.K. Bailey as one well-known example of an African American preacher doing good exegesis which is then applied experientially; an emotional experience of the text isn't in place of an intellectual understanding, but *as well as*. Jones draws his preaching students' attention to the mood and voice of the text, encouraging students to "catch" the emotion of the speaker by asking them to perform it in character: *how does the biblical author "sound" as they communicate?*

Smith emphasized the importance story, since stories naturally involve the listener anyway. He retells the biblical stories in such a way as to identify viscerally with the oppressed in the narrative, showing how their present mirrors the situation of the text. With the epistles, he tends to "narrative" the rhetorical situation, not merely speaking *about* the church in Corinth but *telling their story* in a way that it becomes our story.[11] The preacher is thus an "exegetical escort," helping the audience understand and experience the text for themselves.[12]

---

8. E.g., Aristotle, *Ars rhetorica* 2.1.9.

9. E.g., Quintilian, *Institutio oratoria* 6.2.20–26; Cicero, *De oratore* 2.189–192.

10. See my discussion in *Preaching the New Testament as Rhetoric*, 168–71; also Kraftchik, "Πάθη in Paul," 50–56.

11. For some published examples of this, by white authors, see the imaginative fiction by Witherington, *A Week in the Life of Corinth*, and the narrative reconstruction of the Corinthian situation in Pogoloff, *Logos and Sophia*, 275–81.

12. For more on this image, see Smith and Massey, *Doctrine That Dances*.

A feature of much African American preaching is the active response from the congregation. As the preacher paints the picture, the audience makes audible agreement to let the preacher know: *I see that; I feel that!*[13] This arose from the church service being the one place where African Americans could have freedom to publicly express themselves, while out in the wider society they were told to "know their place," firstly as slaves, and then as a segregated and disenfranchised minority.[14] The church was "the one place where African Americans had freedom and could celebrate the goodness of God regardless of their present circumstances."[15] It reminded them that others were going through the same experiences of oppression and marginalization. Although, as we've stressed before, the situations are in no way comparable in severity, we may find that more vocal participation happens throughout the church in the West as the secular environment begins to place subtle limits on how we can express our faith in public.

In learning from African American preaching, Jones cautioned not to see minority preaching as "entertainment" for majority culture Christians; it shouldn't be embraced merely for the novelty factor. However, there is much for Anglo preachers to learn from their African American counterparts, particularly in how they go about helping their congregations see themselves in the text, and finding their identity within God's big story. But this won't happen from gaining a few quick tips from practitioners, nor simply from reading books by or about African American preachers.[16] Just like the emotion of the text, it's more caught than taught, and involves regularly listening to preachers from other minority cultures and experimenting with how approaches and techniques might be adapted for use in other settings.[17] Although this might be criticized in some places as "cultural appropriation"—and it could easily devolve into that if not done thoughtfully—to my three conversation partners, the wisdom contained in the African American preaching tradition was seen more as a gift to their white brothers and sisters, if only they would have the sense and humility to unwrap it.

13. Jones.
14. Smith.
15. Calvert.
16. Intentionally platforming more minority voices in conferences about preaching, while insufficient in itself, would be an important step forward. Organizers need to see this as being more than just "optics"; it's about living out the scriptural vision of a multi-ethnic, united people, as well as making use of *all* of the resources with which God has equipped his church.
17. For an intentional and systematic approach to adopting and adapting from other preachers, see Demond, "Still Learning to Preach—Imitative Practice."

## Opposition brings opportunity

Asked directly for advice for the white church as it's pushed from its previous position near the center of the majority culture, Jones said, "it's gonna be hard for y'all," with just the hint of a wry smile. It will entail giving up the sense that "we are right and control what's right" and any suggestion of entitlement because of who we are—or because of what our nation might have been in the past. In its place, we need to foster an attitude of humility which, when it comes, will be the work of the Spirit.

As that happens, Jones said we will probably rediscover the role of suffering and affliction in conforming our character to that of Jesus'—something more recognized at present in African American theology, and among minorities generally. Rather than seeing present suffering as an aberration which must be fixed *now*, we will grow to see it as a reality by which God is glorified as we become more like Jesus in his suffering (Phil 3:10). We may also find a greater sense unity as what unites us (our experience of opposition for the sake of Jesus) becomes more significant than issues that divide us.

Some of the changes, while distressing initially, should be seen as opportunities to be welcomed. No longer having an automatic seat at the table, we will be liberated to be faithful to God, rather than always having one eye to keeping our access to power and influence. Jones pulled no punches when discussing how a future removal of financial privileges ought to be welcomed:

> I think, in America at least . . . that tax breaks are a cloaking device for censoring the church . . . The church ought to give up its politically protected status so it can preach . . . Render unto Caesar what is Caesar's so that we can render unto God what is God's.

Calvert agreed, noting that the church had become too comfortable with culture in the past, since it allowed us to say what we wanted to say without experiencing much in the way of backlash. We've been able to preach "the biblical story [of God liberating his people] without identifying with it. I think this is the time for the church to find its identity with the persecuted church and not the church of convenience." It's time for the church to take up its cross.

Mainstream opposition in recent years has also given the church the opportunity to refine how it presents its message, sorting out what needs to be offensive (because the gospel is offensive) and what doesn't. Calvert said that it had helped him personally to become more sensitive in how he communicates the same gospel truths, but in a less confrontational and judgmental manner. Knowing that the wider culture is no longer supportive or indifferent to our message, but is increasingly hostile to it, ought to be a welcome factor in heeding Peter's call to communicate with gentleness and respect.

Calvert also warned of the some of the difficulties, particularly as increased disapproval encourages some to assimilate back into the majority culture, or compromise in some way in order to foster its approval. Within the African American church, he noted that prosperity theology can be an attractive alternative, offering a (mostly unrealized) path to acceptance among the wider culture on the basis of improved socio-economic status. And for those who do climb the socio-economic ladder, there is the temptation to migrate to a majority culture church rather than show solidarity with their brothers and sisters. A responsibility of our preaching will be to encourage faithfulness to the group, and point out the destructive consequences of compromising in order to maintain our tenuous positions of influence. Such prophetic preaching risks becoming divisive; however, Jones makes it clear that our primary responsibility is to call out such behavior in our own Christian "tribe"—much like Israel's prophets were usually sent to their own people—rather than attacking perceived deficiencies in how other groups are going about it.

Finally, it needs to be pointed out that all three preachers I spoke to didn't claim that the African-American churches had all of the answers about how to be a faithful, Jesus-following minority. They were mostly reluctant to give too much in the way of advice to the Anglo church, despite being more than equipped and entitled to do so. Instead, there seemed to be an anticipation of greater mutual understanding and a genuinely equal partnership in working it out together as aliens and exiles.

# 16

## Conclusions
### *What Next?*

WHEN I BOUGHT A new Honda Jazz a few years ago, I was surprised at how many of them I then saw on the road. It's not that there were any more of them than before. It's just that now I was subconsciously primed to notice them since I owned one myself. It was like my eyes had been opened and I couldn't help but spot them.

The purpose of this book has been to prime you to notice minority group rhetoric whenever it turns up in the pages of the New Testament. Hopefully, you won't be able to read it *without* spotting the explicit and implicit references to the first readers' minority status, and how it sought to encourage the response of attractive difference we've discussed at length. Nor, I trust, will you be able to ignore how it connects with our own increasingly marginalized reality and guides us in perhaps some "old new ways" of responding and interacting with the majority culture. You now have a new set of lenses through which to read both Scripture and our everyday experience as followers of Jesus.

I'm going to resist the temptation here, in this concluding chapter, to provide a systematized summary of the New Testament's minority group rhetoric. That's firstly because chapter 2 already did that in a preparatory sense. But also, perhaps more importantly, because producing a systematized minority group rhetoric drawn from the various New Testament texts would be reductionistic. Once formed and articulated, it risks leaving the inspired biblical text behind; to borrow Scot McKnight's metaphor, once we've "solved" the puzzle, who needs the individual pieces anymore?[1] If we detach the minority group strategies from the texts in which they are present—and from the particular contexts into which those texts spoke— we lose the inspired essence of what they were doing in the first place.

---

1. McKnight, *The Blue Parakeet*, 49–52.

This would be open to the same kind of critique that Abraham Kuruvilla rightly levels at "big idea" preaching, which distils the irreducible text into a set of propositions, and it's the distillate which is then preached.[2] Or, as Fred Craddock put it many years beforehand, "the minister boils off all the water and then preaches the stain in the bottom of the cup."[3] God didn't give us a systematized theology, or a systematized rhetoric; he gave us a set of particular texts which employ theology and rhetoric to *do something* to their original audiences. As preachers, it's our task to harness the applied theology and rhetoric of each unique biblical text to *do something similar* among our own audiences.

It's my hope that the lenses provided here will facilitate such an approach. In line with our six key questions (see chapter 2), such a reading of the New Testament ought to:

1. Keep us focused on God as our source of what is right and honorable, not the prevailing winds of culture.

2. Help us deal with an environment of increasing hostility, shaping our response so that we neither cave in to the pressure, nor create an isolated Christian enclave.

3. Form our identity, increasing our sense of belonging to one another and of being part of a much bigger story.

4. Sharpen our behavior so that our difference is, in fact, attractive.

5. Inculcate a Christian worldview that sees us as part of God's plan to redeem his creation and restore us as his image-bearers, insulating us from the default narratives of the majority culture such as global consumerism and human progress, and providing a theocentric framing for our participation in other narratives such as environmental catastrophe and the abuse of power.

6. Heighten our sense that this is all more relevant now than perhaps at any time in the history of the Western church.

Such a reading will have implications for how we engage with culture in general, and politics in particular. As our minority brothers told us in the previous chapter, we'll need to give up our sense that we're entitled to our seat at the table as a key participant in shaping culture; instead, we'll need to settle for living out counter-cultural values in an attractive way, leading from the margins rather than trying to hold on to the center. And as we do

---

2. Kuruvilla, "Time to Kill the Big Idea?," 825–46.
3. Craddock, *Preaching*, 123.

that, we may find that we actually enjoy the freedom that comes with not worrying about having to be liked by everyone!

That freedom will be essential if we're going to transform the way Christians engage in politics. Because a lot of the time we *do* worry about being liked; not by everyone, but by those in our own political tribe. Belonging, as we do, to the same Jesus-following minority should unite us no matter what our natural tribal affiliation might be; in social scientific terms, the church ought to be the *superordinate* group whose collective identity overrides other social, ethnic, gender, and political groupings (cf. Gal 3:28). Too often, it seems, we treat these other groupings as superordinate—particularly in our political engagement—which has been a significant obstacle to our witness. We've grafted our version of the gospel onto one or other of the political tribes and then uncritically aligned ourselves with its people and policies.

Yet for us there should be neither right nor left, conservative nor progressive, Republican nor Democrat, for we all are of the one civic body in Christ Jesus. More than that, the message of the kingdom is *both* conservative *and* progressive, while being truly neither. It seeks to conserve that in human society which is in line with God's plan for humanity as his image-bearers; but it refuses to conserve oppressive, abusive, and self-serving sources of power. It also seeks to progress the values of the kingdom which are about freedom from oppression, the valuing of all people and people groups, and meeting the needs of the marginalized and disadvantaged; but it doesn't confuse progress with a humanist, secularist agenda that sees God (and his lack of tolerance for sinful behavior) as being part of the problem. Yet the kingdom also operates outside the power structures of the majority culture; it seeks not to legislate its agenda, but embody its attractive difference in the individual and collective lives of its members.

If we continue to show greater allegiance to political, social, and ethnic groupings than we do to God and his people, our witness will be increasingly imperiled. But if, in an increasingly partisan age, we can follow the lead of the New Testament in making those differences subordinate to our oneness in Christ—that may well prove refreshingly attractive.

# Bibliography

Adamson, James B. *The Epistle of James*. New International Commentary on the New Testament. Grand Rapids: Eerdmans, 1976.
Alexander, Loveday. *The Preface to Luke's Gospel: Literary Convention and Social Context in Luke 1.1-4 and Acts 1.1*. Society of New Testament Studies Monograph Series 78. Cambridge: Cambridge University Press, 1993.
Ashcraft, Morris. *Revelation*. Broadman Bible Commentary. Nashville: Broadman, 1969.
Aune, David E. *The New Testament in Its Literary Environment*. Library of Early Christianity 8. Philadelphia: Westminster, 1987.
———. *Revelation 6-16*. Word Biblical Commentary 52B. Nashville: Nelson, 1998.
———. *Apocalypticism, Prophecy, and Magic in Early Christianity: Collected Essays*. Wissenschaftliche Untersuchungen Zum Neuen Testament 199. Tübingen: Mohr/Siebeck, 2006.
Bartlett, David. "An Exegesis of Matthew 25:31-36." *Foundations* 19 (1976) 205-22.
Bassler, Jouette M. "Mixed Signals: Nicodemus in the Fourth Gospel." *Journal of Biblical Literature* 108 (1989) 635-46.
Bauckham, Richard. *The Gospels for All Christians: Rethinking the Gospel Audiences*. Grand Rapids: Eerdmans, 1998.
Beale, G. K. *The Book of Revelation: A Commentary on the Greek Text*. New International Greek Testament Commentary. Grand Rapids: Eerdmans, 1999.
———. *Revelation: A Shorter Commentary*. Grand Rapids: Eerdmans, 2015.
Bennema, Cornelis. *Encountering Jesus: Character Studies in the Gospel of John*. 2nd edition. Minneapolis: Fortress, 2014.
Blomberg, Craig L., and Mariam J. Kamell. *James*. Zondervan Exegetical Commentary Series on the New Testament. Grand Rapids: Zondervan, 2008.
Boring, M. Eugene. *Revelation*. Interpretation. Louisville: John Knox, 1989.
Brant, Jo-Ann A. *John*. Paideia. Grand Rapids: Baker Academic, 2011.
Brewer, R. R. "The Meaning of *Politeuesthe* in Philippians 1:27." *Journal of Biblical Literature* 73 (1954) 76-83.
Brown, Raymond E. *The Community of the Beloved Disciple*. New York: Paulist, 1979.
———. *The Epistles of John*. Anchor Bible. Garden City, NY: Doubleday, 1982.
Bruce, F. F. *The Epistle to the Hebrews*. Rev. ed. New International Commentary on the New Testament. Grand Rapids: Eerdmans, 1990.

———. *The Epistles to the Colossians, to Philemon, and to the Ephesians.* New International Commentary on the New Testament. Grand Rapids: Eerdmans, 1984.
Bultmann, Rudolf. *The Gospel of John: A Commentary.* Translated by G. R. Beaslley-Murray. 1971. Reprint, Johannine Monograph Series. Eugene, OR: Wipf & Stock, 2014.
Carnegie, Dale. *How to Win Friends and Influence People.* New York: Simon & Schuster, 1937.
Carr, David. *Time, Narrative, and History.* Studies in Phenomenology and Existential Philosophy. Bloomington: Indiana University Press, 1986.
Carrier, Hervé. *The Sociology of Religious Belonging.* New York: Herder & Herder, 1965.
Carson, D. A. *The Gospel according to John.* Grand Rapids: Eerdmans, 1991.
Carter, Edward J. "Toll and Trouble: A Politcal Reading of Matthew 17.24–27." *Journal for the Study of the New Testament* 25 (2003) 413–31.
Carter, Warren. "Paying the Tax to Rome as Subversive Praxis: Matthew 17.24–27." *Journal for the Study of the New Testament* 76 (1999) 3–31.
Chan, Sam. *Preaching as the Word of God: Answering an Old Question with Speech-Act Theory.* Eugene, OR: Pickwick Publications, 2016.
Chester, Tim, and Steve Timmis. *Everyday Church: Gospel Communications on Mission.* North American edition. Wheaton, IL: Crossway, 2012.
Cialdini, Robert B. *Influence: The Psychology of Persuasion.* Rev. ed. New York: Harper Collins, 2007.
———. "The Science of Persuasion." *Scientific American* (2001) 76–81.
Ciampa, Roy E., and Brian S. Rosner. *The First Letter to the Corinthians.* Pillar. Grand Rapids: Eerdmans, 2010.
Classen, Carl J. *Rhetorical Criticism of the New Testament.* Boston: Brill Academic, 2002.
Clifford, Ross, and Philip Johnson. *The Cross Is not Enough: Living as Witnesses to the Resurrection.* Grand Rapids: Baker, 2012.
Cockerill, Gareth Lee. *The Epistle to the Hebrews.* New International Commentary on the New Testament. Grand Rapids: Eerdmans, 2012.
Collins, Adela Yarbro. *Crisis and Catharsis: The Power of the Apocalypse.* Philadelphia: Westminster, 1984.
Condor, S. "Social Identity and Time." In *Social Groups and Identities: Developing the Legacy of Henri Tajfel*, edited by W. P. Robinson and Henri Tajfel, 285–316. Boston: Butterworth-Heinemann, 1996.
Copenhaver, Adam. *Reconstructing the Historical Background of Paul's Rhetoric in the Letter to the Colossians.* Library of New Testament Studies. New York: Bloomsbury T. & T. Clark, 2018.
Coser, Lewis A. *The Functions of Social Conflict.* Glencoe, IL: Free Press, 1956.
Covey, Stephen R. *The 7 Habits of Highly Effective People: Restoring the Character Ethic.* Rev. ed. New York: Free Press, 2004.
Craddock, Fred B. *Preaching.* Nashville: Abingdon, 1985.
Creamer, Jennifer M. *God as Creator in Acts 17:24: An Historical-Exegetical Study.* Eugene, OR: Wipf & Stock, 2017.
Culpepper, R. Alan. *Anatomy of the Fourth Gospel: A Study in Literary Design.* Philadelphia: Fortress, 1983.
Danker, Frederick W. *Benefactor: Epigraphic Study of a Graeco-Roman and New Testament Semantic Field.* St. Louis: Clayton, 1982.

Davies, W. D., and Dale C. Allison. *A Critical and Exegetical Commentary on the Gospel According to Saint Matthew.* International Critical Commentary. Vol. 1. London: Bloomsbury Academic, 1997.
———. *A Critical and Exegetical Commentary on the Gospel according to Saint Matthew.* International Critical Commentary. Vol. 2. London: Bloomsbury Academic, 1991.
———. *A Critical and Exegetical Commentary on the Gospel According to Saint Matthew.* International Critical Commentary. Vol. 3. London: Bloomsbury Academic, 2004.
De Botton, Alain. *Status Anxiety.* New York: Pantheon, 2004.
Demond, Allan. "Still Learning to Preach—Imitative Practice." https://www.academia.edu/659796/Still_Learning_to_Preach_Imitative_Practice.
DeSilva, David A. "Despising Shame: A Cultural-Anthropological Investigation of the Epistle to the Hebrews." *Journal of Biblical Literature* 113 (1994) 439–61.
———. *Honor, Patronage, Kinship & Purity: Unlocking New Testament Culture.* Downers Grove, IL: InterVarsity, 2000.
———. *An Introduction to the New Testament: Contexts, Methods & Ministry Formation.* Downers Grove, IL: InterVarsity, 2004.
———. *The Letter to the Hebrews in Social-Scientific Perspective.* Cascade Companions. Eugene, OR: Cascade Books, 2012.
———. *Perseverance in Gratitude: A Socio-Rhetorical Commentary on the Epistle "to the Hebrews".* Grand Rapids: Eerdmans, 2000.
———. *Seeing Things John's Way: The Rhetoric of the Book of Revelation.* Louisville: Westminster John Knox, 2009.
Dever, Mark. *The Message of the New Testament: Promises Kept.* Wheaton, IL: Crossway, 2005.
Dodd, C. H. *The Johannine Epistles.* Moffatt. London: Hodder & Stoughton, 1946.
Doriani, Daniel M. *James.* Reformed Expository Commentary. Phillipsburg, PA: P&R, 2007.
———. *Putting the Truth to Work: The Theory and Practice of Biblical Application.* Phillipsburg, NJ: P & R, 2001.
Elliott, John H. "Disgraced yet Graced. The Gospel according to 1 Peter in the Key of Honor and Shame." *Biblical Theology Bulletin* 24 (1995) 166–78.
———. *A Home for the Homeless: A Social-Scientific Criticism of 1 Peter, Its Situation and Strategy.* Philadelphia, PA: Fortress, 1990.
———. "The Jewish Messianic Movement: From Faction to Sect." In *Modelling Early Christianity: Social-Scientific Studies of the New Testament in Its Context*, edited by Philip F. Esler, 75–95. London: Routledge, 1995.
———. "Social-Scientific Criticism of a Biblical Text: 1 Peter as an Example." In *Social-Scientific Approaches to New Testament Interpretation*, edited by David G. Horrell, 339–58. Edinburgh: T. & T. Clark, 1999.
Eriksson, Anders. "Fear of Eternal Damnation: Pathos Appeal in 1 Corinthians 15 and 16." In *Paul and Pathos*, edited by Thomas H. Olbricht and Jerry L. Sumney, 115–26. SBL Symposium Series 16. Atlanta: Society for Biblical Literature, 2001.
Esler, Philip F. "Community and Gospel in Early Christianity: A Response to Richard Bauckham's *Gospels for All Christians.*" *Scottish Journal of Theology* 51 (1998) 235–48.
———. *Community and Gospel in Luke-Acts: The Social and Political Motivations of Lucan Theology.* Society for New Testament Studies Monograph Series 57. Cambridge: Cambridge University Press, 1987.

———. *The First Christians in Their Social Worlds: Social-Scientific Approaches to New Testament Interpretation*. London: Routledge, 1994.

———. "Group Norms and Prototypes in Matthew 5.3–12." In *T&T Clark Handbook to Social Identity in the New Testament*, edited by J. Brian Tucker and Coleman A. Baker, 148–71. London: Bloomsbury T&T Clark, 2014.

———, ed. *Modelling Early Christianity: Social-Scientific Studies of the New Testament in Its Context*. London: Routledge, 1995.

———. "An Outline of Social Identity Theory." In *T&T Clark Handbook to Social Identity in the New Testament*, edited by J. Brian Tucker and Coleman A. Baker, 13–40. London: Bloomsbury T. & T. Clark, 2014.

Farrelly, Nicolas. "An Unexpected Ally." *Trinity Journal* 34 (2013) 31–43.

Fee, Gordon D. *The First Epistle to the Corinthians*. New International Commentary on the New Testament. Grand Rapids: Eerdmans, 1987.

———. *Paul's Letter to the Philippians*. New International Commentary on the New Testament. Grand Rapids: Eerdmans, 1995.

Fitch, David E. *The Church of Us vs. Them: Freedom from a Faith That Feeds on Making Enemies*. Grand Rapids: Brazos, 2019.

Flew, Antony, and Roy Abraham Varghese. *There Is a God: How the World's Most Notorious Atheist Changed His Mind*. New York: HarperOne, 2007.

Fowl, Stephen E. *Philippians*. Two Horizons New Testament Commentary. Grand Rapids: Eerdmans, 2005.

French, David. "Another Pop-Culture Christian Loses His Faith." *National Review*, 13 Aug 2019. https://www.nationalreview.com/2019/08/another-pop-culture-christian-loses-his-faith.

Frost, Michael, and Alan Hirsch. *The Shaping of Things to Come: Innovation and Mission for the 21st-Century Church*. Rev. ed. Grand Rapids: Baker 2013.

Furnish, Victor Paul. *1 Thessalonians, 2 Thessalonians*. Abingdon New Testament Commentaries. Nashville: Abingdon, 2007.

Garland, David E. *Luke*. Zondervan Exegetical Commentary on the New Testament. Grand Rapids: Zondervan, 2011.

Gentry, Kenneth L. *Before Jerusalem Fell: Dating the Book of Revelation*. Fort Worth: Dominion, 1989.

Good, Dierdre. "The Verb Ἀναχωρεω in Matthew's Gospel." *Novum Testamentum* 32 (1990) 1–12.

Goulder, Michael D. *Midrash and Lection in Matthew: The Speaker's Lectures in Biblical Studies, 1969–71*. London: SPCK, 1974.

Green, Joel B. *1 Peter*. Two Horizons New Testament Commentary. Grand Rapids: Eerdmans, 2007.

———. *The Gospel of Luke*. New International Commentary on the New Testament. Grand Rapids: Eerdmans, 1997.

———. "Internal Repetition in Luke-Acts." In *History, Literature, and Society in the Book of Acts*, edited by Ben Witherington III, 283–99. Cambridge: Cambridge University Press, 1996.

Greenberg, Eric H., and Karl Weber. *Generation We: How Millennial Youth Are Taking over America and Changing Our World Forever*. Emeryville, CA: Pachatusan, 2008.

Gregg, Steve. *Revelation, Four Views: A Parallel Commentary*. Rev. ed. Nashville: Nelson, 2013.

Grene, Clement. *Cowardice, Betrayal and Discipleship: Peter and Judas in the Gospels.* Edinburgh: University of Edinburgh Press, 2018.

Griffith, Terry. "A Non-Polemical Reading of 1 John: Sin, Christology and the Limits of Johannine Christology." *Tyndale Bulletin* 49 (1998) 253–76.

Gundry, Robert H. *Matthew: A Commentary on His Literary and Theological Art.* Grand Rapids: Eerdmans, 1982.

Hagner, Donald A. *Encountering the Book of Hebrews: An Exposition.* Grand Rapids: Baker Academic, 2002.

———. *Matthew.* Vol. 1, *Matthew 1–13.* 2 vols. Word Biblical Commentary 33A. Dallas: Word, 1993.

Hakola, Raimo. "The Burden of Ambiguity: Nicodemus and the Social Identity of the Johannine Christians." *New Testament Studies* 55 (2009) 438–55.

———. "'Friendly' Pharisees and Social Identity in the Book of Acts." In *Contemporary Studies in Acts*, edited by T. E. Phillips, 181–200. Macon, GA: Mercer University Press, 2009.

Hansen, G. Walter. *The Letter to the Philippians.* Pillar. Grand Rapids: Eerdmans, 2009.

Hanson, K. C. "How Honorable! How Shameful! A Cultural Analysis of Matthew's Makarisms and Reproaches." *Semeia* 68 (1996) 81–111.

Harding, Susan. "Representing Fundamentalism: The Problem of the Repugnant Cultural Other." *Social Research* 58 (1991) 373–93.

Harnack, Adolf von. *The Mission and Expansion of Christianity in the First Three Centuries.* Edited and translated by James Moffatt. 1962. Reprint, Eugene, OR: Wipf & Stock, 1998.

Harvey, A. E. *Jesus on Trial: A Study in the Fourth Gospel.* Atlanta: John Knox, 1977.

Hauser, Gerald. "Aristotle on Epideictic: The Formation of Public Morality." *Rhetoric Society Quarterly* 29 (1999) 5–32.

Hays, Richard B. *First Corinthians.* Interpretation. Louisville: Westminister John Knox, 2011.

Hemer, Colin J. *The Letters to the Seven Churches of Asia in Their Local Setting.* Biblical Resource Series. Grand Rapids: Eerdmans, 2001.

Hogan, Lucy Lind. "Rethinking Persuasion: Developing an Incarnational Theology of Preaching." *Homiletic* 24/2 (1999) 1–12.

Holwerda, David E. "Suffering Witnesses—to What End? A Sermon on Revelation 11:1–14." *Calvin Theological Journal* 41 (2006) 127–32.

Horsley, Richard A. *Jesus and Empire: The Kingdom of God and the New World Disorder.* Minneapolis: Fortress, 2003.

Hoskyns, Edwyn Clement, and Noel Davey. *The Fourth Gospel.* London: Faber & Faber, 1940.

Hunter, A. M. *The Gospel according to John.* The Cambridge Bible Commentary. Cambridge: Cambridge University Press, 1965.

Jao, Greg. "Honor and Obey." In *Following Jesus without Dishonoring Your Parents: Asian American Discipleship*, edited by Jeanette Yep and Peter Cha, 43–56. Downers Grove, IL: InterVarsity, 1998.

Johnson, Luke Timothy. *Brother of Jesus, Friend of God: Studies in the Letter of James.* Grand Rapids: Eerdmans, 2004.

———. *Hebrews: A Commentary.* New Testament Library. Louisville: Westminster John Knox, 2006.

———. "The New Testament's Anti-Jewish Slander and the Conventions of Ancient Polemic." *Journal of Biblical Literature* 108 (1989) 419–41.
Johnson, Luke Timothy, and Daniel J. Harrington. *The Gospel of Luke*. Sacra Pagina. Collegeville, MN: Liturgical, 1991.
Judge, Edwin Arthur. "Paul's Boasting in Relation to Contemporary Professional Practice." *Australian Biblical Review* 16 (1968) 37–50.
Keener, Craig S. *A Commentary on the Gospel of Matthew*. Grand Rapids: Eerdmans, 1999.
———. *The Gospel of John: A Commentary*. Peabody, MA: Hendrickson, 2003.
———. *Revelation*. NIV Application Commentary. Grand Rapids: Zondervan, 2000.
Kemmler, Dieter Werner. *Faith and Human Reason: A Study of Paul's Method of Preaching as Illustrated by 1-2 Thessalonians and Acts 17, 2-4*. Novum Testamentum Supplements 40. Leiden: Brill, 1975.
Kennedy, George A. "The Genres of Rhetoric." In *Handbook of Classical Rhetoric in the Hellenistic Period, 330 B.C.—A.D. 400*, edited by Stanley E. Porter, 43–50. Leiden: Brill, 1997.
———. *A New History of Classical Rhetoric*. Princeton Paperbacks. Princeton, NJ: Princeton University Press, 1994.
———. *New Testament Interpretation through Rhetorical Criticism*. Studies in Religion. Chapel Hill, NC: University of North Carolina Press, 1984.
Kinnaman, David, and Aly Hawkins. *You Lost Me: Why Young Christians Are Leaving Church—and Rethinking Faith*. Grand Rapids: Baker, 2011.
Koester, Craig R. *Hebrews: A New Translation with Introduction and Commentary*. Anchor Bible 36. New York: Doubleday, 2001.
———. *Revelation and the End of All Things*. Grand Rapids: Eerdmans, 2001.
———. *Revelation: A New Translation with Introduction and Commentary*. Anchor Yale Bible 38A. New Haven: Yale University Press, 2014.
———. *Symbolism in the Fourth Gospel: Meaning, Mystery, Community*. 2nd ed. Minneapolis: Fortress, 2003.
Kuruvilla, Abraham. *A Manual for Preaching: The Journey from Text to Sermon*. Grand Rapids: Baker Academic, 2019.
———. "Time to Kill the Big Idea? A Fresh Look at Preaching." *Journal of the Evangelical Theological Society* 61 (2018) 825–46.
Kwon, Oh-Young. *1 Corinthians 1–4: Reconstructing Its Social and Rhetorical Situation and Re-Reading It Cross-Culturally for Korean-Confucian Christians Today*. Eugene, OR: Wipf & Stock, 2010.
Kysar, Robert. "Coming Hermeneutical Earthquake in Johannine Interpretation." In *What Is John? Readers and Readings of the Fourth Gospel*, edited by Fernando F. Segovia, 1:185–90. 2 vols. SBL Symposium Series 3. Atlanta: Scholars, 1996.
Lane, William L. *Hebrews 1–8*. Word Biblical Commentary 47A. Dallas: Word, 1991.
Larson, Jennifer. *Understanding Greek Religion: A Cognitive Approach*. Understanding the Ancient World. London: Routledge, 2016.
Larzelere, Robert E., et al. "Children and Parents Deserve Better Parental Discipline Research: Critiquing the Evidence for Exclusively 'Positive' Parenting." *Marriage & Family Review* 53 (2017) 24–35.
Lennox, John C. *God and Stephen Hawking: Whose Design Is It Anyway?* Oxford: Lion, 2010.

Lewis, C. S. "Myth Became Fact." In *God in the Dock: Essays on Theology*, edited by Walter Hooper, 63–67. London: Collins, 1979. Reprint, 2001.

Lewis, C. S., and Walter Hooper. *The Collected Letters of C.S. Lewis*. 3 vols. San Francisco: HarperSanFrancisco, 2004.

Litfin, A. Duane. *St. Paul's Theology of Proclamation: 1 Corinthians 1–4 and Greco-Roman Rhetoric*. Society of New Testament Studies Monograph Series 79. Cambridge: Cambridge University Press, 1994.

Harding, Mark, and Alanna Nobbs, eds. *Into All the World: Emergent Christianity in Its Jewish and Greco-Roman Context*. Grand Rapids: Eerdmans, 2017.

MacBride, Tim. "Aliens and Strangers: Minority Group Rhetoric in the Later New Testament Writings." In *Into All the World: Emergent Christianity in Its Jewish and Greco-Roman Context*, edited by Mark Harding and Alanna Nobbs, 301–33. Grand Rapids: Eerdmans, 2017.

———. *Catching the Wave: Preaching the New Testament as Rhetoric*. Nottingham: Inter-Varsity, 2016.

———. "Imitators of the Lord in Severe Suffering." In *Divine Suffering: History, Theology, and Church Mission*, edited by Andrew Schmutzer. Eugene, OR: Wipf & Stock, 2020.

———. "Preaching Paul's Epistles to Australians." In *Preaching with an Accent: Biblical Genres for Australian Congregations*, edited by Ian Hussey, 162–88. Sydney: Morling, 2020.

———. *Preaching the New Testament as Rhetoric: The Promise of Rhetorical Criticism for Expository Preaching*. Australian College of Theology Monograph. Eugene, OR: Wipf & Stock, 2014.

———. "Preaching to Aliens and Strangers: Preaching the New Testament as Minority Group Rhetoric." *Journal of the Evangelical Homiletics Society* 16/2 (2016) 5–14.

———. "To Aliens and Strangers." In *Not in Kansas*, edited by David Starling and Darrell Jackson, 87–103. Sydney: Morling, 2020.

MacMullen, Ramsay. *Paganism in the Roman Empire*. New Haven: Yale University Press, 1981.

Malina, Bruce J. *The New Testament World: Insights from Cultural Anthropology*. 3rd ed. Louisville: Westminster John Knox, 2001.

Marshall, I. Howard. *The Epistles of John*. New International Commentary on the New Testament. Grand Rapids: Eerdmans, 1978.

Martyn, J. Louis. *History and Theology in the Fourth Gospel*. New York: Harper & Row, 1968.

McAlpine, Stephen. "The Beguiling Technicolor of OZ." In *Not in Kansas*, edited by David Starling and Darrell Jackson, 1–21. Sydney: Morling, 2020.

McCartney, Dan. *James*. Baker Exegetical Commentary on the New Testament. Grand Rapids: Baker Academic, 2009.

McKnight, Scot. *The Blue Parakeet: Rethinking How You Read the Bible*. Grand Rapids: Zondervan, 2008.

———. *Galatians: From Biblical Text—to Contemporary Life*. NIV Application Commentary. Grand Rapids: Zondervan, 1995.

———. *Kingdom Conspiracy: Returning to the Radical Mission of the Local Church*. Grand Rapids: Brazos, 2014.

Meeks, Wayne A. *The First Urban Christians: The Social World of the Apostle Paul*. New Haven: Yale University Press, 1983.

Michaels, J. Ramsey. *The Gospel of John*. New International Commentary on the New Testament. Grand Rapids: Eerdmans, 2010.

———. "The Gospel of John as a Kinder, Gentler Apocalypse for the 20th Century." In *What Is John? Readers and Readings of the Fourth Gospel*, edited by Fernando F. Segovia, 1:191–98. 2 vols. SBL Symposium Series 3. Atlanta: Scholars, 1996.

Mischel, Walter. *The Marshmallow Test: Mastering Self-Control*. New York: Little, Brown, 2014.

Mischel, Walter, et al. "Cognitive and Attentional Mechanisms in Delay of Gratification." *American Psychological Association* 21/2 (1972) 204–18.

Mitchell, Margaret M. *Paul and the Rhetoric of Reconciliation*. Louisville: Westminster John Knox, 1993.

Moo, Douglas J. *The Letter of James: An Introduction and Commentary*. Tyndale New Testament Commentaries 16. Grand Rapids: Eerdmans, 1985.

Morrison, Michael. *Enthymemes in Hebrews*. Kindle Edition. 2010.

Mosser, Carl. "Rahab Outside the Camp." In *The Epistle to the Hebrews and Christian Theology*, edited by Richard Bauckham, et al, 383–404. Grand Rapids: Eerdmans, 2009.

Mounce, Robert H. *The Book of Revelation*. New International Commentary on the New Testament. Grand Rapids: Eerdmans, 1977.

Moxnes, Halvor. "Honor and Shame." In *The Social Sciences and New Testament Interpretation*, edited by Richard L. Rohrbaugh, 19–40. Peabody, MA: Hendrickson, 1996.

Murray, Stuart. *Post-Christendom: Church and Mission in a Strange New World*. 2nd ed. After Christendom Series. Eugene, OR: Cascade Books, 2018.

Neyrey, Jerome H. *Honor and Shame in the Gospel of Matthew*. Louisville: Westminster John Knox, 1998.

Oropeza, B. J. *In the Footsteps of Judas and Other Defectors: The Gospels, Acts, and Johannine Letters*. Apostasy in the New Testament Communities. Eugene, OR: Cascade Books, 2011.

Osborne, Grant R., and Clinton E. Arnold. *Matthew*. Zondervan Exegetical Commentary on the New Testament. Grand Rapids: Zondervan, 2010.

Painter, John, and Daniel J. Harrington. *1, 2, and 3 John*. Sacra Pagina 18. Collegeville, MN: Liturgical, 2002.

Pate, C. Marvin. *The Writings of John: A Survey of the Gospel, Epistles, and Apocalypse*. Grand Rapids: Zondervan, 2011.

Paul, Ian. *Revelation: An Introduction and Commentary*. Tyndale New Testament Commentaries 20. Downers Grove, IL: InterVarsity, 2018.

Perdue, Leo G. "Paraenesis and the Epistle of James." *Zeitschrift für die neutestamentliche Wissenschaft* 72 (1981) 241–56.

Perkins, Pheme. *First Corinthians*. Paideia. Grand Rapids: Baker Academic, 2012.

———. *Peter: Apostle for the Whole Church*. Studies on Personalities of the New Testament. Columbia: University of South Carolina Press, 1994.

Piper, John. *Desiring God: Meditations of a Christian Hedonist*. 25th anniversary reference edition. Colorado Springs, CO: Multnomah, 2011.

———. *Don't Waste Your Life*. Wheaton, IL: Crossway, 2003.

Pitt-Rivers, Julian. "Honor and Social Status." In *Honor and Shame: The Values of Mediterranean Society*, edited by Jean G. Péristiany, 19–77. Chicago: University of Chicago Press, 1966.

Pogoloff, Stephen M. *Logos and Sophia: The Rhetorical Situation of 1 Corinthians.* SBL Dissertation Series 134. Atlanta: Scholars, 1992.
Porter Stanley E., ed. *Handbook of Classical Rhetoric in the Hellenistic Period, 330 B.C.– A.D. 400.* Leiden: Brill, 1997.
Quicke, Michael J. *360-Degree Preaching: Hearing, Speaking, and Living the Word.* Grand Rapids: Baker Academic, 2003.
Reddish, Mitchell. *An Introduction to the Gospels.* Nashville: Abingdon, 1997.
———. *Revelation.* Smyth & Helwys Bible Commentary. Macon, GA: Smyth & Helwys, 2001.
Reicher, Stephen, and Nick Hopkins. *Self and Nation: Categorization, Contestation, and Mobilization.* Thousand Oaks, CA: Sage, 2001.
Resner, André. *Preacher and Cross: Person and Message in Theology and Rhetoric.* Grand Rapids: Eerdmans, 1999.
Robinson, W. P., and Henri Tajfel, eds. *Social Groups and Identities: Developing the Legacy of Henri Tajfel.* Boston: Butterworth-Heinemann, 1996.
Ropes, James Hardy. *A Critical and Exegetical Commentary on the Epistle of St. James.* International Critical Commentary. New York: Scribner, 1916.
Sales, Nancy Jo. *American Girls: Social Media and the Secret Lives of Teenagers.* New York: Vintage, 2017.
Scaer, David P. *James, the Apostle of Faith: A Primary Christological Epistle for the Persecuted Church.* St. Louis: Concordia, 1983.
Schenck, Kenneth. *Understanding the Book of Hebrews: The Story behind the Sermon.* Louisville: Westminster John Knox, 2003.
Schmidt, T. "Moral Lethargy and the Epistle to the Hebrews." *Westminster Theological Journal* 54 (1992) 167–73.
Sittser, Gerald L. *Resilient Faith: How the Early Christian "Third Way" Changed the World.* Grand Rapids: Brazos, 2019.
Smith, Christian, and Melinda Lundquist Denton. *Soul Searching: The Religious and Spiritual Lives of American Teenagers.* Oxford: Oxford University Press, 2005.
Smith, Murray J. "The Book of Revelation: A Call to Worship, Witness, and Wait in the Midst of Violence." In *Into All the World: Emergent Christianity in Its Jewish and Greco-Roman Context*, edited by M. Harding and A. Nobbs, 334–71. Grand Rapids: Eerdmans, 2017.
Smith, Robert, and James Earl Massey. *Doctrine That Dances: Bringing Doctrinal Preaching and Teaching to Life.* Nashville: B & H Academic, 2008.
Stanton, Graham. *A Gospel for a New People: Studies in Matthew.* Louisville: Westminster John Knox, 1993.
Starling, David. "Preaching on Sex in a Post-Christendom World." Paper presented at Morling College Preaching Conference, 2018.
Stott, John R. W. *The Letters of John: An Introduction and Commentary.* 2nd ed. Tyndale New Testament Commentaries 19. 1988. Reprint, Nottingham: Inter-Varsity, 2009.
Suggit, J. N. "Nicodemus—the True Jew." *Neotestamentica* 14 (1981) 90–110.
Tajfel, Henri. "The Achievement of Group Differentiation." In *Differentiation between Social Groups: Studies in the Social Psychology of Intergroup Relations*, edited by Henri Tajfel, 77–98. London: Academic, 1978.
Talbert, Charles H. *Ephesians and Colossians.* Paideia. Grand Rapids: Baker Academic, 2007.

Tanner, Cullen. "Climbing the Lampstand-Witness-Trees: Revelation's Use of Zechariah 4 in Light of Speech Act Theory." *Journal of Pentecostal Theology* 20 (2011) 81–92.

Thompson, James W. *Hebrews*. Paideia. Grand Rapids: Baker Academic, 2008.

———. *Preaching Like Paul: Homiletical Wisdom for Today*. Louisville: Westminster John Knox, 2001.

Thompson, Leonard L. *The Book of Revelation: Apocalypse and Empire*. New York: Oxford University Press, 1990.

Trebilco, Paul R. *The Early Christians in Ephesus from Paul to Ignatius*. Wissenschaftliche Untersuchungen zum Neuen Testament 166. Tübingen: Mohr/Siebeck, 2004.

Trites, Allison A. *The New Testament Concept of Witness*. Society for New Testament Studies Monograph Series. 31. Cambridge: Cambridge University Press, 1977.

Turcan, Robert. *The Cults of the Roman Empire*. Ancient World. Oxford: Blackwell, 1996.

Turner, John C., et al. *Rediscovering the Social Group: Self-Categorization Theory*. Oxford: Blackwell, 1987.

Twenge, Jean M. *iGen: Why Today's Super-Connected Kids Are Growing Up Less Rebellious, More Tolerant, Less Happy—and Completely Unprepared for Adulthood*. New York: Atria, 2018.

Walsh, Brian J., and Sylvia C. Keesmaat. *Colossians Remixed: Subverting the Empire*. Downers Grove, IL: InterVarsity, 2004.

Waltke, Bruce K. *A Commentary on Micah*. Grand Rapids: Eerdmans, 2007.

Watson, Duane F. "Amplification Techniques in 1 John: The Interaction of Rhetorical Style and Invention." *Journal for the Study of the New Testament* 51 (1993) 99–123.

———. "An Epideictic Strategy for Increasing Adherence to Community Values: 1 John 1:1–2:29." Paper presented at the Eastern Great Lakes and Midwest Biblical Societies, 1991.

Weima, Jeffrey. "What Does Aristotle Have to Do with Paul? An Evaluation of Rhetorical Criticism.". *Catholic Theological Journal* 32 (1997) 458–68.

Welborn, Larry L. *Politics and Rhetoric in the Corinthian Epistles*. Macon, GA: Mercer University Press, 1997.

White, Leland J. "Grid and Group in Matthew's Community: The Righteousness/Honor Code in the Sermon on the Mount." *Semeia* 35 (1986) 61–90.

Wilson, Bryan R. "An Analysis of Sect Development." *American Journal of Sociology* 24 (1959) 3–15.

Winter, Bruce W. "Is Paul among the Sophists?" *Reformed Theological Review* 53 (1994) 28–38.

———. *Seek the Welfare of the City: Christians as Benefactors and Citizens*. First-Century Christians in the Graeco-Roman World. Grand Rapids: Eerdmans, 1994.

Witherington, Ben, III. *1 and 2 Thessalonians: A Socio-Rhetorical Commentary*. Grand Rapids: Eerdmans, 2006.

———. *The Acts of the Apostles: A Socio-Rhetorical Commentary*. Grand Rapids: Eerdmans, 1998.

———. *Conflict and Community in Corinth: A Socio-Rhetorical Commentary on 1 and 2 Corinthians*. Grand Rapids: Eerdmans, 1995.

———. *Friendship and Finances in Philippi: The Letter of Paul to the Philippians*. Valley Forge, PA: Trinity, 1994.

———. *John's Wisdom: A Commentary on the Fourth Gospel*. Louisville: Westminster John Knox, 1995.

———. *Letters and Homilies for Hellenized Christians: A Socio-Rhetorical Commentary on Titus, 1–2 Timothy and 1–3 John*. Vol. 1. Downers Grove, IL: IVP Academic, 2006.

———. *Letters and Homilies for Hellenized Christians: A Socio-Rhetorical Commentary on 1–2 Peter*. Vol. 2. Downers Grove, IL: IVP Academic, 2007.

———. *Letters and Homilies for Jewish Christians: A Socio-Rhetorical Commentary on Hebrews, James and Jude*. Downers Grove, IL: IVP Academic, 2007.

———. *Matthew*. Smyth & Helwys Bible Commentary. Macon, GA: Smyth & Helwys, 2006.

———. *New Testament Rhetoric: An Introductory Guide to the Art of Persuasion in and of the New Testament*. Eugene, OR: Cascade Books, 2009.

———. *Revelation*. New Cambridge Bible Commentary. Cambridge: Cambridge University Press, 2003.

———. *A Week in the Life of Corinth*. Downers Grove, IL: IVP Academic, 2012.

Wright, N. T. *Colossians and Philemon: An Introduction and Commentary*. Tyndale New Testament Commentaries 12. Nottingham: Inter-Varsity, 2008.

———. *Jesus and the Victory of God*. Christian Origins and the Question of God 2. Minneapolis: Fortress, 1996.

———. *Simply Good News: Why the Gospel Is News and What Makes It Good*. San Francisco: HarperOne, 2015.

Yeo, Khiok-Khng. "The Rhetorical Hermeneutic of 1 Corinthians 8 and Chinese Ancestor Worship." *Biblical Interpretation* 2 (1994) 294–311.